THE SILENT VOICE

THE SILENT VOICE

John Woolmer

HODDER AND STOUGHTON
LONDON SYDNEY AUCKLAND TORONTO

All biblical quotations are taken from the New International Version, unless otherwise stated in the text.

British Library Cataloguing in Publication Data

Woolmer, John
   The silent voice.
   1. Christian life. Guidance
   I. Title
   248.4

   ISBN 0-340-51866-9

Published by Hodder and Stoughton, a division of Hodder and Stoughton Ltd, Mill Road, Dunton Green, Sevenoaks, Kent TN13 2YA. Editorial Office: 47 Bedford Square, London WC1B 3DP.

Photoset by Avocet Robinson, Buckingham.

Printed in Great Britain by Cox & Wyman Ltd., Reading.

DEDICATION

To Jane with grateful thanks for her love and help
and to Rachel, Susanna, Timothy and Katharine,
with the hope that one day they will enjoy reading it.

CONTENTS

	INTRODUCTION	5
1.	INQUIRE OF THE LORD	7
2.	CONFUSION AND SILENCE	23
3.	LIVING WORD ·	41
4.	JESUS AND GUIDANCE	56
5.	GUIDANCE AND THE HOLY SPIRIT	72
6.	WORSHIP AND THE VOICE OF GOD	93
7.	LISTENING AND THE BODY OF CHRIST	108
8.	PRAYER – GOD'S SILENT VOICE	117
9.	CREATION SPEAKS	133
10.	CIRCUMSTANCES GUIDE	150
11.	GUIDANCE IN RELATIONSHIPS	166
12.	GUIDANCE AND HEALING	186
13.	GUIDANCE AND THE QUEST FOR HOLINESS	207
14.	GUIDANCE AND THE APPROACH OF DEATH	226
15.	THE MYSTERY OF GUIDANCE	249
16.	THE SILENT VOICE TODAY	264

ACKNOWLEDGMENTS

My grateful thanks to the parishes of Shepton Mallet, Doulting, Cranmore, and Prestleigh for their support and encouragement. Especially to all who have supplied material for the book, or given permission to mention their experiences. Also to the Community at Stanton House, the household of Richard and Kay Thwaites, and the Diocesan Retreat House at Glastonbury, where the book was written, and to David Prior for his helpful criticism, and, finally, to Joyce Martin for typing innumerable drafts of the manuscript.

FOREWORD

by the Bishop of Lewes

This is a book about personal guidance. It explores many ways in which guidance may come to us, but it is not a catalogue, for there is always a great refreshment in hearing stories in theological and spiritual writing. There is a wealth of stories in this book which join spiritual possibilities to the lives of us Christians who long for guidance, and confirm our belief that God has a purpose and a plan for each of us. It is urgent that we should know this today when there is so much that seems to be out of control in the environment, and in the lemming-like rush of the Western world towards more and more wealth and the desire to do what 'I like'.

The guidance which this book is about comes to us and is lived within God's overall purpose for His Creation and for Christians within the Church, which is the instrument to bring this to light. Personal guidance is always set within God's overall purpose and it is important that we give this vision priority over our own hopes if we are to be obedient to our guidance.

Let me say a little more about this purpose, which is two-fold: first, it is to reveal the community of faith and love which we call the Church: second, it is the transfiguring of the Creation by this Easter community of faith, though others also will have a part in this purpose. I purposely use the word 'reveal' rather than 'build up' or 'create' with respect to this community because there is a sense in which His Church, the Body of Christ, is always perfect and complete, whether there be any members within it on this earth or not. Guidance gains its importance from God's call to us to share in the work of perfecting and transfiguring the Church. There can be nothing more urgent and nothing more thrilling than this; today the possibilities of co-operating by grace with God have never been more exciting, for modern life goes on revealing more and more of the secrets of His universe and showing how everything can shine more and more with His glory. There are all the wonders of medicine allowing us to have better bodies; there are all the resources for education and art and craft and sport which can draw out the splendours of our humanity and the beauty of the universe. Yet unless we listen to the guidance of God these things can become our disaster: the break-up of marriages, the rise of abortions, the ever-increasing desire for more possessions are but a few examples of this, so it is urgent that we are not only willing to listen but are also given guidance about guidance.

We must always be sure, though, that however great the danger and pressures of today we Christians are never frantic, never dismayed into thinking that anything will ever disturb God's ultimate purposes. They have already been perfected in the Resurrection of Jesus Christ.

We all long to know what God has in store for us, we all long to have clear guidance in particular circumstances and at particular times, we all long to hear what God is saying to us through particular events and through our friendships and intuitions. We all long that our prayer should be so real that we can rise from it every morning with a new sense of how to live that life which is life indeed. But guidance which is not set within the life of the Church and within God's overall purposes will quickly become an individualistic game, probably narrowing its vision of what is significant. We shall end up by wanting guidance about whether or not we ought to do up our shoelace, whether there is a significance in the blackbird sounding somewhat bronchial this morning, or in the number 11 bus being late.

So John Woolmer sets guidance firmly in the revelation of Scripture, which he says must be the sure and firm testing rod for any guidance, for being certain that the silent voice is the voice of the Holy Spirit and not our own concoction. Of course, like Holy Scripture, the book has come through the minds of men and women who are not sinless. The voice of God has been heard down the ages, and we can know that with the word of Scripture that voice can never be telling us to sin, nor to go aside from the inferred teaching of the Church when it is consistent with Scripture. Though John Woolmer covers almost every way in which we may hear the inner voice, we are never given that awful assurance that we won't make a mistake or mishear. We are helped greatly in this area by a thorough examination of the blocks that may be set up which make it impossible for us to hear that voice: complacency, bitterness, guilt, cares of the world, and even involvement in strange or occult practices.

Perhaps I may be allowed to spell out, however, what this book makes possible, though perhaps never says explicitly: that in the end what we have to do is to trust and get on with living. This is a record of the saints and I look forward to perhaps another book in which the author will draw more of his examples from the lives of the saints. Their acknowledged lives of holiness give us more confidence in the way guidance came to them, and what they had to suffer in the clearing and the purifying of their hearts and minds so that they could hear clearly. But without doubt the glorious wealth of material drawn from modern experience and told as modern stories does help us to know that God's voice is still clearly heard today and can be heard by us. This is enriching and helpful.

How should this book be used? As I have said it is essentially personal (though never individualistic) so we must not be disappointed that it does not tackle some of the key texts of Scripture about hearing the Church in its more hierarchical and conciliar way. There is material about living in the Body in its more personal aspect; I suggest it is more important that we read the whole book through first, perhaps as quickly as possible, so that we get an overall picture. This is important, for it is also a very helpful reference book and we shall be tempted to use it simply in this way. Once we have read the book we shall be immensely helped to read again those passages which speak to us at the moment: guidance in relationships, perhaps, or guidance in our approach to death. We are beautifully trusted by the author not simply to find answers in his book, but to use it so that we may be encouraged to listen for the voice of God, knowing that He does speak personally to His beloved disciples. By reading the book we shall have a deep understanding of discernment and therefore a great confidence to perform God's holy will in our lives and to go on and on seeking His will and listening to His silent voice. I am sure that is why this book was written and I tingle with delight at the thought that God's message will come to His people. So He will be glorified and we shall live richly and in holiness within His Holy Church.

Peter Ball
Bishop of Lewes

INTRODUCTION

I am standing at the window of a guest room at Stanton House, Stanton, near Oxford. It is a house set aside for missionaries on furlough and others in need of spiritual refreshment.

Looking far away to the East, I can see the Chilterns; in the middle distance is the great expanse of Bernwood Forest, home of many of Britain's rarest butterflies; in the foreground are the trees of Stanton House's spacious garden. To the left, a towering Canadian redwood soars above the house, to the right an unusually elegant flowering lime; elsewhere, massive beech trees, horse-chestnuts, slim silver birches, all blend together to make a breathtaking landscape.

On the edge of the garden, a little stream flows swiftly, coots come quietly out of it looking for food on the lawn. Over the garden fence, a ripe cornfield awaits the reaper.

Closing my eyes, I can hear the occasional burst of traffic through the village, distant farm machinery, the cooing of the pigeons, the insistent tap of a woodpecker, the buzz of one or two flies, the gentle rhythm of the stream, and the rustling of the wind in the great trees.

Keeping deeper silence, I seem to hear the silent voice of God. I realise how fortunate I am to have a job which includes a time like this – and bishops who insist that priests take time to retreat each year. I begin to repent of my ingratitude to my Father for His calling which keeps me so desperately busy so much of the time. I remember my family enjoying the end of their summer holidays in different ways. I begin to remember how easily my eyes have become shut and my ears deaf, not only to God's silent voice, but to the wounded voices of His children.

The words of a haunting chorus 'Thank you, O my Father, for giving us your Son' repeat themselves over and over again in my mind. My prayer becomes urgent that anyone who reads this may not be distracted by my words, by my errors, by my prejudices, but despite them, may find something new of the Father whose silent voice is there for all to hear . . .

1

INQUIRE OF THE LORD

Some years ago, I returned to Oxford for the wedding of a friend. The bride looked beautiful, the church was full, and the wedding was a glorious blend of Anglican liturgy and exuberant spontaneity. The preacher started to read, and then to speak on, Psalm 27. One word stood out — Inquire. God's servants need to seek His face, behold His beauty, be taught, but above all to inquire of the Lord to discover His will for their spiritual journey.

I sat spellbound. I thought of the radiantly happy bride and remembered the times she had agonised over God's will — about church, about baptism and, above all, about marriage. I remembered her bewilderment at God's apparent silence and her steadfast faith amid so much uncertainty.

As I listened, the Lord seemed to speak to me. 'If you ever write another book, this is the subject on which I want you to write . . .' His silent voice spoke deep into my heart in a way that I have known before and have known since. I felt that inner certainty which, in the same church, had driven me towards commitment to Christ years earlier.

Then the sermon was over, the worship continued, the marriage vows were taken, and the wedding party began. The bride's father, a suffragan bishop, spoke movingly of his time in Kenya during the Mau Mau uprising. He spoke of God's protection of his baby daughter. In a quiet and dignified way, he gave a marvellous testimony to God's guidance and protection in times of extreme danger.

Just behind me in the church sat a man of whom, with good reason, I had been terrified. That day he, too, looked radiantly happy and wonderfully changed. Yet not long afterwards, he seemed to lose his way again, and his life disintegrated once more into chaos. I hope and pray that he will again hear the silent voice of God and rediscover the peace that he appeared to have found that day.

People ask 'Why don't I hear God's voice?' 'What's so special about you?' 'I envy your faith', 'Why should God want to speak to me?' The more searching add 'How do I recognise that it is God's voice – it may be my imagination, or even the Devil's voice?'

A CLASSIC CASE

For many of us, the story of the call of Samuel is an early childhood memory, one of those Old Testament stories beloved of children's picture Bibles and Sunday School teachers. It all seems so simple and so clear.

> Samuel was lying down in the temple of the Lord, where the ark of God was. Then the Lord called Samuel.
> Samuel answered 'Here I am.' And he ran to Eli and said 'Here I am; you called me.' But Eli said 'I did not call; go back and lie down' (1 Samuel 3: 3-5).

The rest of the story is equally familiar. Three times the Lord calls, three times Samuel wakes up old Eli. At last, Eli understands and tells the boy Samuel what to say:

> 'Speak, Lord, for your servant is listening.' So Samuel went and lay down in his place. The Lord came and stood

there calling as at the other times 'Samuel! Samuel!'
Then Samuel said 'Speak, for your servant is listening.'

It is seldom emphasised in either childhood or adult
lessons, that the Lord had a pretty terrible message for this
boy. The Word of the Lord had become rare, Eli was old
and feeble, his sons were a disgrace. God's message to Eli
(to some extent a repeat of that given by a 'Man of God'
in 1 Samuel 2) was that disaster was about to fall upon him
and his household. Not surprisingly, Samuel didn't want to
give this message to Eli. Eli, however, was still sufficiently
a man of God to want to hear, and commanded Samuel in
no uncertain terms to speak the truth.

After that 'The Lord was with Samuel as he grew up, and
he let none of his words fall to the ground.' (1 Samuel 3: 19).

We cannot know why the Lord chose to speak to Samuel.
There is a mystery in the sovereignty of God's dealings with
us. Nevertheless, there are several important clues. Samuel
had an exceptionally godly mother. Hannah had prayed
desperately for a child — so desperately that Eli thought
she was drunk. Poor Eli, so used to his sons' dissolute
behaviour, couldn't recognise a godly woman when he saw
one. Nevertheless when Eli recognised his mistake, he gave
Hannah his blessing and prayed that God would answer her
prayer. Very soon afterwards, Hannah conceived, and in
due course gave birth to a son. She named him Samuel which
means 'heard of God'. She also determined, with her
husband's consent, that he should be given to the Lord.

After this good beginning, 'Samuel continued to grow in
stature and in favour with the Lord and with men' (1 Samuel
2: 26) until the time when the Lord was ready to speak to
him for the first time. After that encounter, Samuel was
unflinching in his obedience to God, he was careful to listen
to all that God had to say, and God continued to reveal

Himself to Samuel in various ways.

It is extremely easy to despair at this point! We haven't had a believing parent, let alone an exceptionally godly one. We haven't heard God's voice. We wouldn't know what it would sound like. We don't like the idea of God speaking directly to us. We feel like Bishop Butler who, when confronted by the young John Wesley and his friend George Whitefield, was reduced to saying 'Mr Wesley, I will deal plainly with you. I once thought you and Mr Whitefield well meaning men; but I cannot think so now. For I have heard more of you: matters of fact, sir. And Mr Whitefield says in his journal "There are promises still to be fulfilled in me." Sir, the pretending to extraordinary revelations and gifts of the Holy Spirit is a horrid thing — a very horrid thing!'

But the point is, that although it is God's choice how, and when, and if, He chooses to speak to us, He nevertheless encourages us — commands us — to seek Him!

A MORE NORMAL STORY

Hannah began in despair. Her godly husband had two wives. Hannah seems to have been his favourite wife, but she was childless while her rival produced children with extraordinary regularity. The other wife provoked her and drove her to a state where she couldn't eat and spent her time crying.

Hannah went up to Shiloh, the holy place of the day, with Elkanah, her husband, her arch rival Peninnah, and all the children. At Shiloh Hannah prayed 'in bitterness of soul'. But at least she prayed! She had no idea of how God would answer, but she prayed and she made a vow. A pretty dramatic vow. She longed for a child; but if she received a son, she would give him to the Lord.

Hannah, not Samuel, I would suggest is a typical model

for us to follow. She faced not only barrenness, one of the worst social stigmas of the day, but also she had an impossible home situation. Furthermore, she lived in an age when the 'church' was in sharp decline and the Word of the Lord was rare! The Lord's chief servant, Eli, was hardly one to inspire faith.

In that situation, Hannah could easily have said 'My situation is hopeless, I've prayed for years and nothing has happened. My church is useless, its leaders are feeble, and things are going to get worse . . .'

But she didn't — she prayed. True, it was in bitterness of spirit. But it was sincere, heartfelt prayer. Prayer from the depths of a despairing, sad heart. Prayer that was backed with a sincere promise to God. Despite the circumstances both at home and in the church, Hannah 'inquired of the Lord'. She sought Him in the only place she knew, and He answered her. She heard His voice, she had only the rather tentative blessing of Eli, but she felt encouraged. She ate some food, felt better, and looked better. Next morning she worshipped God with the rest of the family, and soon afterwards Elkanah played his part, and the Lord answered her prayers.

It could scarcely be less dramatic. A modern counsellor might be tempted to say it was just a coincidence. Hannah looked better, felt better, and then the chemistry of her body changed. But Hannah knew differently. She had sought the Lord, and the Lord had given her the desire of her heart. (See Psalm 37: 4)

GOD'S LOVE FOR THE INDIVIDUAL

The Scriptures are very clear. We can, and must, seek the Lord. We can, and must, inquire in His temple. He may speak to us, clearly and audibly, as He did to Samuel. More probably, He will speak silently to our hearts, as He did to Hannah. But speak He will; if only we will take the trouble to search, and learn to listen for His silent voice.

I often meet people who think it rather arrogant, or absurd, to imagine that God should speak to them as individuals. They feel their problems are too small, or too big. They feel that God should be dealing with the really big problems — nuclear disarmament, drought, floods, apartheid, the greenhouse effect, the chaos in the Middle East, the affluence of the West . . . Individual guidance, individual communication from God to man, sounds like a theology that should be avoided by decent thinking people.

Now, I don't doubt for one moment that God is greatly concerned about all these major issues. I don't doubt for one moment that the Risen Lord is constantly driving individuals and churches towards greater prayer and greater action on these matters. I believe that the Archbishop of Canterbury's initiative over *Faith in the City* and The Church Urban Fund are under the direct inspiration of the Holy Spirit. But I would also dare to believe that God wants to communicate with, and work through, all individuals.

Jeremiah, that sad, lonely, haunted prophet, who has to bring God's message to a people who don't want to know, or hear, has a glorious message for the future:

'This is the covenant that I will make with the house of Israel after that time,' declares the Lord. 'I will put my law in their minds and write it on their hearts. I will be their God, and they will be my people. No longer will a man teach his neighbour, or a man his brother, saying "Know the Lord", because they will all know me from the least of them to the greatest,' declares the Lord. 'For I will forgive their wickedness and will remember their sins no more' (Jeremiah 31: 33-34).

God still wants to meet people at their point of need; He wants to redirect their lives through repentance and faith; He wants to send them out into the world to live and work for His glory. God would be God to the Hannahs of this world — surrounded by apparently insuperable domestic problems! God would be God to the Samuels of this world — men or women who will rule nations and influence, for good or ill, the prosperity of thousands.

'The fool says in his heart "There is no God" '(Psalm 53:1). A different sort of fool imagines that God doesn't want to guide his life. It is somewhat arrogant to imagine that we can organise our lives without reference to God — yet how many Christians get married, change jobs, move house, even change church, with little or no serious attempt to discover God's will for their situation?

Many people feel that God is only available at crises — it may be a 'good' crisis like marriage or baptism, or after a safe childbirth. More usually it is a 'bad' crisis like divorce, unemployment, serious illness, or bereavement. It is undeniable that God does find many people at such a point in their lives; but that is very different from seeking Him day by day, or inquiring in His Temple.

Sadly, many serious people, and this includes church-goers and church officers, have little idea of how to seek God. They try to live their lives according to the Christian code — the Ten Commandments, the Sermon on the Mount, sporadic, or even regular, Sunday worship, being a good neighbour and a responsible citizen, interspersed with occasional bursts of enthusiasm — yet in the midst of it all, they have little or no sense of God's presence.

Not surprisingly, they feel frustrated. Uninspired by safe worship, which doesn't impinge on their daily life, threatened by some more direct approaches which can seem irreverent and out of place; yet deep down, they still have an intuitive faith. Deep down, they would like to know . . .

GUIDELINES FOR THE SEARCH

So, how do we begin to 'inquire of the Lord'? What does it involve? I am going, at this stage, to identify six principal areas where the search may begin – the Bible, worship, the Body of Christ, prayer, creation or nature, and the circumstances of our lives.

Many people start their search with the Scriptures. In a real sense, there is no better place to begin. Unfortunately, the Bible is a very difficult book. People, especially children and prisoners, start with Genesis and get lost in Exodus (or certainly in Leviticus). Others start with the Gospels and feel they've read it all before (which is probably untrue), or else they are out of their depth in the Epistles, or bewildered by the spiritual experiences in Acts.

Of course, God has spoken to many people directly through the Bible. My hope is that this book will constantly drive you back to the Bible! Prisoners have been converted through Gideon Bibles in their cells – Vic Jackopson, author of many books, Bible reading notes, and pioneer of Hope Now Ministries, is a classic example. Patricia St John[1] gives an example of someone converted through a few fragments of Scripture bought casually in a wayside market. Other such examples abound.

Sadly, for most English people, the Bible still remains an effectively closed book (if you don't believe me, look at any congregation with Bibles in their pews trying to find the Epistle to the Romans). Some have struggled, in childhood, with the Family Bible – the Authorised Version. Despite

its magnificent English and godly translators, it is difficult
to read without a good literary background, or a strong
religious upbringing. Some have been put off at school by
cavalier methods of biblical criticism which have questioned
the historicity of parts of the Bible without giving any real
answers or encouragements to persist.

It was a great moment for me when an afternoon nurture
group consisting (as I think they would agree!) of some very
ordinary people, started to read Mark's Gospel in the Good
News Bible. They read the whole of it, and came back
thrilled. They came with lots of questions, and inspired me
to read the whole of St Mark in three services at Evensong.

Perhaps one of the best starting places would be Isaiah
55. Not only is there the encouragement to seek the Lord,
but there is also the invitation 'Come, all you who are
thirsty, come to the waters, and you who have no money,
come, buy and eat! Come, buy wine and milk without
money and without cost.' (Isaiah 55: 1)

WORSHIP

Many people, perfectly reasonably, start searching for God
in church. They come to services and expect to find Him
there. Now, undoubtedly, God does meet many people
through worship. Indeed, I believe that if a church is truly
worshipping God, newcomers will either find God fairly
quickly, or will turn away because they don't really want
to hear God's voice. I am sure that God meets people
through the most traditional services, and also through the
freer, less traditional forms of worship. I shall look at this
question more thoroughly in Chapter 6. For the moment,
I am concerned with our attitude when we come to worship.
Do we come to 'get something out of the service'? Do we

come because we like the music (or the vicar, or our neighbour who goes)? Do we come because we are lonely and hope to meet a few friendly people?

All these motives are quite common, and are not necessarily bad. Most people came to hear Jesus because they had needs, or because they were attracted by the crowds and His reputation, not because they thought He was the Messiah.

Sadly, many people are put off from searching for God via worship for fairly trivial reasons.

'They've changed the services — they've altered the time — the church is cold — last time I went nobody spoke to me (I was first out of the church) — I don't like the vicar — the church is full of hypocrites (come and make one more!) — I can't stand the modern hymns — I don't want to change — I haven't time — I can worship God on my own . . .'

God has appointed worship as a prime way in which 'we may seek His face', and His Son, Jesus Christ, commanded us 'This is my body given for you; do this in remembrance of me' (Luke 22:19). Worship is not an optional extra, nor is it an unfortunate duty added to the lives of over-busy Christians. It is one of the essential ways of discovering God and His will for us.

THE BODY OF CHRIST

God has organised His people so that they are dependent on one another. 'As you come to him, the living Stone — rejected by men but chosen by God and precious to him — you also, like living stones, are being built into a spiritual house to be a holy priesthood, offering spiritual sacrifices acceptable to God through Jesus Christ ' (1 Peter 2: 4-5).

We may not like it, but we need one another. People are

always surprised by how hard it is to pray for healing for oneself (see Chapter 12), and how necessary is the guidance and ministry of others. 'Inquiring of the Lord' may sound like a very individualistic occupation, yet we shall certainly need to allow what we hear to be tested by others; and, sometimes, we shall only hear through the wisdom and insight of others.

It is desperately easy to be put off by others! They may scoff, and dampen the Lord's voice, they may enthuse and run far ahead of the Lord, but frequently they will provide some much needed wisdom and confirmation to what we think we've received.

PRAYER

Many of us begin our search for God with some desperate prayer at a crucial stage of our lives. 'Lord, please get me out of this mess − Lord, please help me through this exam (even though I haven't worked very hard) − Lord, please make X fall in love with me − Lord, please make my wedding day fine − Lord, please save my marriage − Lord, what do you want me to do? − Lord, why do I feel so ill? − Lord, why can't I control this bad habit? − Lord, please find me a job . . .'

We soon discover that realistic, regular prayer is unbelievably difficult. The world we live in (and the church we worship in) seems so noisy, we are so busy, so tired, how can we find time and space to seek God through prayer?

Prayer is the way, above all other ways, to hearing God's silent voice (see Chapter 9). It was Jesus' way. It was the way of the great men and women of the Bible. It was the way of the great saints. James Montgomery in his hymn puts it most eloquently:[2]

Lord, teach us how to pray aright
With reverence and with fear.
Though dust and ashes in Thy sight,
We may, we must, draw near.

Prayer requires a strange mixture of spontaneity and discipline. Without discipline, we shall seldom pray,[3] we shall seldom find time, and when we do, we shall be disorganised and ill-prepared. Without spontaneity, we shall lapse into dry repetitions of 'Our Father', personal shopping lists, and desperate confessions of our continued failings.

True prayer may require a very long time − our Lord spending a night on the mountain before choosing the twelve (Luke 6:12), or just an opportune second − Nehemiah's arrow prayer before answering Artaxerxes' searching question (Nehemiah 2:4).

Prayer ultimately should become a way of life, something as natural as breathing. Yet even those who experience prayer whatever they are doing − washing up, or worshipping in a traffic jam, or on the mountainside, teaching or learning − know that they need special times of prayer and sometimes special places.

THE VOICE OF THE CREATOR

Many people most naturally find God in their garden, or in the countryside. There is nothing wrong with that. The Bible, and Christian history, are full of people who have found God in such natural ways. I have often found that the beauty of nature compels a spiritual response. I used to have rooms just above a most glorious magnolia tree. For most of the year it was just a mass of untidy green leaves, then each spring it would burst into a few weeks of breath-taking glory. Nearby was the garden of a Diocesan Retreat House with perfectly proportioned copper beeches. Surveying these from a first floor chapel led me to meditate on the permanence of the Church of God. Many branches, millions of leaves, yet one great vertical trunk reaching inexorably towards the sky. The magnolia seemed to stand for the burst of glory and cheering on Palm Sunday, the beech for the eternal certainty of the faith. We need both!

God has often used nature to speak to me, and there is a long tradition for this in Christian writing, and in Scripture. There is a danger that we shall construct God in our own image. There is a danger that we will settle for a vague pantheism and miss the glory of the Lord's revelation in Jesus. Nevertheless, for many people nature, despite its redness in tooth and claw, is a gateway to a real experience of the silent voice of God.

CIRCUMSTANTIAL GUIDANCE

Circumstances often lead people to God. They move next to a godly neighbour. At a point of crisis, someone turns up to help, and they wonder at the source of his/her inner source of strength. They fall in love with a Christian. They become parents and start to wonder about the meaning of life, and their responsibilities to their newborn baby. A friend or relative dies, and they wonder about the possibility of a future life. They have a real need, and someone offers to pray. Sometimes the circumstances are more unusual.

A man I know used to speak to people about his faith on railway journeys. Surprisingly, this led to many good conversions, until one day he shared his faith and tried to evangelise an elderly gentleman. He turned out to be a bishop. My friend was offered the job as Diocesan Evangelist! I made a permanent friend on a railway journey. He was even responsible for my first book, written twenty years after our first meeting.

Circumstances led me to an even more important meeting. I had been writing a dramatic reading based on the life of John Wesley. I was very struck by his depressed words:

'I went to convert the Indians, but who will convert me?'

I wrote along these lines to Canon Keith de Berry, then Rector of St Aldate's, my chief spiritual director. He summoned me on an Oxford working party at Lee Abbey. There, like others before and since, I met my wife to be!

The Christian doesn't look for signs in the sky (see Jesus' teaching in Matthew 16: 1-4), but he does learn that God is the master of his circumstances. Once he believes that, life becomes much more positive. There is a hymn which expresses this perfectly – 'Thy way, not mine, O Lord.'[4] One verse runs:

> I dare not choose my lot
> I would not if I might
> Choose Thou for me, my God
> So shall I walk aright.

That was a favourite hymn of a very dear member of our church. I remember getting a very clear spiritual nudge to visit him in hospital. I discovered that, unexpectedly, he was dying. He asked me to bring him communion, and as we prayed, I sensed his complete and gentle surrender to God as his life ebbed away.

In conclusion, I believe that God does want to speak to us, guide us, and reveal His will to us. Sometimes the way will be dramatic and clear like His call to Samuel, sometimes it will be painful and through something totally natural like His answer to Hannah. The main avenues are the Bible, worship, the Body of Christ, prayer, creation or nature, and circumstances. Before we begin experiencing His guidance over particular issues, we will need to have established a living relationship with Him. Until we have responded to His covenant love, it is unwise to expect too much in the way of guidance. God's providence is available to all, His silent voice to those who, through repentance and faith, have learnt what it means to 'inquire of the Lord'.

But, before we proceed too far, there is one great question – *How can I know if it is God's voice?*

In an absolute sense we can't. We have to respond to it in faith, and any step of faith involves a measure of stepping into the unknown. Nevertheless, there are a number of ways in which guidance can and should be tested.

(1) *Is the guidance in agreement with the overall teaching of Scripture?*
Too often I have met people whose instincts and emotions have led them into situations which are clearly contrary to Scripture. This is especially true in the difficult area of relationships.

(2) *What is the spiritual standing of the person claiming to offer guidance (or to having been guided)?*
Obviously, God does sometimes use strange messengers – Balaam and his ass, for instance! (Numbers 22:20 ff). But far too many immature people race around with 'words from the Lord' for unsuspecting bystanders. It requires a great deal of maturity, and due humility, to offer guidance to others.

(3) *What do our closest spiritual advisers think?*
They won't always be right, but usually God will use our closest Christian friends and trusted leaders to confirm or

block some course of action. We need to learn to be dependent upon the Body of Christ.

(4) *What is the inner witness in our own hearts?*
God's voice is usually gentle and persistent, not loud and instantaneous. The world, the flesh and the Devil may all try to manipulate us into taking instant decisions, God usually allows us time. If His voice is urgent, it will usually be confirmed with independent and unexpected signs.

(5) *Am I prepared to admit that I may be wrong?*
The greatest pastoral tragedies seem to occur when people insist that they've heard God's voice, and then conclude that everyone else is wrong!

Notes and references

1 St John, Patricia. *Would you believe it? You can grow to know God*. Pickering, 1983, pp26-28.
2 Hymns Ancient and Modern Revised. No 317.
3 Foster, Richard J. *Celebration of Discipline: the path to spiritual growth*. London, Hodder & Stoughton, 1984.
4 Hymns Ancient and Modern Revised. No 356.

2

CONFUSION AND SILENCE

People often complain that they have no sense of God's presence. They pray and get no help, they seek guidance and get more confused, they try to worship and feel nothing.

Many people describe their attempts at prayer as like trying to break through a brick wall. Often the brick wall seems to symbolise a spiritually closed in person who doesn't have any real commitment to Christ. Many perfectly normal 'good' people find that they cannot pray and they wonder why. Isaiah has some blunt words 'Your iniquities have separated you from your God' (Isaiah 59:2). At this stage it is not usually a particular sin, but rather the sin of leaving God out of one's life. For some, this is increased by the knowledge that promises made to God at confirmation, weddings, family baptisms, times of trouble and illness, have not been kept.

Frequently, a real commitment to Christ has led to the brick wall being demolished and an effective prayer life beginning.

One woman said she used to feel God's presence, but now felt absolutely nothing. She had professed faith as a teenager, somewhat lapsed, and had recently started to try and find God by reading the Bible. But she felt a total block and compete lack of God's presence. A retired missionary discovered that her Bible was a version produced by a sect for their own doctrinal purposes. The missionary felt that this was a block and so it proved. The book was thrown out, the question of rededication to Christ and a real desire to receive afresh the Holy Spirit was prayed about and a period of tremendous spiritual growth ensued.

We all need to get on our knees before God, and consider prayerfully the barriers which prevent us from enjoying His presence and hearing His voice. I have identified seven — need for conversion, bitterness, guilt, complacency, despair, dangerous paths and the cares of the world.

THE NEED FOR CONVERSION

Unless we get conversion sorted out, the rest of our communication with God will inevitably be a mixture of muddle and disappointment.

First, a negative point, people can have spiritual experiences which are not from God.

> Dear friends, do not believe every spirit, but test the spirits to see whether they are from God, because many false prophets have gone out into the world. This is how you can recognise the Spirit of God: Every spirit that acknowledges that Jesus Christ has come in the flesh is from God, but every spirit that does not acknowledge Jesus is not from God. This is the spirit of the antichrist which you have heard is coming and even now is already in the world (1 John 4: 1-3).

For a somewhat extreme example, read the story of Madam Zelda in Chapter 13.

Second, God often gives people genuine experiences before they are converted. I can remember listening to

Lenten addresses at school when I was about fourteen. I was sure that I heard God speaking, but I didn't know what to do or how to respond.

Third, people at crisis points – good crises like marriage, or the birth of children, or painful crises like illness, unemployment, or bereavement – often experience God's love in a new way. This is often a preparation for a life-changing encounter soon afterwards.

Fourth, each person's spiritual path is unique. Samuel (see Chapter 1), was dedicated to God from the time of conception. Some people grow up in a Christian family, always hearing and trusting God's voice. There will be a time of public commitment, such as adult baptism or confirmation, yet there may be no clear moment of conversion.

Fifth, it is most unhelpful to tell someone they are within God's kingdom when there is no real evidence. I was a regular church-goer, lesson reader, Bible reader, member of Christian Union, and when I faced a spiritual crisis, my local vicar was sympathetic, but said 'They're trying to convert you, you don't need that!' although he was a godly man, he failed to discern my need and was unable to guide me at a crucial moment in my life.

After conversion, there is often a honeymoon period for the new Christian, we seem to hear God's voice in a fresh and wonderful way. Prayers are answered, but then the blocks reappear. We now examine a few more!

BITTERNESS BLOCKS THE SPIRIT

As we learn to pray, so we will begin 'to inquire of the Lord' and as we begin to inquire, so He will begin to speak. But like the Israelites of old, we may find when we come to the springs, hoping for sweet water, they actually taste bitter

(Exodus 15:23). And that bitterness is not in God, it is in us!

So many of us cannot truly say the Lord's prayer. 'Forgive us our trespasses, as we forgive those who trespass against us.' Time and again, as I talk to people who are making no spiritual progress, I come up against this bitterness. Sometimes it is deep in the past. One friend had a mother who was always devaluing her and putting her down. The effect was devastating. Slight hurts got exaggerated, unintended remarks were misconstrued, and a fruitful Christian discipleship was full of painful pauses. We shall look at this question in more detail later in the book. Meanwhile, a practical suggestion – ask God, through His Holy Spirit, to show you any people from the past who have hurt you, whose conduct you need to forgive. It may be parents, it may be schoolteachers, it may be bullies at school, it may be friends. Then begin to pray to forgive them.

Bitterness does not only lie locked in the past. It is easy to allow present bitterness to creep into our spiritual life. We are easily jealous of others in the church and this can lead to a most unattractive bitterness about life in general and the church in particular. Clergy are jealous of contemporaries, or juniors, who are promoted. Lay members of the congregation are jealous as others take responsible positions in the local church. This is increasingly a problem in churches which have a shared ministry. This 'second tier' of leadership – vital to the growth and health of every church – can leave others feeling disillusioned and rejected.

Then a root of bitterness creeps in (Hebrews 12:15). Once that root is present, like ground elder in a garden, it spreads everywhere. Bitterness against one individual becomes multiplied to bitterness against all authority figures and ultimately becomes bitterness with the whole church and even with the Lord.

We have valiantly battled with the ground elder in our garden. The solution seems to be vigorous attacks in the spring, followed by extensive planting so that the ground is put to better use. I have battled with individuals in some churches. The solution seems to be radical repentance in the spiritual springtime, followed by extensive opening to God's grace and new learning and new work in His field.

Of course there are many other causes of bitterness; painful illness, divorce or marital troubles, unemployment, being swindled, slander, being passed over for promotion and so on. These, and many other things, can make us bitter. But they need not! Just as Moses, under God's instruction, could make the waters sweet (Exodus 15:25), so we, under God's direct instruction or through the help of a spiritual adviser, can find the waters sweetened – or at the very least made drinkable!

But make no mistake, 'Without holiness no one will see the Lord' (Hebrews 12:14) and, as the writer to the Hebrews makes plain, bitterness is an immediate and total block to holiness.

GUILT

Guilt is another great barrier to hearing God. Sometimes, our guilt is correct, our feelings are deserved, and we will not hear God's voice until we repent and as far as possible put the matter right.

I remember feeling out of fellowship with a member of a congregation. I was about to preach. During the hymn before the sermon, I knew that I had to make a long walk down the church aisle to start to put the matter right! Feeling guilty, convicted of sin (John 16:8), led me to the right action.

A man feels a hypocrite in church. He feels that God isn't pleased with him. He knows that he is taking his spiritual life for granted. God has blessed him greatly in the past, but now he is ignoring God. Rightly, he feels guilty. Then he begins to stay away from church. This affects his family, it affects his church.

'If one part suffers, every part suffers' (1 Corinthians 12:26). As I write with a painful finger, my whole body suffers. If one church member stays away, all are diminished.

Now, in a way, God is speaking to our absent friend. He is teaching him not to take Him for granted. God is showing him a way forward. Communication isn't broken, but it has become somewhat blocked and confined to just one issue. Sometimes, through guilt or some other means, God has to speak to us about just one issue in order to re-open wider channels of communication. The true solution , of course, is not for my friend to go on feeling guilty, but rather for him to swallow his pride, confess his sin, return to the church fellowship, thereby encouraging the Body of Christ, his family, and himself, by one right action.

The divorcee continues to feel guilty for his or her part in a failed marriage. Again, this may initially be correct. But in the end, if forgiveness is genuinely sought, then guilt is no longer justified. So often the feeling of guilt is compounded by the consequences of the action. The mistakes which I have made as a teacher, as a priest, as a father, are liable to continue to trouble me, if I have to live with their consequences. Yet the God of the Scriptures declares quite clearly that He wants to forgive me. Satan, on the other hand, stands revealed (Revelation 12:10) as the 'accuser of the brethren'.

Guilt and depression are closely associated. People like me who have a naturally depressive nature, are prone to feelings of false or excessive guilt. Again and again, we need to understand the nature of God and believe His word.

'If we claim to be without sin, we deceive ourselves and the truth is not in us. If we confess our sins, he is faithful and just and will forgive us our sins and purify us from all unrighteousness' (1 John 1: 8-9).

False guilt, like bitterness, often has its roots in the past. Exacting parents with Victorian standards of conduct, but lacking the compensating love, will produce guilt-ridden children. Sometimes we parents, like certain schoolteachers, make our offspring feel that they can do nothing right.

Although the God of the Bible spends much Divine Energy pointing out the sins of His people, He always has time for praise and acceptance — of Solomon (1 Kings 3:10) — of Jeremiah (Jeremiah 1: 7-8) — of Paul (2 Corinthians 12:9 and Acts 23:11). And there is joy in heaven over one sinner that repents (Luke 15: 7-10). God does not want His people riddled with unnecessary guilt. There is enough sin in the world without us adding to the pile of misery. We are very unlikely to have committed unpardonable apostasy — if we had we wouldn't be seeking help from Christian counsel, books or prayer. We are almost certain not to have committed the unforgivable sin. Mark makes it clear that this was the ultimate sin of saying that Jesus' power came from Beelzebub — the prince of the devils. Have you or I, even in our wildest moments, accused Jesus of that?

COMPLACENCY

Outside the church, and on the fringes of the church, for every guilt-ridden person there are probably a dozen complacent ones. I well remember a scene at my theological college. The editor of a popular daily newspaper had come to meet us. He sat in the common room, puffing a cigar, talking to and questioning us. Then he produced the immortal line 'I admire you chaps for all you're trying to do; but I've got my yacht, I've got my paper, and I've got my wife!'

And that, in a way, is the Church's biggest problem. So many people apparently have all that they need. So many Christians apparently have all that they need. They're comfortably off, they have a pleasant home, good friends, work and the Christian faith as a comforting insurance policy in the event of death or some other disaster.

Talk of renewal, direct intervention by God or the like, is met by amused scorn. We don't need those sort of naive ideas (and, as the Church ordination selector said to me, 'We hope you will grow out of them!'). Complacency allows churches to ignore the social problems at their doorstep. Complacency, allied with a decent bit of misinformation, allows churches to duck out of Third World and political issues. Complacency deadens the individual's conscience, keeps God at a safe distance, dismisses revelation as an unnecessary enthusiasm, and gently pours scorn on those who think otherwise.

Complacency was the spiritual undoing of the Pharisees (Luke 18:9); complacency allowed the German church to succumb virtually without a murmur to Hitler in the 1930s. Complacency sees no need for sermons, doesn't wish to be challenged by the Word of God, regards fasting and spiritual discipline as a foolish foible. Complacency talks at length in platitudes, finds good reasons for inaction, rejoices in the status quo, regrets the decline of the Church, but has little to offer.

Complacency creeps up on middle-aged clergy – especially those with growing congregations. Complacency ignores the wounded sheep — it's their fault! Complacency has no time to listen to God. Complacency does little wrong — and even less right. As I started writing I read the words of a complacent prophet.

> In the fifth month of that same year, the fourth year, early in the reign of Zedekiah, King of Judah, the prophet Hananiah son of Azzur, who was from Gibeon, said to me in the house of the Lord in the presence of the priests and all the people: "This is what the Lord Almighty, the God of Israel, says: 'I will break the yoke of the king of Babylon. Within two years I will bring back to this place all the articles of the Lord's house that Nebuchadnezzar king of Babylon removed from here and took to Babylon. I will also bring back to this place Jehoiachin son of Jehoiakim king of Judah and all the other exiles from Judah who went to Babylon,' declares the Lord, 'for I will break the yoke of the king of Babylon' "
>
> (Jeremiah 28:1-4).

Smooth words, comforting words, just what the people wanted to hear. Not, however, the true word of the Lord. It was left to Jeremiah, a lonely and haunted man, to reply. In no uncertain terms, he denounced Hananiah, prophesied further doom for Jerusalem and personal disaster for Hananiah. A few months later he was vindicated. Hananiah died, and there was no sign of a return of the exiles or their treasure. In fact, worse was to follow. Jerusalem was besieged, Zedekiah captured, and many more were taken into captivity.

With hindsight, it is easy to see that Jeremiah was right, just as it is easy to see that Winston Churchill was right when, almost alone, he stood out in 1938 against Neville Chamberlain's declaration of 'Peace in our time'.

But what are we to make of someone whom many call a modern prophet, Dr Clifford Hill, who at a meeting called by Action for Biblical Witness to our Nation in March 1988, tore his clerical stock and collar in two in symbolic demonstation of how the Lord would rend the Church of England for misusing its position and failing to proclaim God's word faithfully (unless, that is, the church visibly repents).

Is this God's word to me today? Is it wholly true? Partly true, or man's exaggeration expressing the frustration felt by many at the confused and vacillating stance of the Church of England on so many important issues? None of us likes real prophets! I didn't enjoy Jeremiah's denunciation of Hananiah's smooth words. I liked even less Dr Clifford Hill's Jeremiah-like acted parable. Later on we must consider what God may be saying to us through creation (Chapter 10). It's all too easy to accept the beauty of nature, and yet totally ignore what is being said to us about the destruction of the environment. Prophets have a hard journey through life. They are not infallible! Even Jeremiah was hardly right to curse the day that he was born (Jeremiah 20:14). Dr Clifford Hill might be wrong. But, as a man of God, much that he prophesies will be from the Lord. Few will thank him for that. Complacency is our natural defence against the Word of God. 'Did God really say that?' is a common sceptical reaction.

If we want to 'inquire of the Lord', we must be prepared for our complacent spirituality to be shaken, we must be prepared for new adventures, new directions, new responsibilities. When I first prayed about the question of ordination, the Lord didn't answer for nearly a year. When He did, it began to shake my complacent satisfaction about my spirituality – or lack of it – and where my life was going.

DESPAIR, DISILLUSIONMENT, AND FEAR

A fifth block is despair, or its close ally disillusionment; both these often stem from an ungodly fear. We've prayed for a loved one's illness – and they've got worse and died. We've struggled to bring our children up to go to church and they've rebelled. We read about the goings on in General Synod, and we wonder whether the church we belong to stands for anything. We've made occasional excursions into piety – attended Lent courses, even been on retreat, joined the inevitable church house group – and we've found little help. God may speak to other people, but He certainly doesn't seem to speak to me. Thomas is the classic disillusioned disciple (John 11:16; 20:24 ff). Faced with the news of friend Lazarus' death, he produces the most nihilistic of comments – 'Let us also go (to Judea) that we may die with him.' With an outlook like that, it is hardly surprising that Thomas wasn't there after the Resurrection, when Jesus showed himself to the remaining ten. Despairing disciples never are there at the right time. They hear the wrong sermons, they read the wrong biblical texts – time and again I've counselled those in despair who pick out from a Bible reading the one thing that needn't apply to them. It's as though I, reading Jeremiah 28 for Matins on the day I started writing decided that I was like Hananiah with a false word for the people. Rationally, it is at least as likely that I am a Jeremiah figure with a true word from the Lord. But if I'm a despairing, Thomas-like disciple, I shall misread the situation. Despairing disciples invariably find the wrong counsellors, read the wrong books and drive others towards despair.

Some, like Thomas, escape by presenting God with a direct challenge. Unless . . . I will not believe! This is scarcely a recommended method, as it comes dangerously close to blackmailing God. Peter, in his despair, learnt first to weep and then to accept Jesus' threefold restoration. Paul, in prison and awaiting almost certain death, could reasonably have despaired. Instead he sought practical help from Timothy, Mark, Luke and, above all, the Lord.

Disillusioned disciples need discernment. We may feel troubled by the state of our Church, either national or local. But part of the answer will be with us. Our local church can only be revitalised by our own renewal. As we seek with others to hear God's voice and to follow His way, great things can happen. When dead bones live it is invariably because a few saints have taken time to pray, to praise and to keep faith. Many a 'renewed' church, humanly, owes its renewal to a few insignificant, unseen members battling in prayer.

For others, however, some great personal anguish causes complete despair. They've watched a loved one decline and die. God apparently did nothing. Here, then, is a real religious crux. We will not go far in evangelism, in healing, or even in social action, without finding this sort of crisis. Canon Vanstone's masterpiece *The Stature of Waiting*[1] helps — especially in his majestic story of the bishop lying helpless and blind in bed as his life ebbed away.

'As one stood beside him on a particular morning, some weeks before his death, one had a sudden and overwhelming impression that something of extraordinary significance was going on before one's eyes.' The significance, the stature of waiting, lay not in the bishop's courage (he was past that) but in his helplessness. Open only to the world, the ravages of death, and God.

God understands despair! The Psalmist knew it frequently (Psalm 40, for example), the prophets knew it (not only Jeremiah!), Jesus knew it as He wept over Jerusalem (Luke 19:41 ff) and as He agonised in Gethsemane (Luke 22:39

ff), Christians throughout history have known it. God is very close to us when we suffer — if only we will learn to look for signs of His presence.

I was an only child. The night of my mother's funeral was particularly poignant. My father was bearing up quite well — a false dawn, he was soon to relapse into utter despair — but I felt terrible. Through tears I read these words:

'I tell you the truth, you will weep and mourn while the world rejoices. You will grieve, but your grief will turn into joy' (John 16:20).

God had spoken, and the next verse, about the joy of a woman after the suffering of childbirth, seemed to show how my particular sorrow would be overcome. So it proved.

Fear is one of the most negative of all emotions. Fear leads to lying, cheating, distorted relationships, paralysed inactivity, disobedience to God's word, and a host of other problems.

Fear gets some Christians in a terrible tangle. We are afraid of hurting people, so instead of talking directly to them, we gossip and hurt them and others far more. Christians forming relationships (see Chapter 11) get into amazing twists. We are afraid to say what we really feel and leave people deeply and unnecessarily hurt.

When we are afraid, we cannot hear God's voice and our faith disappears. The disciples were full of fear during the storm at sea (Matthew 8:23 ff); Jesus slept calmly.

There is, of course, a proper holy fear which calls for reverence and awe on our part (Hebrews 12: 25-28).

DANGEROUS PATHS

There are many dangerous paths in seeking to inquire of the Lord. I shall cover this topic more fully in Chapter 13.

Suffice it to say at this stage that all mediumistic paths are
forbidden. Deuteronomy 18:9 ff is quite clear! Divination,
sorcery, spiritism . . . are all out. Tarot cards and ouija
boards are out. All cause confµsion, and are liable to bring
a chain of false guidance, spiritual depression, and even
demonisation.

Christians are particularly vulnerable. Baptism contains
a prayer of exorcism. Those who turn to Christ after baptism
and confirmation need to renounce all occult practices. It
is particularly dangerous to receive prayer for the 'baptism
of the Holy Spirit' without prior renunciation of all occult
links. This can apply (Exodus 20:5) to previous generations
in our family tree. Occultism is like a poisonous ivy which
creeps up our family tree harming one generation and then
another.

But if all that is obvious, other dangerous perils are less
easily recognised. Many have a seemingly gentle slope which
can suddenly turn into a spiritual precipice.

Freemasonry has been much debated recently. While I
don't doubt that there are sincere Christians who are
Masons, I believe them to be misguided. Rituals with strange
names for 'god', strange ceremonies and the alleged danger
of inner networks in business, police, or church are to be
avoided. Each Mason must judge these and other practices
with his own conscience. But I've known Christians who,
as they've really listened to hear the Lord's voice, have felt
that they must renounce the Masonic way.

Yoga and Transcendental Meditation (TM) are other
dangerous paths. Yoga practised purely as a physical form
of release can apparently do much good and little obvious
harm. Yet the underlying philosophy is in Eastern religion.
Those learning yoga are liable to be given a 'mantra' −
often the name of a Hindu deity to repeat. Is it surprising
if this causes a spiritual block?[2]

Meditation is an important part of the Christian's prayer life. I shall have more to say about this. But TM, or any other meditation technique, is not usually under the direction of the Holy Spirit. It may help to sweep the room clean — but what does it let in? (Luke 11:24 ff).

The Christian who wishes to love His Lord will want to please Him in every way. Psalm 119 presents a marvellous picture of spiritual purity — the result is:

'Your word is a lamp to my feet and a light for my path' (Psalm 119:105).

Dare we ask for less? Dare we be neutral about other lamps which light other paths?

Such words seem hard, such words are harsh to write. They are written not to condemn these ways — Freemasonry may bring friendship to lonely people, yoga and TM may bring rest to the weary — but to warn those seeking the Lord that these do not appear to be His ways.

In *Pilgrims' Progress* Christian and Faithful wandered into Doubting Castle because they took an attractive looking short cut. The path disappeared, night came, the storm crashed down, and in the morning they were a sitting target for Giant Despair and his wife Diffidence.

THE CARES OF THE WORLD

Finally, and most important of all, the cares of the world remain the greatest potential barrier. In the parable of the sower (Mark 4:1 ff), and similarly in the Sermon on the Mount, Jesus described them as the worries of this life, the deceitfulness of wealth, and the desires for other things. What a penetrating description of life today! Worries about this life fill doctors' waiting rooms with anxious, guilt-ridden patients who need, above all, to find God's peace. The deceitfulness of wealth causes many to work long hours and ignore their families and the voice of God. It must be admitted that some have to work like this even to make ends meet. Even more than in Britain, I was struck by the situation in Yugoslavia where everyone seemed to need a second, moonlighting, job to help cope with the ravages of inflation. The desire for other things, especially success, can lead clergy and church leaders away from the voice of God. Sadly, we are full of cares, anxieties and wrong priorities.

Most church programmes are concerned with survival — of the building and the congregation. We have little vision, or time, for spiritual growth and listening to the Lord. Our numbers are falling — let's have a mission! Our buildings are crumbling — let's have an appeal! We want to be successful, we want to be listened to, so we are full of schemes and plans. We need to listen to some of Jesus' strongest warnings — 'Not everyone who says to me, "Lord, Lord," will enter the kingdom of heaven, but only he who does the will of my Father who is in heaven. Many will say to me on that day, "Lord, Lord, did we not prophesy in your name, and in your name drive out demons and perform many miracles?" Then I will tell them plainly, "I never knew you. Away from me, you evildoers!" ' (Matthew 7: 21-23).

Yet there is time, if only we'd all realise it and make the right use of it. At its most basic, time spent in prayer and quiet will refresh and release us in such a way that we get far more done, far better and far faster.

Michel Quoist puts it beautifully:[3]

I went out, Lord.
Men were coming out.

They were coming and going,
Walking and running.
Everything was rushing, cars, lorries, the street, the whole
    town.
Men were rushing not to waste time.
They were rushing after time . .
To catch up with time,
To gain time . . .

And so all men run after time, Lord.
They pass through life running – hurried, jostled,
    overburdened, frantic, and they never get there.
    They haven't time.
In spite of all their efforts they're still short of time,
    of a great deal of time.
Lord, you must have made a mistake in your calculations.
There is a big mistake somewhere.
The hours are too short,
The days are too short,
Our lives are too short . . .

Lord, I have time,
I have plenty of time,
All the time that you give me,
The years of my life,
The days of my years . . .

I am not asking you tonight, Lord, for time to do this
    and then that,
But your grace to do conscientiously, in the time that you
    give me, what you want me to do.

God has a plan for each of us and for our families, for
our church, even, dare I say it, for our national Church and

our nation. But if our concern is to make more money − or even just enough money to live in the way to which we are accustomed − if our concern is our concerns; if our mind is ever on the daily round, the common task, then we will not stop to listen for the still, small voice. And if we don't stop to listen, we shall fail to hear it when we really need to.

God wants to speak to us! He wants to begin to teach us to listen. Tomorrow? In twenty years' time when we retire? No, He intends His voice to be heard by each one of us − today.

Notes and references

1 Vanstone, W H. *The Stature of Waiting*. London, Darton, Longman and Todd, 1982, p 67.
2 Green, Michael. *I believe in Satan's downfall*. London, Hodder & Stoughton, 2nd edn, 1988.
3 Quoist, Michel. Extract from: 'Lord, I have the time' In: *Prayers of Life*. Dublin, Gill and Macmillan, 1983. Reproduced with permission of the publishers.

3

LIVING WORD

(Some Old Testament examples)

The Old Testament contains a wonderfully varied series of instances where God speaks to people, and where people seek God. The means of communication may be extraordinary, surprising, commonplace, even puzzling and confusing. Sometimes the communication seems to be utterly lacking, at others it seems no more than a series of guidelines.

We shall look briefly at Abraham, Jeremiah, Nehemiah, a few Psalms, and at Ecclesiastes. I hope this may encourage us to search other parts of the Old Testament and discover the remarkable ways in which God's ancient dealings with men and women throw light on His dealings with us today. Very recently, I listened to a series of addresses on Jacob and was amazed at how his twisting series of encounters with God and his family could be applied to today's world.

It is easy to look for extraordinary encounters. They are found in some of the most well-known parts of the Bible, they are memorable, and most of us long for them to be repeated in our own experience.

ABRAHAM – DIRECT COMMUNICATION

Abraham's life contains many such examples: 'The Lord

had said to Abram, ''Leave your country, your people and your father's household and go to the land I will show you. I will make you into a great nation and I will bless you; I will make your name great, and you will be a blessing. I will bless those who bless you, and whoever curses you I will curse; and all peoples on earth will be blessed through you'' ' (Genesis 12: 1-3). How did the Lord speak to Abraham? It sounds so simple. (Abram went, as the Lord had told him!) Yet we know perfectly well that it can't have been! Even so, it profoundly affected the spiritual destiny of us all. Later there are plagues, which make us very uneasy, especially when the reason given is sexual immorality; there are visions, a miraculous birth, angels, an extraordinary Dutch auction in prayer, a tremendous test of faith, and a classic type of coincidence guidance for Abraham's servant when securing a wife for Isaac.

Small wonder that both Paul, in Romans 4, and the writer of Hebrews, in Chapter 11, see Abraham as the most amazing example of someone with whom God communicated. Above all, they saw Abraham as a man of faith, who obeyed God's voice in the many and various ways that he heard it. Much of Abraham's life must have been very ordinary. He faced the sort of problems that we all can face. Does God really want me to move house? (Genesis 12) How do I sort out a business dispute? (Genesis 13) How can I communicate with my more sceptical wife (or more usually in our case — husband) what God is saying? (Genesis 18) How can I prevent people of whom I am afraid taking advantage of me? (Genesis 20) (A singularly unedifying story which, if nothing else, teaches us how easily even great saints ignore God's commands through fear.) How can I trust the apparent promises of God when there seems to be so little sign of fulfilment? (Genesis 17 ff).

Abraham was given some extraordinary means of

guidance; but he was also a man of remarkable faith and courage. The signs and wonders confirmed the way that God was leading him. Once he obeyed the initial call, the whole great adventure was set in motion. What I would love to know, is how God spoke to him in the first place. Was it in an audible voice? Was it an inner conviction? Was it through a dream? Was an angel involved? We don't know! We just aren't told! We don't even know if Abraham was seeking God, or whether God spoke to him as one who was as yet completely unaware of God's existence. We do know that Abraham from the beginning recognised one huge problem (Genesis 11:30) — his wife, Sarai, was barren. We can only wonder if it was this that led Abraham to inquire of the Lord.

Later, Abraham is described by God as 'my friend' (Isaiah 41:8). Abraham did not earn that friendship. He responded to God's call, he let God down on a number of occasions, and yet he remained God's friend. Guidance becomes a much less fearful matter if we understand that God's silent voice in our hearts is for our good and for the extension of His Kingdom. 'If God is for us, who can be against us?' (Romans 8:31).

JEREMIAH — SIGNS FROM DAILY LIFE

Jeremiah's life and ministry was full of many surprising means of communication from God. His call was somewhat similar to Abraham's. 'The word of the Lord came to me, saying, "Before I formed you in the womb I knew you, before you were born I set you apart; I appointed you as a prophet to the nations" ' (Jeremiah 1:5). His response was more equivocal, but the Lord gave him two natural phenomena to think about — the almond rod and the boiling pot. Natural phenomena usually leading to an acted parable seemed to be the main means of God's communicaton to Jeremiah and then through Jeremiah to the people.

In Jeremiah 13: 1-11, the uncomfortable business of the soiled waistcloth clearly spoke of God's displeasure with the pride of Judah. There was nothing very remarkable in the soiled cloth — it would have been much more a cause for wonder if it had been pure and white after being dug into a cleft in the rock! Nevertheless the message was clear and unacceptable to most of his hearers.

The potter's wheel (Jeremiah 18: 1-11) was a more hopeful parable. The potter was not deliberately destroying the unsuccessful pots, but rather remaking the useless into something useful. Here again, the natural action of the potter is used to communicate a simple and a profound message. If Judah were to repent, the Lord would change his plans from judgment to mercy. This is one of the many examples of conditional guidance in the Bible. God gives His people a genuine choice — a choice which in some cases can lead to spiritual life or death.

The yoke (Jeremiah 27 and 28), to which I have already referred in Chapter 2 was an acted parable against which there was a simple action. A false prophet breaks the yoke! Unfortunately for Hananiah, prophecy is dangerous enough when it is true, doubly dangerous when it is man-made and false. The Book of Deuteronomy (Chapter 13) warns against false prophecy. As this book had just come into prominence with its discovery (2 Kings 22:8) it was particularly inept of Hananiah to be unaware of the dangerous ground on which he was treading.

The Anathoth field (Jeremiah 32: 6-25) is a glorious example of an acted parable of hope. Jeremiah buys a field which, because it lay well outside besieged Jerusalem, was practically useless as well as being very expensive. Jeremiah could doubtless have used his seventeen shekels of silver to buy bread and other necessities, but he obeyed the voice of the Lord, and gave everyone hope with the moving words 'For this is what the Lord Almighty, the God of Israel says: "Houses, fields and vineyards will again be bought in this land." ' Perhaps here is an important incident for those who feel they've made shipwrecks of their lives. Jeremiah saw hope in the long term for Judah (cf Jeremiah 29). For many of us there may be a severe penalty to be paid for sin, but ultimately there is always hope. God will put our lives back on the rails, but usually the consequences of our sin have to be worked out.

Finally, the scroll (Jeremiah 36) which actually belongs to an earlier part of Jeremiah's ministry, was used to communicate God's word to a rebellious people. Jeremiah couldn't go to the temple, but he was determined that God's word should be heard. Jeremiah had to wait over a year to get his message heard (cf 36:1 and 36:9). Despite the emotive nature of the message, which can probably be found in Chapter 25: 1-14, Jeremiah was prepared to wait for the silent voice of God to guide him as to when to speak.

How often do we speak at the wrong time, even when we have the right message!

The sequel was highly dramatic. Poor Baruch the scribe had to obey Jeremiah and read the scroll in public, then he was forced to read it to the leaders, and finally to the King.

The King displayed an almost unequalled contempt for God's word and destroyed the scroll piece by piece after each portion had been read. Jeremiah was well equal to the situation and the luckless Baruch had to rewrite the scroll with many similar words added to it!

Here in a real sense it was the King who acted out the Divine Parable. Jeremiah merely dictated the appropriate words, but the King gave them additional force by his contemptuous and fearless destruction of them. It would have been more forgivable if he had simply burned the scroll — but he preferred to listen to a few columns, then destroy what he had heard and repeat the procedure until it was finished. His attitude to God and His servants could scarcely have been clearer.

At the end of it all, there is one great question. We know that God spoke to Jeremiah; we know that the words Jeremiah spoke were fulfilled — not only in the historical sense of the defeat of Jerusalem, but also in the profound spiritual sense of the New Covenant (Jeremiah 31: 31-34). But how did God speak to Jeremiah?

Was it through visions? Was it through a quiet inner certainty? Again, like Abraham, we are not told, but the fact that God used so many natural things as visual aids suggests to me that God spoke quietly into Jeremiah's heart and that he knew, with utter certainty, what words he had to speak.

NEHEMIAH – PRAYER AND ACTION

Nehemiah is probably the greatest figure in Jewish spiritual history in the post-exilic period. His, too, is a wonderful story of Divine communication and tremendous action. It is also a story of unusual spiritual success. A story of ruins rebuilt and spirituality beginning to be restored. Nehemiah's way of 'inquiring of the Lord' would seem quite straightforward to us, and although his achievements seem superhuman, the method seems normal.

It all began with bad news. 'In the month of Kislev in the twentieth year, while I was in the citadel of Susa, Hanani, one of my brothers, came from Judah with some other men, and I questioned them about the Jewish remnant that survived the exile, and also about Jerusalem. They said to me, "Those who survived the exile and are back in the province are in great trouble and disgrace. The wall of Jerusalem is broken down, and its gates have been burned with fire" ' (Nehemiah 1: 1b-3).

Nehemiah's response was to break down. He wept, mourned, fasted and prayed. His prayer (Nehemiah 1: 5-11) is a model of effective intercessory prayer. He showed his sincerity by his actions, and showed spiritual insight by confessing his own sins, his family's sins, as well as the nation's sins. He reminded God of his promises both of judgment and of mercy. He produced a practical prayer asking for God to help in the sight of his employer — the King!

After that the drama moves fast. Nehemiah is given an opportunity to speak to the King, prays quietly and quickly (Nehemiah 2:4) and makes some very practical requests. While it may have been inspirational, it must also have been well prepared in his long time of prayer recorded in the first chapter.

Nehemiah's whole approach is that of practical common sense undergirded by a sense of God's destiny. Arriving in Jerusalem, he has a secret tour of inspection. Instead of upbraiding the officials in Jerusalem for the state of the wall (Nehemiah 2:17) he encouraged them with his spiritual testimony and the obvious signs of his own organisational skills. The opposition, Sanballat and company, started to laugh. Nehemiah replied prophetically. The work continued without any further direct communication from God, and the opposition grew sharper (Nehemiah 4: 7-8).

In fact it wasn't the opposition which brought the work to a halt, but a deep social injustice (Nehemiah 5). Again Nehemiah's response was practical, fair, and supported by his own example. It is significant that he didn't hide behind the wall and use it as an excuse for ducking the potentially explosive social issue. How easy it would have been to say 'The Lord says that this wall is His project, and that it must be completed, and if you trust Him in this matter, your financial troubles will be sorted out.'

Nehemiah had enough spiritual understanding to avoid a nasty trap (Nehemiah 6:10). Having avoided the obvious assassination assignment on the Plain of Ono (Nehemiah 6:2) he avoided a much more subtle one. The prophet, Shemaiah, suggested that they went and walled themselves up in the Temple. Nehemiah rightly realised that his enemies would then have been given cause to mock, and discerned that Shemaiah was in Sanballat's pay. The wall was finished amazingly quickly. (The only comparable saga I have heard was from an Intourist guide at the Moscow underground who said that foreigners offered them help to build it in a year with machines, but we built it with our bare hands in a few months.)

Then there was a great celebration and a great spiritual challenge. Again the book of the Law was read (Nehemiah 8) and the response was much repentance, reform and realism. God's ancient Word had not lost its power. The book concludes with another great celebration 'Come, let us dance round the walls of the City' and further spiritual challenges. Finally, Nehemiah asks God to remember him for good (Nehemiah 13:31).

Nehemiah had guided Jerusalem from ruin to relative safety and spiritual order. But he did it without any of the direct communication, of the type that the older leaders had received, from the Lord. His inquiry of the Lord was based on sound principles, practical common sense, supported by one glorious moment of answered prayer when the King released him from his duties as cupbearer and sent him on his way with timber, letters of authority and a bodyguard.

PSALMS – CLEAR AND OPAQUE

The Psalms which presumably span the lifetime of David to the exile and beyond, can be quite puzzling in the whole matter of guidance. Three examples will have to suffice. Psalm 27, the inspiration of this book, begins with a confident assertion of the Lord as the writer's light and salvation. He declares that he needn't be afraid – of evildoers, slanderers, or enemies. He longs to dwell in the house of the Lord and to inquire in His temple (27:4). He is confident that he can worship God who will protect him (27:5) and lift him above his enemies (27:6). He knows that God has told him to seek His face (cf Isaiah 55:6) – but he suddenly loses his confidence. Verses 9-12 of the Psalm are a most depressing turnabout. He seems to face the serious possiblity of God abandoning him (27:9) and then much more tentatively he prays for protection (27:10-12) and reasserts his faith (27:13-14).

What has happened? Does this well-loved Psalm reflect David's longing to serve God in the temple, only to discover that it isn't even God's will for David to build the temple? Whatever the true circumstances, this change of mind is one that overtakes most people who believe in the direct guidance and protection of God. Very few, possibly none save Jesus Himself, seem to be able to experience God without falling back into natural fear and doubt. Paul's tirade against the spiritual declension of the Galatian church (Galatians 3: 1-4) would seem to be a case in point.

Psalm 40, which I would like to think of as the 'anti-depressant' Psalm has a similar uncertainty. It begins with a classic testimony of gloom and despair turned to worship and testimony (40:1-3). It continues with even more testimony, delight of God, and many hearers (40: 4-10). It has all the makings of a 'prison to praise' type of testimony, and then, quite unexpectedly, it too collapses.

Disaster has struck (40:12), mockery has resulted (40:15), believers are liable to be confused (40:16), hurry up Lord — I know you will help — but it's getting desperate (40:17).

And there is no happy ending. We are left in suspense. What happened? Did the mockers continue to mock, or did the Lord again set his feet upon the rock?

Psalm 84 is a great favourite of mine. Nevertheless it, too, poses a theological conundrum. It begins with a great affirmation of God's goodness. 'Even the sparrow has found a home and the swallow a nest for herself, where she may have her young — a place near your altar, O Lord Almighty, my King and my God. Blessed are those who dwell in your house; they are ever praising you' (84: 3-4). It ends with the glorious truth that he would rather be a doorkeeper in the House of the Lord than to dwell in the tents of the ungodly (84:10). But what of this strange verse in the middle (84:6) which talks of those who 'Going through the vale of misery, they use it for a well' (Book of Common Prayer translation)?

Here there seems to be another acted parable. Many of the pilgrims on the way to some festival in the temple would pass through a dry valley. In it, they would find a well — provided they knew the route, or had a good guide. So it is with the Christian pilgrimage. The destination is Zion, there is much confidence, even singing on the way, but even the doorkeepers will find the vale of misery at various stages of their journey. We cannot always walk in the clear light of God's direct guidance, we will be called to walk through the wilderness — whether it be in temptation, disease, deep sorrow, or whatever.

Recently, we as a family, went to a Christian Conference. Timothy, our son, then almost aged seven, celebrated his arrival by breaking his leg in the Adventure Playground. After a painful visit to hospital, he was unable to sleep at night. We borrowed a Christian tape called 'The Power' by Don Franscisco. I lay through the night with him listening to it over and over again. One of our favourite songs 'One thing I would ask of the Lord' is really a commentary on Psalm 84. It certainly made an amazing difference to Timothy's vale of misery. It has helped him spiritually and together with other tapes from the same source, has helped us as a family on many potentially tedious car journeys.

The wilderness was the place of Israel's grumbling and failure; by contrast, it was the scene of Jesus' successful preparation for His ministry. It will almost certainly be our lot at various times on our spiritual journey. How we fare there will do much to determine our ability to continue to hear God's voice.

ECCLESIASTES – THE APPARENT ABSENCE OF GOD

The wisdom literature, especially Ecclesiastes, gives us another picture of what happens when people use their minds to search for the Lord. His experience leads him perilously close to atheism. There is little sense of God's revelation or guidance. He is a very twentieth-century writer whose key words are not right and wrong, but better and but. He begins by asserting the meaninglessness of life.

'Meaningless! Meaningless!' says the Teacher. 'Utterly meaningless! Everything is meaningless ' (Ecclesiastes 1:2).

If that isn't bad enough, he comments wearily on the futility of work (1:3), and the endless cyclical nature of life

(1: 4-11). Even wisdom, his apparent aim in life, is an unsatisfying pursuit.

'For with much wisdom comes much sorrow; the more knowledge, the more grief' (Ecclesiastes 1:18).

This is actually important to our whole theme. It is possible to take a very simplistic view of the guidance of God — based for instance on Psalm 37: 1-7 — which is superficially very satisfying. A more mature Christian walk, while respecting the promises contained in that Psalm and similar passages, allows for radical uncertainty and a measure of questioning. For instance, guidance in the whole matter of healing (see Chapter 12) would seem to be far more complex than some current thinking will allow. And so it goes on; see especially Ecclesiastes 3: 16-22 which laments the absence of justice and Ecclesiastes 4: 1-3 where justice is actually perverted. The righteous and the unrighteous suffer the same fate (Ecclesiastes 9: 1-2) — that fate is death. But at least the righteous are in God's hands. Most of the book is a long catalogue of observations about the fate of men. Yet there is a glimmer of faith in God's justice:

'Although a wicked man commits a hundred crimes and still lives a long time, I know that it will go better with God-fearing men, who are reverent before God. Yet because the wicked do not fear God, it will not go well with them, and their days will not lengthen like a shadow' (Ecclesiastes 8: 12-13);

and in some sort of future life:

Remember him — before the silver cord is severed,
    or the golden bowl is broken;
before the pitcher is shattered at the spring,
    or the wheel broken at the well,

and the dust returns to the ground it came from,
and the spirit returns to God who gave it
(Ecclesiastes 12: 6-7).

But still the awful cry of 'Meaningless! Meaningless!'. There
seems more than an echo of Ecclesiastes in Samuel Beckett's
famous play *Waiting for Godot*. What are we to make of
this? The writer of Ecclesiastes seems to have little sense of
God or guidance. He doesn't hear the silent voice, for him
the voice is silent. He observes, and what he observes he
records with a measure of distaste.

This is a vital part of the record of Scripture. It should
deliver us once and for all from an unrealistic view of God.
There is suffering, there is tragedy, there is injustice.
Christians pray and suffer, Christians pray and face tragedy
(did the Early Church pray any less hard for James the
brother of John than for Peter? See Acts 12:1 ff); Christians
pray and face injustice (many prayers have been offered for
several years for Terry Waite. We know we must pray, we
don't know the answer. Doubtless Mr Waite felt God's
guidance as he left his protectors on that fateful January
day, doubtless he would do the same again). What is
important is that Ecclesiastes returns to the mystery and
sovereignty of God.

a time to be born and a time to die,
a time to plant and a time to uproot,
a time to kill and a time to heal,
a time to tear down and a time to build
(Ecclesiastes 3:2-3).

He does advise us to seek God early in our lives, so that
in the crisis of a lost youth we can look back and have
something to hold on to:

Remember your Creator in the days of your youth,
before the days of trouble come
and the years approach when you will say,
'I find no pleasure in them' –
before the sun and the light
and the moon and the stars grow dark,
and the clouds return after the rain (Ecclesiastes 12: 1-2).

Today we hear his voice on all sides. But it is the voice of
the despairing teacher (of say Chapter 9), and not the teacher
who is prepared to wait for God's time. He sensed the old
theology – crudely called reward and punishment – was
inadequate. Together with Job, he prepared the way for a
theology of the Resurrection. Theologically, Ecclesiastes
was, perhaps, walking in the 'vale of misery', but the whole
journey must end at Jerusalem. Much modern theology
seems to have left Jerusalem – like the disciples walking
to Emmaus – and is firmly stuck on the vale of misery
facing in the wrong direction.

In the end there is a purpose; the voice of God can be
heard. We have just touched the wonderful kaleidoscope
of spiritual experiences in the Old Testament. Yet time and
time again, the Israelites lost their way because they failed
to seek advice from the Lord. One incident, recorded in
Joshua 9 is particularly revealing. The leaders, including
Joshua, were deceived by a trick played by the Gibeonites
(reading with twentieth-century eyes we might be very glad
that the trick worked, but that is not the point). 'The men
of Israel sampled their provisions, but did not enquire of
the Lord' (Joshua 9:14). Perhaps Isaiah 55 should have the
last word:

Seek the Lord while he may be found;
call on him while he is near.

Let the wicked forsake his way
and the evil man his thoughts.
Let him turn to the Lord, and he will have mercy on him,
and to our God, for He will freely pardon.
'For my thoughts are not your thoughts,
neither are your ways my ways,' declares the Lord.
'As the heavens are higher than the earth,
so are my ways higher than your ways
and my thoughts than your thoughts.
As the rain and the snow
come down from heaven,
and do not return to it
without watering the earth
and making it bud and flourish,
so that it yields seed for the sower and bread for the eater,
so is my word that goes out from my mouth:
It will not return to me empty,
but will accomplish what I desire
and achieve the purpose for which I sent it'

(Isaiah 55: 6-11).

4

JESUS AND GUIDANCE

'I and the Father are one' (John 10:30).

Jesus took the nature of a servant (Philippians 2: 6-11). He gave the disciples an unforgettable lesson in servanthood (John 13: 1-17). He told his followers to learn from His example.

'Take my yoke upon you and learn from me . . .' (Matthew 11:29). As a servant, Jesus had a perfect union with God, which enabled Him to accomplish everything that was required of Him until the last great cry on the cross 'It is finished' (John 19:30).

We may wonder at the sheer impossibility of following His example, yet we are meant to learn from Him. We may marvel at the level of guidance that he received (in a real sense, none was needed, such was His relationship with God); but we may learn with Him and from Him.

Jesus heard the voice of God; Jesus met God in prayer; Jesus ministered God's love, healing, and forgiveness to individuals in all walks of life; Jesus recognised and confronted the powers of darkness; Jesus gave very careful teaching on signs; Jesus allowed Himself to be subjected to the ultimate darkness − and the apparent absence of God − on the cross.

Jesus gave us the most astonishing ethical teaching. Teaching that we shall not look at directly, but teaching which must be used as a basis for testing our own claims to be guided.

JESUS AND THE VOICE OF GOD

On just three recorded occasions Jesus heard the voice of God. At His baptism (Mark 1:11), at His transfiguration (Mark 9:7), and in Jerusalem (John 12:28). At the baptism, the Father's voice was an encouragement. Jesus' real walk was beginning, the years of preparation were over. It is unclear whether anyone else heard the voice. Probably they didn't, otherwise it would be hard to account for John the Baptist's later uncertainty:

'Are you the one who was to come, or should we expect someone else?' (Matthew 11:2).

At the Transfiguration, the Father's voice was heard by Peter, James and John. Peter seems to allude to this experience in 1 Peter 1, and refers quite definitely to it in 2 Peter 3: 16-18. I am aware of the doubts about the authority of 2 Peter, but this is outside the scope of this book. The message here is not only of the Father's love, but of the necessity of listening to the Son. For the apostles, Jesus' voice was the voice of God. Thus Jesus could make the most amazing claims – 'I am the way, the truth and the life' (John 14:6) – and the apostles could accept them.

In Jerusalem, God's voice was heard indistinctly by the crowd. They were uncertain whether it was thunder or an angel. The Word was about glory. Jesus had asked 'Father glorify your Name'. The voice from Heaven replied 'I have glorified it and will glorify it again'. Inexorably, suffering and glory are linked in the New Testament. The Transfiguration experience comes in the middle of Jesus' attempts to prepare the disciples for His future suffering (Mark 8:31 ff; 9:12 ff; 10:32 ff).

The voice of God is a preparation for the suffering of the servant. After the baptism, there is the wilderness; after the Transfiguration there is the walk to Jerusalem; after the voice on Palm Sunday there is Holy Week.

There was no voice to comfort Him on the cross, no voice in the garden, no voice in the tomb.

JESUS AND PRAYER

For the rest of Jesus' ministry, His walk with God was so close that He didn't need the visions, prophecies, signs, that all the other great biblical leaders received. But He did need to be quiet and to pray.

From many notable occasions I would mention just one.

That evening after sunset the people brought to Jesus all the sick and demon-possessed. The whole town gathered at the door, and Jesus healed many who had various diseases. He also drove out many demons, but he would not let the demons speak because they knew who he was.

Very early in the morning, while it was still dark, Jesus got up, left the house and went off to a solitary place, where he prayed. Simon and his companions went to look for him, and when they found him, they exclaimed: 'Everyone is looking for you!'

Jesus replied, 'Let us go somewhere else — to the nearby villages — so that I can preach there also. That is why I have come.' So he travelled throughout Galilee, preaching in their synagogues and driving out demons (Mark 1: 32-39).

It had been an amazing day by any standard. Exorcism, with an unheard of authority; healing of Peter's mother-in-law — so complete that she got up off her bed of sickness to serve a meal; multiple healings and exorcisms in the darkness after sunset. Jesus must have been tired, and elsewhere we read of His physical tiredness (John 4:6). But, He was up early to pray. Healing and exorcisms after sunset, prayer before dawn!

Those of us privileged occasionally to see the power of God in healing and exorcism usually sense an amazing elation at God's presence. We often wonder at the authority of the name of Jesus, but if we work far into the night, we are seldom good for much the next morning. How different was the Master!

What was He praying about? We are not told, but I think we may presume He was seeking to confirm God's leading that the priority was to preach the kingdom and that healing the sick was of secondary importance.

Poor Peter — he got up early, too! The crowds were doubtless already gathering; mother-in-law was, perhaps, showing signs of relapse, but anyway Jesus was needed! Peter didn't yet know how to pray for the sick, he must fetch Jesus. Circumstances dictated that Jesus must return to the house in Capernaum. Necessity dictated that Jesus must return to the house in Capernaum. But Jesus knew otherwise! He needed those silent hours of prayer to regain His physical strength for the next stage, He needed prayer to confirm that He had heard the Father's voice aright. He could not be manipulated by people's needs.

Jesus often withdrew to pray (Luke 5:16); sometimes he was so busy that He hadn't time to eat (Mark 3:20). His family thought he was mad and there is a hint that they wanted to lock Him up (Mark 3:21). The pressure, even in the successful Galilean springtime of His ministry, must have been colossal; but Jesus remained the master of circumstances. He knew, either instinctively or from His prayer times, when to be involved and when to withdraw. He knew when to confront and when to slip away (see, for instance, Luke 4: 14-30 and John 6: 1-15).

We, His disciples, must make time to pray. Not only do we need to pray every day (Jesus introduced His teaching on prayer in the Sermon on the Mount with the words 'When you pray', not 'if you pray' – (Matthew 6:5 ff); but we also need real periods of withdrawal and retreat. If Jesus was occasionally exhausted by ministry, if He sometimes felt power leave His body (Mark 5:30; Luke 6:19), how much more will we feel tired and in need of spiritual rest and refreshment.

I am very grateful to a parishioner who tries, usually successfully, to insist that once a month I have a day of retreat away from the parish to pray, listen, and occasionally, to write.

JESUS AND PEOPLE
(The Question of Faith)

Jesus' understanding of people is quite breathtaking. Time after time, He discovers their real needs; time after time, He discerns their spiritual state; time after time, He heals and/or amazes them with His perception. He doesn't spend long with them. A few minutes and a life is transformed; a few seconds and an opponent is discomfited.

Jesus saw the faith of the paralytic man's friends (Mark 2: 1-11). He knew that the man needed forgiveness more than healing. He discerned the attitude of the teacher of the law. He gave them all a sign of healing to confirm His word of forgiveness. Everyone was amazed, and presumably the owner of the house was happy to mend his flat roof.

Jesus knew that unpleasant men like Levi (Mark 2:13) and Zacchaeus (Luke 19:1 ff) could be changed. He singled each of them out for a direct challenge — in the one case to follow, in the other to restore his ill-gotten gains. By eating in their houses, and thereby causing a lot of muttering, Jesus confirmed Levi's call and showed Zacchaeus the way of repentance and salvation. Jesus, instinctively, knew 'who the Father had given Him'. This is a precious insight that a few gifted evangelists seem to share.

Jesus could deal very gently with unbelief and with sin. He came down from the mountain of the Transfiguration into a situation of chaos, doubt and argument (Mark 9:14 ff). The father was desperate, he had sought help from the nine remaining disciples and they had failed. The crowd, and the teachers of the law, were busy arguing with the disciples. The boy was no better; probably, if the evil spirit was active, somewhat worse.

Jesus asked to see the boy. As soon as he came into Jesus' presence the evil spirit threw the boy into a convulsion. Mark[1], in particular, makes it clear that there was an inevitable violent clash between the powers of darkness and Jesus. Frequently in this gospel we meet this reaction. The evil powers recognise Jesus. Their dark nature cannot stand the light of Christ. Desperately they attack — naming Him, convulsing people, destroying pigs . . . On this occasion, Jesus doesn't immediately perform the exorcism. He asks the father about the boy. The father's reply included the essence of unbelief; 'But if you can do anything, take pity on us and help us.' Jesus' reply contained a gentle rebuke 'If you can? Everything is possible for him who believes.' The father's reply was despairingly honest. 'I do believe, help me overcome my unbelief.' That was enough. Jesus took command of the situation, discerned a deaf and mute spirit, and commanded it to come out and never to return.

There was violent conflict which left the boy looking as though he were dead. Jesus knew better and took the boy's hand and lifted him up.

The disciples asked for guidance as to why they had failed. Mark records the somewhat enigmatic reply: 'This kind can only be driven out by prayer.'

Matthew gives this answer:

'Because you have so little faith. I tell you the truth, if you have faith as small as a mustard seed, you can say to this mountain, "Move from here to there" and it will move. Nothing will be impossible for you' (Matthew 17:20).

The twelve had already been given authority over evil spirits (Mark 6:7 ff); they had been victorious (Mark 6:13) and had seen many evil spirits driven out and many healed. But here they had failed. Why? Jesus was teaching them a number of things for their future guidance. They had inadequate faith and inadequate preparation. Clearly this exorcism was particularly difficult, even Jesus expressed a real measure of conflict. This sort of faith required a prayer relationship with God which they hadn't yet established. Jesus had just experienced one of the most remarkable times of His earthly life on the mountain — through prayer (Luke 9:29), and through experiencing the glory and hearing the voice of God.

The disciples' faith would be built through learning to listen to the voice of God in prayer. It is important to see that Jesus quietly accepted the very tentative faith of the boy's father, but rebuked the disciples' lack of faith. Throughout His ministry, Jesus marvelled at the faith of some of the individuals that He helped. He didn't demand their faith, but certainly encouraged it. On the other hand, he was often distressed by the disciples' lack of faith, and on the celebrated occasion in His home town (Mark 6: 1-5) was severely limited by the unbelief of His neighbours.

JESUS AND PEOPLE (THE GIFT OF KNOWLEDGE)

Jesus' encounter with Simon the Pharisee and the sinful woman (Luke 7:36 ff) is particularly instructive. At the beginning of the story, the Pharisee was highly judgmental.

'If this man were a prophet, he would know who is touching him and what kind of a woman she is — that she is a sinner'. Leaving aside Simon's annoyance at the interruption to his dinner party, we can see that he expected a 'man of God' to react violently when touched by someone unclean.

Jesus' discernment was far deeper. Not only did He know exactly with whom He was dealing 'Therefore I tell you her *many* sins have been forgiven', but He also knew, theologically and socially, what she needed — forgiveness and acceptance. He also knew that there was another present at the table who was just as much in need of God's forgiveness and that he was painfully unaware of it!

At the end, Jesus said to the woman 'Your faith' (and it must have taken a great deal of faith and courage to seek Jesus out and behave in such an extravagant way) 'has saved you; go in peace!'

On this occasion He didn't add 'and sin no more', but certainly that is the implication. Obviously, we cannot know if the woman was Mary Magdalene (who appears for the first time two verses later). If she was, she was not only forgiven, but released from many evil spirits, and had the privilege of travelling around with Jesus' team.

Jesus discerned the heart, the mind, the state and the needs of many individuals. He amazed the Samaritan woman at the well: 'You are right when you say you have no husband. The fact is you have had five husbands, and the man you have is not your husband. What you have said is quite true' (John 4:17). This led to her conversion; to a remarkable harvest of faith in her village. Who knows, she may have prepared the way for Philip's remarkable evangelistic visit (Acts 8).

He astonished the rich young man (Mark 10:17 ff): 'One thing you lack. Go, sell everything you have and give to the poor and you will have treasure in heaven. Then come, follow me.' Jesus loved that young man. He could have been a wonderful disciple. But Jesus wouldn't offer cheap grace by demanding anything less than total commitment.

Very few of us have heard that command. But those, like Francis of Assisi, and some missionaries who truly live by faith, have left an example that leaves the rest of us far behind.

He astonished Legion, most of all, with his final word (Mark 5:1 ff). 'Go home to your family and tell them how much the Lord has done for you, and how He has had mercy on you' (Mark 5:19). Jesus could have received Legion as a true follower. He would have had a 'wonderful testimony' and doubtless have had a powerful 'ministry'. But Jesus knew his real need and guided him back to witness to the amazed and fearful residents of his local town. The depth of Legion's new found freedom can be gauged by his obedience. He did exactly what Jesus told him to! Most of those healed by Jesus did the exact opposite (*viz*. Mark 1:45).

Jesus expected, and still expects, complete obedience when He speaks. So often we hear God's call, and then like Jonah run in the opposite direction.

He gave precious time to the woman 'with the issue of blood' (Mark 5:21ff). On this occasion, there was a real crisis. A little girl was dying. Jesus' help was needed urgently. As usual, a large crowd gathered. There was jostling, pushing, and probably the sort of chaos that we see today as politicians do their political walkabouts. The disciples, more gentle than security chiefs, were nevertheless just as anxious. Jesus must get to the girl's home as quickly as possible!

As He walks, Jesus feels a release of power from His body. He knows that someone has been healed. The disciples can't believe it. Don't be ridiculous, Master! You see the crowds! They're all around you, pushing and shoving, and then you ask 'Who touched me?' But Jesus knew that someone had. Interestingly, He doesn't seem to have known who it was.

But Jesus kept looking around to see who had done it. He wanted the woman to come forward freely. When she did, He knew that as well as being healed physically, she could also be declared ritually clean (no small matter — she was probably about as unacceptable in Jewish society as many AIDS victims feel today).

The mystery of the power leaving Jesus' body is one that we will consider later in Chapter 12 — Guidance and Healing. Suffice it to say that many Christians involved in the healing ministry experience these feelings. But we must never use these sorts of signs as tests to seek vindication of a ministry. 'By their fruit, you will recognise them' (Matthew 7:20) says Jesus, and immediately goes on to warn us that neither prophesying, nor performing miracles or exorcism, even in His name are a guarantee of His approval (Matthew 7: 22-23).

Obedience to Him is the only safe test! And for Jesus, obedience to the inner voice of the Father was the way He discerned how to react in each and every situation.

JESUS AND THE POWERS OF DARKNESS

Jesus, as we have already seen, recognised and took authority over the powers of darkness. They, in their turn,

recognised and confronted Him. To suppose that Jesus was
merely using 'the thought forms of His day' seems highly
insulting. If Jesus was wrong on this issue, or the gospel
writers misinformed, a substantial part of His teaching and
authority are completely undermined. Equally, to suppose
that Jesus saw demons everywhere, or worse still, that they
exist everywhere, but that He didn't teach about them, is
even more dangerous.

Jesus discerned demons when they were present. He
released people from their power — there is no record of
His exorcising places. He also healed many people without
exorcism. Jesus instinctively knew what approach was
necessary. Occasionally, at a very different level, He saw
His friends, notably Peter (Mark 8:31 ff) playing the part
of the adversary.

The ultimate mystery of Jesus' choice of Judas, whom
He later described as a devil (John 6:70), is not fully
explained.

Jesus gave His disciples authority and practice in the area
of exorcism (Luke 10:1 ff). We may not like it, but it is an
area in which He appears to expect His followers to continue
to act.

Personally, while making some mistakes, it is an area in
which I have been more aware of God's silent voice guiding
me than almost any other.

JESUS AND SIGNS

Jesus' teaching on signs is sharp and to the point!

The Pharisees and Sadducees came to Jesus and tested
Him by asking Him to show them a sign from heaven.
He replied, 'When evening comes, you say, "It will be

fair weather, for the sky is red,'' and in the morning, "Today it will be stormy, for the sky is red and overcast." You know how to interpret the appearance of the sky, but you cannot interpret the signs of the times. A wicked and adulterous generation looks for a miraculous sign, but none will be given it except the sign of Jonah.' Jesus then left them and went away (Matthew 16: 1-4; see also Matthew 12: 38-43).

Jesus was not giving signs to unbelievers to authenticate His ministry. To those with eyes to see there were plenty of signs. The disciples saw the miracle at Cana and 'He thus revealed His glory and His disciples put their faith in Him' (John 2:11 ff). He gave them a veiled answer to their request for a sign to prove His authority.

'I will destroy this man-made temple, and in three days will build another not made by man.' His opponents completely misunderstood, and indeed seem to have used this statement as part of the false witness at His trial (Mark 14:58), and even His disciples only understood what He was talking about after the Resurrection.

Once only, Jesus gave a 'miraculous' sign for no obvious spiritual purpose. The strange incident of the fish with the coin in its mouth (Matthew 17:24 ff) — so strange that one feels compelled to believe it — was a sign to Peter.

Throughout Christian history there have been many similar stories of poor Christians, missionaries living by faith, and others who have received amazing provision by some remarkable means which have exactly met their needs.[2]

I believe that Jesus would be horrified by the teaching today of the so-called 'prosperity gospel'. The gospels advocate a holy poverty, a promise to find essential needs, not 'showers of blessings' which lead to material prosperity.

Of course, God does bless some people materially, thereby putting a huge responsibility on how they use their wealth.

Perhaps the most remarkable sign was the feeding of the five thousand. This miracle, alone recorded in all the gospels (cf John 6:1 ff), offers no rational explanation. It is a stupendous sign. It has provoked all sorts of understandable scepticism – the little boy's action in producing the bread and the fish provoked everyone else to share their sandwiches (a nice moral story!) – it is a laser beam miracle *par excellence* (why not turn all the stones into bread and solve the world's hunger problem?) – but for our purposes, it is the reaction of Jesus in withdrawing from the crowd which is significant.

He knows they intended to make him a king by force; He knew that was far from God's purpose. He withdrew into the silence of the mountains to pray and to escape.

Jesus saw the miracles as signs authenticating His ministry. John the Baptist (Matthew 11:2 ff), imprisoned, uncertain, facing death, asked 'Are you the one who was to come, or should we expect someone else?' Jesus' reply is not a rebuke at his lack of faith; but a list of signs which fulfilled the Messianic prophecies of Isaiah (Isaiah 35:4-6). Some would see these signs and conclude they were the work of the Devil (Matthew 12: 22-32). Some, like Herod, would long to see the signs for themselves. Some would receive the blessing from the signs and go on their way apparently unmoved (Luke 17:11 ff). A few, like Bartimaeus (Mark 10:46 ff) would see, believe, and follow Him even to Jerusalem.

So it remains today. The church has, to some extent, recovered its belief in a God who performs miracles. Throughout the world, especially in parts of Latin America, Africa and Asia, there are amazing accounts of miracles. But the world's reaction remains much as before.

JESUS AND THE APPARENT ABSENCE OF GOD

Ultimately, Jesus allowed Himself to be 'handed over' to face the final hours of pain and darkness.[3] Here we touch a mystery too deep for words — things into which angels long to look (1 Peter 1: 10-12). In John's gospel there seems to be a double crux. First 'it was night' (John 13:30) when Judas left the last supper to fulfil his fateful purpose. The daylight was gone, the Messianic signs were over, thick darkness lay ahead. Second, Jesus said 'I am he' (John 18:6) and His opponents drew back and fell to the ground.

Vanstone[4] makes the profound point that neither John, nor any reader of his gospel who was at all familiar with the Greek translation of the Jewish Scriptures, the Septuagint, could be unaware that 'I AM' is also the sacred name of God, the name disclosed to Moses. Jesus' reply to the armed men should be heard and understood as the most awesome disclosure of His divinity. It is in this way that the men do hear and understand it. They draw back, for a moment, and fall to the ground overwhelmed.

In between these two key points comes the terrible spiritual ordeal in the garden. I remember once walking on a Maundy Thursday evening from the lights of Jerusalem, past the restored temple, out through a little gate, down the steep valley of the Kidron, and up into the garden area of Gethsemane. It may be a moving way for a pilgrim, but what a terrible way for the Lord.

Luke's is the most graphic account of all (Luke 22: 39-45).

'Father, if you are willing, take this cup from me; yet not my will, but yours be done.'

Words are profoundly inadequate. Our darkness, our indecision, our need of guidance, our fears, all seem as nothing when we enter that garden and hear the Lord at prayer. He, who had always been certain of the Father's will, is now battling to be absolutely certain that *now* is the moment for the 'handing over' and that *now* is the time when His power is to be bound. A little earlier He had prepared for the raising of Lazarus with these words:

'Are there not twelve hours of daylight? A man who walks by day will not stumble, for he sees by this world's light. It is when he walks by night that he stumbles, for he has no light' (John 11:9-10).

Now it is Jesus who will stumble, bearing His cross, as He walks through His time of spiritual night.

Jesus knew that this was to be His fate, He had prophesied it many times.[5] It was one thing to prophesy, but it was another to fulfil. Especially when the cost of fulfilment was so terrible.

For Jesus, we may dare to say, the voice of God became silent. He had to walk to Calvary alone. Bound, silent, beaten, mocked, deserted. Yet in that suffering there is an awful majesty and amazing gentleness.

If we had only the seven sayings from the cross, we would have witness to an extraordinary death. If we had only the forgiveness of Peter, the acceptance of help from Simon of Cyrene and the penitent thief, we would have a sign of forgiveness of almost unbelievable poignancy; but we also have the darkness and the great cry:

'My God, my God, why have you forsaken me?' (Mark 15:34).

Some would see in this the ultimate cry of one whose source of guidance has failed; some would see a quotation from

Psalm 22, full of crucifixion prophecies. We would be wise to join the apostles in recognising this as the ultimate mystery of the gospel.

'God made Him who had no sin to be sin for us, so that in Him we might become the righteousness of God' (2 Corinthians 5:21). Jesus was walking through His 'valley of the shadow'. A far deeper and more terrible valley than any which others are called to walk in. A valley in which the voice of God became silent. A valley which opened the way, not only for our forgiveness, but for our righteousness, (1 Peter 2:24) and thus for any guidance, that God, in His grace, might choose to give us (1 Peter 2:25).

Jesus, in His dereliction, opened the way for His people to hear God's silent voice.

Notes and references

1 Lane, William. *Gospel of Mark*. New International Commentary of the New Testament Series. Michigan, Eerdmans Pub Co, 1974.
2 See for example the story of Ken Matthew in Chapter 16 of this volume.
3 Vanstone, W H. *The Stature of Waiting*. London, Darton, Longman and Todd, 1982, Chapters 1 and 2.
4 *Ibid*, p75
5 See an interesting discussion of these prophecies and their authority in Lane, William. *Op Cit*, pp 374ff.

5

GUIDANCE AND THE HOLY SPIRIT

'On one occasion, while he was eating with them, he gave them this command: "Do not leave Jerusalem, but wait for the gift my Father promised, which you have heard me speak about. For John baptised with water, but in a few days you will be baptised with the Holy Spirit" ' (Acts 1: 4-5). The disciples obeyed. They waited and prayed and, ten days later, Jesus' promise was fulfilled on the Day of Pentecost.

The apostles, and presumably upwards of a hundred other believers (Acts 1:15), were filled with the Holy Spirit. The Spirit came with a sound like wind, a vision like fire, and a miracle of new speech. Outsiders were amazed and perplexed.

'We hear them declaring the wonders of God in our own tongue!' (Acts 2:11). The testimony of the believers, presumably to Jesus' resurrection, was startling enough; but to hear the Galileans, uneducated men from an insignificant part of Judea, speaking many distinct languages was unnerving.

This gift of the Spirit was no silent voice. It was audible, intelligible, and profoundly challenging. There were only two alternatives – to listen, or to mock.

Most remarkable of all was the power of Peter's preaching. The Church was born as the Holy Spirit convicted Peter's hearers (Acts 2:37). They had to respond! Peter, and the apostles, had a completely new confidence, a new strategy, a new openness to God.

The Holy Spirit guided the Early Church in a number of ways — using prophecy, strategy, common sense, effective witness, visions, victory in spiritual conflict, and the baptism of power.

THE HOLY SPIRIT AND PROPHECY

Peter recognised that the ancient prophecy of Joel (2: 28-32) was being fulfilled on the Day of Pentecost. Prophets were very important in the Early Church. Occasionally, they predicted the future; more significantly, they enabled the church to discover God's will and way forward.

Twice Agabus appears with a prophecy in Acts.[1] The first time, his word concerning a severe famine, caused the first Christian Aid journey when Barnabas and Saul took a gift from the Antioch church to help the Jerusalem church prepare for the famine. The second time his dramatically acted prophecy was to warn Paul of impending disaster in Jerusalem. Interestingly, Paul accepted the warning as from the Lord, but determined to continue his journey. For him, the prophecy brought strength for the trials ahead and was not an excuse to avoid danger.

Luke gives the strong impression that prophecy was a major factor in one of the great expansions of the church — the first missionary journey of Barnabas and Saul (see Acts 13: 1-4). Prophets clearly had a major role in the young church at Antioch. It seems as if the leaders of the church, who were mainly being taught by Barnabas with the help of Saul, had gathered for an extended time of worship. The period was long enough to include fasting, and it seems as if it might have been at least a day. Anyway, during this time the Holy Spirit spoke. We are not told how, but it seems reasonable to assume that one of the prophets said 'I think I have a word from the Lord', or, more confidently, 'The Lord is saying . . .' Anyway, whatever the means, the message was crystal clear.

'Set apart for me Barnabas and Saul for the work to which I have called them.'

After further fasting and prayer, presumably to test and confirm the message (1 Thessalonians 5: 19-21), they laid hands on Saul and Barnabas and sent them off. The church in Antioch willingly released its two greatest leaders but, thanks to the large shared leadership team, the church was not left leaderless. How many of today's churches could lose two leaders and, without replacing them, carry on?

Prophecy has been used to warn Christians of impending persecution. Christian tradition tells us that around AD 67, a prophecy warned the Christian church in Jerusalem of the forthcoming siege by the Romans. The Christian community fled, thereby confirming the break with the Jewish leaders.

In more recent times, as recounted by Demos Shakarian in *The Happiest People on Earth*, a prophecy to the Armenian Christians some 120 years ago warned them of a fierce persecution by the Turks. The original prophecy was given by an illiterate boy of eleven in about 1850. About fifty years later, the prophet announced that the time of fulfilment was near. 'We must flee to America, all who remain here will perish.' The instructions proved correct. In 1914 a period of unimaginable horror arrived in Armenia. With ruthless efficiency, the Turks exterminated the Armenians. Their pogrom even inspired Hitler. 'The world did not intervene when Turkey wiped out the Armenians,' he reminded his followers, 'it will not intervene now.' Those who heeded the prophecy emigrated to America, almost all those who stayed were killed.

Of course, prophecy can get out of hand. Like any spiritual gift it can be perverted, and the Scriptures are full of warnings against, and examples of, false prophecy. *The Didache*, an early Christian handbook, has some trenchant advice: 'If a prophet claiming to be in a trance says "Give me money", he is not a true prophet of God.'

In my own experience, a prophetic word has once been of vital significance to confirm a choice that was almost made.

Once I spent about six months looking for the right job. I was sure that it was right to leave my current one, and I began to look for the appropriate situation. Various openings came, but none of them felt right. Guidance in this case was indirect and intuitive. Then suddenly I had to come to a decision. Three possible churches were interested in me; two had offered me the job, a third was considering doing so. I had kept one waiting a long time, and now I had to decide.

God spoke in three ways. First, when we applied for one of the posts we received a polite, but firm refusal from the patron – they had plenty of good candidates. A little while later we spent an evening with a couple whom we had asked especially to pray about our future. After much talk and some prayer, James said: 'Father is saying that you will find something significant in the next week.' The next day, Jane received a phone call from the churchwardens of the church that had plenty of candidates asking me to go for an interview! We were offered that job.

Then God spoke again. We had gathered together a group of our friends and leaders in the church which we were leaving. There was a general, but not complete, consensus as to which job was right, then our parish worker saw a picture in her mind of a long, low, grey, stone house. It didn't mean much to me, but Jane said, 'It's the rectory at . . .' The next morning James rang up with a long word of prophecy. The words which stood out were that we were to 'choose this day the church which was right for us as a family, and the church where we could serve the whole community as well as the church'. The church with the grey stone rectory was far more suited to the family in terms of potential friends and situation, and it was a town parish church, whereas the other possibilities had congregations gathered from afar. There was far more opportunity to serve in the community from the centre of a town parish. For final confirmation, I rang up a bishop involved in the appointment of one of the other potential jobs. He listened, then said quietly, 'I also know the parish with the grey stone rectory. That's where you should go!' In some ways it wasn't the natural choice, the churchmanship being rather different from what we were used to, but the prophetic words also mentioned that 'We would be changed', which seemed to cover that point as well. We felt at peace; six months of waiting were over! When, on the night of our induction, our former parish worker actually saw the house, she gasped. It was exactly the house she had seen in her mind!

It might be helpful to include the whole prophecy as given down the telephone that Wednesday morning.

Choose you this day where you will serve.
Choose the place where, as a family, you all will fit most naturally. I want your roots to take a hold with the whole community and not just with the body of the church. For, as you are accepted and become a part – not merely as a minister, but as a man, a wife, a family, within that same community, so shall the deep ground-swell begin that will shake you as well as those you serve,

but not that anyone shall be destroyed, but rather all shall find together that due measure of fulfilment in my Name and in my Word that is according to the need not only of each one, but of the whole community.

So choose where you most naturally fit, for you will serve me there for many years.

Six years on, it would be ridiculous to say that the prophecy has been fulfilled. Some of it has. We have become very happy as a family, we have seen a real measure of growth in the church (but scarcely the groundswell . . .), we have lost a few members (very few, but even the few hurt and one feels a failure). The church is more recognised in the community, but still seems a long way from having the spiritual and social influence that it ought to have.

Probably it would be unwise to expect every detail to be fulfilled. It was a general word to encourage us, which it did, and the unfulfilled part continues to challenge us. Who knows, it might be in God's plan that some successor should see the real fruit. My predecessors were godly and wise people. They, too, saw fruit in their time.

THE HOLY SPIRIT AND STRATEGY

It is tempting to read the Acts of the Apostles and to see the great missionary expansion of the church as unplanned, spontaneous, and entirely controlled by visions, dreams and inspiration.

Yet there are clear signs of a plan — the work is to spread out from Jerusalem, to Judea and Samaria, and out to the ends of the earth (Acts 1:8). The first wave of persecution, following the martyrdom of Stephen, caused the believers to scatter and, almost inadvertently, fulfil the command to go to Judea and Samaria (Acts 8:1 ff). The conversion of Saul of Tarsus (Acts 9) produced the first effective missionary to the Gentiles. The plan became clear, Peter was to head up the Jewish mission, and Paul the Gentile mission (Galatians 2:9).

Paul's missionary work had a strategy. According to Roland Allen, [2] Paul established his churches in centres of Roman administration, of Greek civilisation, centres of Jewish influence, and centres of world commerce. More important than that, when he established a church it was with the purpose that the mission should radiate out from the centre and establish the faith in the surrounding country.

Paul was also determined, strategically, to come to Rome. Here, of course, a church was already established (Acts 28:15).

It is hard to think strategically, it is much easier to react to circumstances. In our own churches, it would be good to ask if we have a strategy. What do we think the Holy Spirit wants us to achieve in the next five or fifty years? The good chess player knows that most games are won by sound strategy and not by brilliant plans. Brilliant plans, invariably, can only emerge from a well thought-out position. The spontaneous, exhilarating leading of the Spirit usually comes where there is a sound spiritual base and a general sense of direction and purpose.

In my local church, we have been given a strategy for our house groups and a vision for our locality. Whether either can be fulfilled will determine the relative success or failure of the church over the next decade.

THE HOLY SPIRIT AND CIRCUMSTANCES

It would be quite wrong to suppose that all guidance, even in the heady spiritual climate of Acts, is of the direct and dramatic kind. Much of it is circumstantial, unsensational, and so normal that only the eye of faith discerns God's guidance.

One of the first recorded crises in the New Testament church is in Acts 6. The Greek Jews felt that their widows were being unfairly treated and not getting their fair share of the communal food distribution.

One knows the feeling, one group within a church, or one church within a group, feels that it is being treated unfairly. Tension mounts and unpleasantness follows unless there is a quick action.

The apostles' reaction is instructive. They recognise the problem, they realise their priorities – to continue preaching – and they arrange the selection of seven men to sort out the problem. The church sorted the matter out and chose seven men of high quality; notably Stephen, described as a man full of faith and of the Holy Spirit. The seven men were all Greeks, and it was the Greeks who were being discriminated against. In other words, there was a lot of common sense as well as spiritual judgment in the choice. The apostles accepted the choice, prayed for them and laid hands upon them as a sign of their calling to this important work. The consequence of solving this social problem in a spiritual and sensible way was quite simply 'the word of God spread. The number of disciples in Jerusalem increased rapidly, and a large number of priests became obedient to the faith'. Would that all church problems could be approached and solved in such a godly way.

There was, however, one thing the apostolic church seemed to have forgotten. Jesus in His promise about Pentecost had said 'You will receive power when the Holy Spirit comes on you; and you will be my witnesses in Jerusalem, and in all Judea and Samaria, and to the ends of the earth' (Acts 1:8). The Apostolic church seemed somewhat stuck in Jerusalem. However, circumstances which were a direct consequence of Stephen's appointment as a deacon speeded up matters.

Stephen was so successful, not just as a deacon, but as a leader who displayed God's grace and power that trouble was inevitable. The story of his martyrdom is well known. There were two direct consequences. A young man called Saul was witness to these events. In a strange way, they probably prepared him for his conversion. The other was that a fierce persecution arose and the believers were scattered. Philip began an amazing ministry in Samaria, while other believers founded the church in Antioch. Even Peter began an itinerant ministry. The church was on the move! No vision, no prophecy, just a set of circumstances which compelled a new obedience to the Risen Lord's final command.

One could give many similar examples from the church today. The terrible riots in Toxteth and such places a few years ago caused the Church of England to produce its report *Faith in the City*. The Report called for action. The action is the Church Urban Fund, a truly massive response from the national church to a national need.

THE HOLY SPIRIT AND EVANGELISM

Much of the evangelistic success in Acts was achieved by sheer hard work. Acts 18: 1-11 shows that, unusually, Paul stayed eighteen months in one place. With considerable difficulty, he laid the foundations for what appears to have been his most difficult church (see 2 Corinthians 10ff). At Ephesus (Acts 19), Paul laboured for two years with daily discussions in the hall of Tyrannus. The result of this was that a remarkable number of people heard 'the word of the Lord' (Acts 19:10) and after a period of remarkable miracles, many believed.

In other places we can see how miracles led to considerable evangelistic success. Acts 9:32ff shows how Lydda, Sharon and Joppa were evangelised as a result of the miracles wrought for Aeneas and Dorcas.

On Cyprus (Acts 13:4ff), the dramatic confrontation with Elymas the sorcerer led to the conversion of the proconsul; while at Lystra, the healing of the cripple (Acts 14:8ff) initially had the opposite effect — the over-reaction of the crowd was quickly followed by a change of opinion and the near death of Paul. Nevertheless, the apostles returned to Lystra where Timothy was converted.

The church at Philippi (Acts 16:11ff) was founded on the basis of a godly woman's conversion, a slave girl's exorcism, and the amazing conversion of the jailer and his family. Once again, Paul had to leave in a hurry, presumably leaving Luke[3] behind to help the new church on to its feet.

Much the same story could be told today. Fred Smith[4] tells the story of the healing of Dinah Hills. She was a professional dressmaker, who, after slipping on a highly polished floor, was left in great pain and with a useless arm and hand. For over seven years she had to be looked after by her husband. At one of Fred's meetings, they were both converted and she received the most extraordinary healing. The result was a huge turning to Christ in their local village, and a completely new life and ministry for them both.

In many parts of the world, the same story is being told. Effective evangelism accompanied by signs and wonders. You can read about it in many books and magazines.

At the same time, in other places, sheer hard work seems to be required. The Holy Spirit is sovereign. We are commanded to evangelise, we cannot produce the signs and wonders.

THE HOLY SPIRIT AND VISIONS

Visions and dreams were a considerable means of guidance throughout the Scriptures, not least in the Acts. The conversion of Saul, which he sees as a 'resurrection' appearance (see 1 Corinthians 15:8) was accompanied by visions both to Ananias and to him (Acts 9: 11-12). The conversion of Cornelius, which opened the way for the whole Gentile mission, was again accompanied by visions involving both Cornelius and Peter (Acts 10 and 11). Indeed, Peter was so into visions that he had difficulty in distinguishing vision from reality (Acts 12:9)! Paul was led across the Aegean to begin the evangelism of Greece by the famous vision of the Man of Macedonia (Acts 16:10). When things were difficult in Corinth, the Lord spoke to Paul in a vision (Acts 18:9) to such effect that Paul stayed in one place for a year and a half. Again, on board ship, Paul received guidance from an angel to the effect that the ship's company would survive and that he must stand trial before Caesar (Acts 27:23).

However strange we find this sort of guidance, there are many examples in modern Christian literature of dreams, visions and even angels.[5] I have just been reading a wonderful book called *The Road Less Travelled*.[6] The author, a psychotherapist, has a deeply spiritual — though not, at this stage of his career, a specifically Christian approach. He makes the point that, in his experience, dreams which can be interpreted invariably provide helpful information to the dreamer.

Another friend is often given 'pictures' which lead to people's healing. Elizabeth was very ill until about four years ago. She was so crippled with various illnesses, that her husband, a clergyman, couldn't possibly accept a new job because of her physical state. Attending sevices led by Colin

Urquhart on successive nights at Frome and Shepton, she was first healed and then baptised by the Holy Spirit. This has led her into the healing ministry. She often experiences God's direct leading in healing services and on other occasions:

'The first time I experienced the Lord using me in this way at a public time of worship was in September 1987. I have, on many occasions, been given pictures or words to know what the Lord wanted to heal and then, after asking for the gift of wisdom to know how to apply this in prayer, the person has been healed.

This "first" for me followed good teaching from Bishop David Pytches on being obedient and trusting the Lord in the giving of gifts when they are needed.

There were several hundred people present and Bishop Pytches had invited the Holy Spirit to be with us, and had asked for words of knowledge to be called out. I found myself being compelled to call out what the Lord was giving me to say. I "saw" a huge eye, an eyeball so distended and blown up, the socket could barely hold it. I knew it was for a woman. Many other words of knowledge were given and then, as it was at a four-day residential conference, we went on our way until the following morning. Bishop Pytches then asked us to say what healings had been received in response to the words of knowledge on the previous day. At once a woman asked if she could respond to the first word given on the previous day. She told us how she'd been living in East Africa and had been wearing contact lenses. Dust had somehow been trapped under one and oxygen had built up causing oedema of the eye — a grossly distended eyeball. She'd arrived at the conference wearing dark glasses, a hat or sun shield, and avoiding looking at any light or window.

That morning, after hearing the word of knowledge, she had woken and, as her husband drew open the bedroom curtains, she had remarked what a glorious sunny day it was. He looked and saw his wife's eye which had been so badly affected was healed.'

It does seem clear that there are periods of greater and lesser intensity of this sort of experience. We have already considered Samuel's call (Chapter 1) and would do well to remember that during Eli's feeble leadership

'The Word of the Lord was rare, there were not many visions.'

One of the most moving modern visions is recounted by Corrie Ten Boom[7] in *The Hiding Place*. Her sister, Betsie, is dying in Ravensbruck concentration camp; before she dies she has a vision of a future house in Holland, from which Corrie is to work. This vision helped to convince Corrie, a very ordinary, quiet Christian before the war, that God had a world-wide ministry for her afterwards.

In a field in Pilton, the Goode family have erected a striking white cross. At night it is floodlit, and it faces out over the valley where a controversial pop festival takes place most years.

Anne writes: 'Midsummer Day. Fellowship and open air Eucharist in the field beneath the cross. It was the first anniversary of the Pop Festival Witness which had led to two adult baptisms in the field, and other conversions. I was very tired after it all at midnight. Putting out the rubbish at the back of the house, I noticed a luminous "aurora" round the cross, sloping up into a funnel of light which reached outwards and spread like brilliant moonlight over a huge area of the night sky. Intrigued, I went over to the gate in the field, heard some noise and saw some lights in the valley where the festival takes place. Curious to know what was going on, I decided to walk to a vantage point by the cross but I found myself unable to look back down to the valley. I had to walk uphill, towards the cross. Suddenly I saw a huge cross in the sky (much bigger than the one I had seen with a group of people last year). It had its base in the far hedge and it hung right over and above the wooden cross in the middle of the field (and over me, where I had fallen with my face to the ground).'

Next day, Anne told some of her friends at a large Church Urban Fund garden party. There was a distinct lack of enthusiasm, followed the next day by a sharp verbal attack on her lack of commitment to the church and the Body of Christ. She felt bruised and depressed. She struggled through to the weekend, and eventually, on a gloomy wet Monday morning, prayed, 'Lord, you are the Lord; you can't have meant a sign for me alone – yet you obviously did mean it for me in some respect. Please tell me what you want. Speak, Lord, for your servant is trying to listen!'

Anne continues: 'I found myself getting up out of the chair and, as though it was the most natural thing in the world in the middle of prayer, I loaded the washing machine, and picked up the telephone. I rang a neighbour, with whom I had never discussed religion in a really personal way, and said, "You've got to be baptised." She replied, "I've been waiting a year for you to say that." '

The sequel was dramatic, and, I believe, brought spiritual help to her family, some relatives and friends.

She had for years been a hidden believer – a sort of Nicodemus-like figure. She had been intrigued by Christianity as a religious philosophy, but was content to be an onlooker and to pray alone in empty churches. She lives about a mile from the field. In her own words, 'The massive white cross, constructed from telegraph poles, was raised in a field near my home. At first the cross represented a shockingly bold affirmation of faith. Sited as it is, on a hillside, visible for miles around, I could not avoid seeing it. Then it spoke to me most powerfully about the person who erected it, but then it began to provide a centre point to my daily spiritual meanderings. Instead of noticing it, I looked for it; instead of looking at it, I walked consciously towards it. The cross spoke of the need for courage, for public affirmation of faith, and, finally, at a service held in its shadow, I felt the desire to come home, to accept and be accepted.

'The outcome was wonderfully logical. My baptism, which soon followed Anne's challenge, seemed a natural outcome and a tremendous release. I am so grateful to be rescued from spiritual isolation and the futility of endless speculation by the challenge of a simple wooden cross, and the brave outspoken faith of a friend.'

Recently, a very simple picture opened up an unusual period of ministry. I was with the family on a Christian holiday. We were having a marvellous experience of learning, fellowship and worship. The holiday had a profound effect on us all. Family prayers, for instance, were quite transformed by subsequent renderings of 'Be bold', 'Jesus' love is very wonderful' and 'God is not dead', from four usually somewhat reluctant young worshippers. I was quite clearly there to learn, to be quiet, and to listen. Slightly unwillingly, I attended an optional meeting entitled 'One step more'. Towards the close, there was a time of quiet for us to listen to God. I saw a very simple picture – so simple that I was reluctant to share it. It was a path through heathland. The sky was bright, the landscape beautiful and the pathway was clear. Then the path disappeared into deep woodland. It seemed fairly clear that God was reminding us that there are times of considerable light and clarity which can then turn into times of difficulty and darkness. He was reminding us that He is as much the God of the shadowland as of the open heath.

I am not sure that this picture proved of particular help to anyone, but it was what happened afterwards that was truly startling. The obedience of sharing that picture led directly to my being involved in some prayer for a tremendous Christian project in which there were real difficulties. In this situation, and in many others over the next four days, God spoke with a clarity that I've seldom experienced before.

I am certain that many people have much more that they could share; but, like me, they are held back for fear of seeming stupid. Of course, there is the opposite — the exhibitionist Christian who must share something at all costs, often with disastrous results.

THE HOLY SPIRIT AND CONFLICT

None of us likes conflict. It seems far removed from our understanding of 'the fruit of the Spirit' (Galatians 5:22). Yet there is a great deal of spiritual conflict and the guidance of God is often very clear in such situations.

The Acts of the Apostles give us a number of sharp confrontations. Peter recognised Simon Magus for what he was (Acts 8:20), Philip, although mightily used by the Lord, had failed to discern Simon's heart and had baptised him. Peter's confrontation with Simon brought him to the verge of repentance (Acts 8:24), and we do not know the outcome.[8]

Saul, soon to be renamed Paul, had little truck with Elymas (Acts 13:6ff), and bluntly called him 'a child of the devil'. We can only hope that the judgment worked out upon him may have led him, along with the proconsul, to repentance.

In Philippi (Acts 16), a slave girl followed Paul and his companions shouting 'These men are servants of the Most High God, who are telling you the way to be saved'. The message was one of impeccable orthodoxy, reminiscent of the evil spirit who recognised Jesus as 'the Holy One of God' (Mark 1:24). Remarkably, Paul put up with this interference for several days! When he eventually addressed the evil spirit within her, she was set free, her owner's profits from her fortune-telling disappeared, and a different sort of conflict broke out! It is interesting that vested commercial interests twice achieved, here and in Ephesus, what evil spirits couldn't – the removal of Paul from the scene!

I have once experienced this sort of thing. Towards the end of a parish house-party, a few of the leaders gathered in an upper room. We invited people to come for prayer and there was a remarkable sense of expectancy. None of us had really been involved in this sort of prayer before. We knew that some people wanted to receive guidance for the future and the baptism of the Holy Spirit, but we didn't know what to do!

We had just started to pray – there were about a dozen people present – when one lady started to sing. She was singing 'spiritual songs', but something seemed to be wrong. St Paul may have had the grace to put up with this for several days, but I had had enough after a few minutes. Quietly, but firmly, I told her to 'shut up in the Name of the Lord'. Graciously, she left the room. Back home, she was released from an evil spirit connected with her religious background, and, I believe, grew strongly in the Lord.

THE HOLY SPIRIT AND THE BAPTISM OF POWER

Jesus said 'But you will receive power when the Holy Spirit comes on you' (Acts 1:8).

That night, we saw it happen. A number of lives were transformed. At least three of those present were eventually called into full time Christian service.[9]

The sense of God's presence was overwhelming. A number of factors helped. We were together — taking time apart with the Lord. We were genuinely open to the renewing power of the Spirit. The room in which we were praying was a 'holy place'. Many other groups had prayed there over the years. But in the end, it was the Holy Spirit who, sovereignly, led us forward.

However much we seek guidance, however much we claim the promises of Scripture, we must remember that all the gifts 'are the work of one and the same Spirit, and He gives them to each one, just as He determines' (1 Corinthians 12:11).

Many people, including the Ephesian twelve (Acts 19: 1-6), get confused by these matters. It is obviously outside the scope of this short book to make a doctrinal statement on this complicated matter.

Nevertheless, certain things seem reasonably clear:
(1) In the Scriptures, people do receive empowering experiences from the Holy Spirit. These experiences are sometimes one-off (Ananias praying for Paul, Acts 9:17); sometimes repeated (the apostles, Acts 4:31; Timothy, by implication, 2 Timothy 1:6); sometimes ongoing (Ephesians 5:18 which, nearly all commentators agree, means be continuously filled with the Spirit!).
(2) The ultimate purpose of this experience is to assure the individual of the Fatherhood of God (Romans 8: 15-17).[10] The result of this experience is a release of power for the

benefit of the Body of Chirst. People learn to pray for others, people become effective in evangelism, people become much more aware of God and of the leading of His Spirit.

(3) Such experiences are dangerous if sought without truly renouncing evil (see Chapter 13), without a real sense of repentance and understanding of the cross. The very word 'baptism' often associated with this experience, should lead every Christian, seeking such an experience, first to the foot of the cross.

(4) The gift of tongues is *sometimes* given as a confirmatory sign (Acts 10:46 for instance).

The gift of tongues was originally a gift of speaking foreign languages. Such experiences do still occur.

Rex Gardner[11] records a recent incident told to a meeting in 'Sunderland in 1986 where a couple seriously considering abandoning Christian ministry went reluctantly to a service in a Pentecostal church. They didn't enjoy it and would have left if they hadn't been hemmed in. Then they heard an old man speaking in a tongue — he was speaking in a language they had learned in their missionary work in Sri Lanka — and their whole ministry was transformed by the experience which was so similar to Acts 2:6.

I have heard a number of people testify to this sort of experience, and have once been present when it happened.

Nevertheless, in today's church, the gift of tongues is usually used in private prayer, healing prayer, in singing, and occasionally with interpretation as an equivalent to prophecy.

It is controversial[12] for all sorts of reasons. In my own experience, singing in tongues is a deeply moving experience (my wife says I even sing in tune!). On the eve of Pentecost 1988, our Bishop had a 'teach in' in the Cathedral at Wells. After a day of seminars, on everything from the Holy Spirit in architecture to the gifts of the Spirit, we gathered for a short period of worship. Having led seminars on healing for most of the day, I was competely exhausted. Suddenly the Holy Spirit led us into singing in tongues. Well over half the congregation were able to join in. Some of those I spoke to afterwards, who found this outside their experience, were deeply moved, others were not! For me, it crowned a beautiful day – even if the Cathedral School choir did look somewhat puzzled as they walked in to prepare for Evensong.

People often ask 'Of what use is the gift?' I can remember praying for someone's back. She was very intelligent, fairly new to the church, and I felt a bit inhibited. Tentatively, I asked her permission to pray in tongues. 'It helps me when I don't know how to pray,' I explained (*viz.* Romans 8:26). When she returned some time later, she asked me to pray in tongues as she felt that it was far more effective.

Sadly, the gift of tongues causes fear and division. Paul puts it last in his list of spiritual gifts (1 Corinthians 12), and there are many far more vital gifts for the church, administration, for instance, see 1 Corinthians 1: 12-28. Nevertheless, many people who have received this gift, testify to a new sense of the Holy Spirit's presence, leading, and guidance.

Notes and references

1 See Acts 11:27ff and Acts 21:10ff.
2 Allen, Roland. *Missionary Methods: St Paul's or Ours?* Michigan, Eerdmans Pub Co, 1962.
3 The 'we' narrative ends in Acts 16:11 and reappears again at Philippi in Acts 20:6.
4 Smith, Fred and Saunders, Hilary. *God's Gift of Healing.* Chichester, New Wine Press, 1986, p 74ff.

5   St John, Patricia. *Would you believe it? You can grow to know God*. Pickering, 1983, p 141ff, and
    McAll, Kenneth. *Healing the Family Tree*. London, Sheldon Press, 1986, p 1ff.

6   Peck, M Scott. *The Road Less Travelled*. London, Hutchinson, 1983, p 245.

7   Boom, Corrie Ten. *The Hiding Place*. London, Hodder & Stoughton, 1976, p 197.

8   If sub-apostolic literature is to be believed, Simon remained a major thorn in the side of the church.

9   See Chapter 9 of this volume for the stories of two of these people.

10 Lloyd Jones, Martyn. *Roman Series: The Sons of God*. Banner of Truth, 1974. See especially his exposition on 8: 5-17, and
    Smail, Tom. *Forgotten Father*. London, Hodder & Stoughton, 1987.

11 Gardner, Rex. *Healing Miracles: a doctor investigates*. London, Darton, Longman and Todd, 1986, p 143.

12 *Ibid*, p 145.

6

WORSHIP AND THE VOICE OF GOD

In this chapter, we shall consider some of the ways that God speaks to people through worship, some of the blocks that hinder us from hearing His voice, some of the ways in which these can be overcome, and, finally, how God sometimes speaks to the whole congregation rather than just to the individual.

Worship is an expected part of Christian discipleship. It is frequently commanded by God in the Old Testament, Jesus worshipped regularly in the synagogue, and the apostles met regularly for worship.

Jesus commanded His disciples 'Do this in remembrance of me' (Luke 22:19); He taught that 'a time is coming and has now come, when the true worshippers will worship the Father in spirit and truth, for they are the kind of worshippers the Father seeks. God is spirit, and His worshippers must worship in spirit and in truth.' (John 4: 23-24) and the writer of Hebrews stated pointedly 'Let us not give up meeting together, as some are in the habit of doing, but let us encourage one another' (Hebrews 10:25).

Worship is not an optional extra for Christians, it is part of God's covenant with us, and if we do not worship regularly, it is unlikely that our spiritual experiences are Christian. If we are worshipping regularly, we should begin to expect to hear God's voice through scripture, sermon, song, silence . . . or in whatever way the Spirit chooses to communicate with us.

In my experience, however difficult and unsatisfactory some acts of worship may be (and how often it is that we are difficult and unsatisfactory worshippers?), it is a means through which God most frequently speaks to people.

But how do people hear God's voice in worship?

A SENSE OF HIS PRESENCE

Our experience of God is often almost indefinable. A very common experience is of a sense of uplift, joy, awe, comfort, or even of profound grief. While such experiences may not bring direct guidance, they are very important. Their intangible reality helps many people in their 'daily round and common task'. Positive experiences of worship give a balance to our lives, and sense of direction to our work. We may not feel that we have heard God's voice directly, but we are aware of some inward experience which gives us more confidence to believe in God in a personal way, and more openness to seek Him in our daily life.

David understood this well:

One thing I ask of the Lord, this is what I seek:
that I may dwell in the house of the Lord all the days
    of my life,
to gaze upon the beauty of the Lord and to seek him in
    His temple.
For in the day of trouble He will keep me safe in His
    dwelling;

He will hide me in the shelter of His tabernacle and set
    me high upon a rock.
Then my head will be exalted above the enemies who
    surround me;
at His tabernacle will I sacrifice with shouts of joy;
I will sing and make music to the Lord. (Psalm 27: 4-6)

I have often experienced this.

One Ascension Day I arrived in Cranmore, one of the
small village churches in my somewhat complex parish, to
take an evening service. I was tired, hurried, and ill prepared.
I walked into the church. There were over twenty people
there (now, they had been told to make a special effort,
but − for a Thursday evening . . .). More importantly,
there was an immediate atmosphere of praise and
expectancy. This in a church which I had felt a few years
earlier was spiritually dead and possibly should be closed.
The service was amazing. My spirit soared, I preached I
know not what, but it helped many. Another step of preparation for a future mission was taken, I felt the tangible love
and enthusiasm of a small congregation. Even more, I felt
our mutual love and worship of God.

I felt released, recharged, and on fire. I left in a very much
better state than I had come!

By contrast, grief is also part of many worshippers'
experience. It can be caused by human reasons − bereaved
people often feel saddest in church (I still find it difficult
to visit the village church where my family worshipped for
so many happy years). Those who have experienced broken
relationships, or whose home life is profoundly unhappy
often are overcome with tears in church.

Grief may sometimes be sheer indulgence, but more
usually it is God's way of bringing healing into someone's
life. Worship helps us free the pain and allows God to bring

healing, and if need be, forgiveness.

A few weeks earlier, my Aunt had died. She had lived to be ninety-three and, as my only close living relative outside my immediate family, she was very special. She was my godmother, and years ago had sent me a New English Bible. I remember writing to her once, saying something to the effect that 'If someone sent me a modern translation of the Bible, I might start reading it again.' She responded by return of post! After her death, I preached in Cranmore. It was just after Easter. I preached about the Resurrection, but also about my Aunt. I talked of her helplessness, like the dying bishop,[1] I talked of God's grace in her, and her choice of funeral hymn:

> God be in my head,/And in my understanding;
> God be in my eyes,/And in my looking;
> God be in my mouth,/And in my speaking;
> God be in my heart,/And in my thinking;
> God be at my end,/And in my departing.

In particular, I said that I would remember her as she had been in her prime, a gracious, godly woman who had experienced suffering and yet found fulfilment in her life, and not just as the mere shadow that I had known in the last few years.

One visitor was strangely moved. A Norwegian lady, visiting a friend in Cranmore, had an old father who was dying. She had found the church at home unhelpful. Here, in a strange land, with a strange form of service, with a strange speaker, God spoke words of comfort. I can't be certain, but I don't think that I intended to speak about Aunt Hilda's death when I entered that church.

A WORD FROM THE LORD

When we come to church, do we expect to hear the voice of God? Do we really want to hear His voice? Are we prepared to change?

My mother used to tell the story of the country signalman who was found with one level crossing gate open and the other closed. When asked why, he said 'I was half expecting a train'. Half expecting! One gate open, one closed. Isn't that a picture of us − half open to God, yet constructing the gates of our lives so that neither God nor man can get through to us?

I was brought up in a small country village. My mother's faith, shining through difficult circumstances, encouraged me as did the village church. They used to have a rather terrible lesson reader who mumbled, and read with his hands in his pockets. After one service, the Squire's wife could stand it no longer. 'Colonel —, if you can't read the lessons better than that you'd better stop.' He did. I, at some quite young age, became one of the regular readers. But still I hadn't heard His voice. I was confirmed − rather a matter of course, I fear, and I went up to Oxford. I was recommended to St Aldate's and attended for the best part of three years. I was amazed by the size of the congregation; we even used to sit on the window sills on special occasions. I was moved by the preaching, I was somewhat repelled by the reputation of some of the Christians in college, and still I hadn't heard His voice.

I shared digs with an unusual man who used to conduct nightly worship according to the principles of the Free Presbyterian Church of Scotland. His demeanour, and that of his friends, although a constant source of innocent merriment, made a profound impression. I joined them sometimes, but still I hadn't heard the voice of God.

Eventually, in my final term, I did hear His voice. The Sunday service was quite ordinary. The church, as usual, was full. The preacher was to be Mr Ernest Shippam. It didn't sound impressive – St Aldate's usually raked up bishops, celebrities, and even the occasional Archbishop. Once he started to speak I was spellbound. He didn't preach, he told his life history.

It was a story of a religious upbringing, an avoidance of real commitment to Christ, a busy life and a difficult job, drink, more drink, and an alcohol problem. Then, gradually, things started to change. He had a simple prayer answered when he found himself asking for an orange squash instead of a double whisky at an airport bar. Then he hired a coach to take his employees to hear Billy Graham one evening at Harringay in 1953. 'It will do them good!' he thought. At the end of the address, when Dr Graham invited inquirers to come forward, Ernest found himself leading the way. Only later did he notice his wife beside him. His conversion revolutionised his life. Family life, previously ruined by alcohol and all its attendant disorders, was transformed. Christian priorities were introduced into the firm. Some of the work-force became Christians. Ernest became a lay preacher, he ran the firm to the glory of God and he was happier than he had ever been before.

Jesus was so obviously real to him; Jesus so obviously had changed his whole life. I felt an inner turmoil. We sang the hymn 'Jesus calls us o'er the tumult'. We were invited to come forward and talk to the preacher. I tried to escape. But the church was so crowded, I just couldn't get to the door. I went back to the pew, and waited. Very tentatively I went forward. I hoped he might be too busy to talk to me. He wasn't. He asked me why I had come up. I said something about wanting that sort of faith. I added that I wasn't sure my friends at my digs would approve (it was generally held that no good thing could happen in the Church of England). Mr Shippam told me not to worry and gave me a booklet to read. That afternoon, in the quiet of my digs, I made a very tentative prayer of surrender to Christ. It seemed so simple, yet for the next few weeks, I felt in a spiritual whirl. Everything was changing, God seemed so real. Bridge, my god at that time, seemed unimportant. Canon Keith de Berry, the Rector of St Aldate's, made gallant efforts to follow me and help me. Without his friendship, his prayers, his teaching, progress would have been very slow, or even non-existent. I soon discovered that conversion didn't solve all one's problems and created some new ones. My girlfriend, a committed Christian, didn't immediately fall in love with me. It took me a long time to realise that that wasn't God's intention. My parents were bewildered. I was uncertain about worship. My Free Presbyterian friend took me on a tour of Scotland. I was deeply moved by the power and sincerity of their worship, but that didn't seem to be God's way for me. The village church had somewhat lost its attraction. The school that I went to teach in had very formal worship, attended, on the whole, by reluctant and, occasionally, disruptive boys. The voice of God was growing faint.

Again I was rescued by Canon de Berry. He summoned me to his parish holiday – ostensibly as a helper, but in fact to learn. Each year, I again heard something of the voice of God. One year, I wondered if God was calling me to ordination. It was an appalling thought. I enjoyed teaching; I was becoming involved in the school chapel; I was very happy. Not me, Lord? For a year I wrestled and prayed. The voice of God remained silent. Right at the end of a summer term, just before the third parish holiday, I shut the Bible and said to God 'If you want me to be ordained, you'd better make it clear.' As I write now, twenty years later, it sounds an appallingly arrogant and inadequate prayer. But two weeks later He did.

I went to church in Ambleside. It was the middle of the fortnight of the parish holiday. I was again in a turmoil. The night before, God had begun to speak. He told me quite clearly to give up one budding relationship (which was just as well, as the girl concerned had just got engaged and was herself becoming confused). He also told me to give up my teaching career. For good measure, I was directed to Psalm 143:8 which spoke of experiencing God's love in the morning. I went to church in an expectant daze. The first thing that happened was that we sang Psalm 143. The voice of God seemed a little louder. Then Canon Keith de Berry preached. The church was filled with holidaymakers. Normally he would have preached an evangelistic sermon. That year, the Feast of the Transfiguration of Our Lord (celebrated on August 6th), fell on a Sunday. Keith preached a sermon about Jesus on the mountain, and the choice that lay before Him.

'Humanly speaking, Jesus had a choice. He could return to Galilee as a fairly successful minor prophet, or He could go on to Jerusalem and fulfil God's destiny for Him . . . Some of you, in a lesser way, face that sort of challenge. You can stay where you are. . . or you can go forward and do something far more difficult to which God is calling you.'

He didn't know the state that I was in. I hadn't discussed the matter of ordination with him. But, now, I knew. I could have talked my way out of the previous evening (emotion); I could have talked my way out of the sermon (coincidence, meant for others); but I couldn't talk my way out of both. Reluctantly I set off on the trail towards ordination.

Many other times, subsequently, God has spoken to me through worship. Sometimes in the 'great congregation'; sometimes in small, quiet services; occasionally when I'm leading others; more often when I'm being led. A few more examples, and then we must consider the much more important question of how, in general, we can encourage and enable one another to hear God's voice in worship.

AN EXPERIENCE OF CHANGE

One woman came to an evening service because her daughter wanted to be baptised. She came out of duty, and was startled to find an unstructured service with orchestra and open prayer. She was even more startled to hear the sermon preached by Bishop Ban It Chiu[2]. She had entered the church a distant agnostic, she walked out a newborn Christian. God spoke, through Bishop Chiu, with clarity and power and she knew that the word was for her.

Parents often come to church out of a sense of duty. A number of clear adult conversions have taken place in Shepton because children, young and old, have brought their parents to church!

One teenager went to a nearby independent school. He was surrounded by Buddhists and Muslims. They seemed to take religion very seriously. The boy demanded to be taken to church. His father reluctantly complied. His opinion of the church, based on distant memories and professional experiences, was extremely low. To his surprise, he became intrigued. Father and son were both prepared for confirmation. They discovered a great release in their own relationship. Then, one Good Friday, the father was hoovering his house. God gave him a worship song, and a tune. We were thrilled. Not only was it a powerful verse, but it had a hauntingly simple tune. The final line of the first verse contained the line 'Come, follow Me!' which,

unknown to the author, was to be the chosen title of our
Parish Festival.

After a little tidying up of the verse and some musical
pointing, at my request a fourth verse was added to
emphasise the 'Come, follow Me' theme. It became the
centre piece of the Festival and remains a well-loved song
in our church. Here are the words:

> Dark was my life till the Lord spoke to me
> Hard was my heart and no point could I see:
> Jesus spoke clearly to me: glory be!
> 'Lay down your burdens, come follow Me'
> > Now there's
> Love in my heart for the light of my life,
> Peace in my soul now my Saviour is near
> Love everlasting and peace evermore
> O, how I wish I'd listened before
> > I know
> Prayers will be answ'red and all sins forgiv'n,
> Doubts are dispelled and my future is clear
> Now I will worship and serve Him with joy,
> Gladly I'll follow Jesus my King
> > And so
> If you're alone and your heart's full of care,
> If darkness rules in your life, don't despair,
> Seek, look and listen, and soon you will see
> He will say clearly 'Come, follow Me.'

Receiving those words released Tim into a completely new
awareness of God's presence in both worship and his daily
life. There is the link! Lips that confess His name will offer
God a continual sacrifice of praise — in worship and good
works. The people whose discipleship impresses
me — those who hear God's voice and bring practical help

to many people — are usually those who have a natural expectancy in their attitude to worship.

The writer of Hebrews puts it: 'Through Jesus, therefore, let us continually offer to God a sacrifice of praise — the fruit of lips that confess His name. And do not forget to do good and to share with others, for with such sacrifices God is pleased.'

Sometimes God speaks during a service in a very unexpected way. One of my congregation writes: 'I had been trying to cope with a feeling of isolation and alienation from the church in Shepton. In one of your sermons you told us how your daughter, Susanna, was often accused of being idle about the washing-up. Her reply was "I'm an idol — you must worship me!" I saw suddenly my attitude as idolatry. I asked for forgiveness. My request was answered soon afterwards when I heard a voice calling my name. We sang the hymn "Dear Lord and Father of mankind" and "the still, small voice of calm" became a reality.'

A VARIETY OF MEANS

I believe that God speaks to people through a great variety of worship. We may all have our preferences, but since there are remarkably few New Testament directives about forms of worship, we should surely be generous in accepting a wide variety of types of worship, and open to God's voice in unlikely services and places! A few personal examples may help.

Twice recently on holiday, God seemed to speak. The first was during a period of informal worship on a houseparty. We sang 'The Servant King'[3]. I had never heard it before. I am not an emotional person, but tears filled my eyes as we sang about Christ's experience in the garden, and our need to give ourselves to others in service. The result of this song was that God opened me up, so that despite being on holiday and off duty, I was able, in some measure, to be available to others.

Later, on that same holiday, I was agonising over the title for this book. Early one morning I went alone to a small village church to a Prayer Book Communion Service. Not normally a time, or a service, at which I have great expectations. During the reciting of the familiar liturgy (and there is a place for well-known words to help us meditate and listen), my mind moved back to my own village church and my parents. I thought of my father, and how, very gradually, towards the end of his troubled life, he had joined us for worship. Then, quite suddenly, I remembered his one and only published play *The Silent Voice*. Was this the answer to months of uncertainty about a title . . . ?

As a priest I am terribly in bondage to numbers. People's absence can quite unreasonably affect my morale, and my judgment. Perhaps for that reason it is often at the smallest services that God speaks to me most clearly!

BLOCKS TO HEARING GOD'S VOICE IN WORSHIP

Obviously there are as many potential blocks as there are worshippers! Nevertheless, I would want to highlight three major blocks – predictability, chaos, and presumption.

The prophet Hosea had some caustic words about predictable worship:

'Come, let us return to the Lord. He has torn us to pieces but He will heal us; he has injured us but He will bind up our wounds. After two days He will revive us; on the third day He will restore us, that we may live in His

presence. Let us acknowledge the Lord; let us press on
to acknowledge Him. As surely as the sun rises, He will
appear; He will come to us like the winter rains, like the
spring rains that water the earth.

What can I do with you, Ephraim? What can I do with
you, Judah? Your love is like the morning mist, like the
early dew that disappears. Therefore I cut you in pieces
with my prophets, I killed you with the words of my
mouth; my judgments flashed like lightning upon you.
For I desire mercy, not sacrifice, and acknowledgment
of God rather than burnt offerings' (Hosea 6: 1-6).

Jesus twice picked up Hosea's evocative phrase[5], 'For I
desire mercy, not sacrifice'.

The effects of predictable, in this case, sacrificial, worship
were to harden people's hearts and to leave them incapable
of seeing, in Hosea's time, the real repentance that God
required; and in Jesus' time it led His opponents into criticising Jesus' ministry to Matthew's friends and to criticising
the disciples for picking ears of corn on the Sabbath.

Today, sadly, worship is often predictable − both in
liturgical and non-liturgical services − the voice of God is
stifled by the rituals of man.

A different sort of problem is caused by chaos. Children
are a great joy in church, but it has to be admitted that it
is very hard to lead worship (let alone to listen!) against a
babble of small voices. Each church, and each congregation,
will have to seek God's voice about children and worship.

Adults are often as indisciplined as children. I once led
a healing service in a village church where it was impossible
for anyone to prepare themselves before the service because
of the loud voice of one of the praying team gossiping to
a friend.

If the whole congregation would arrive early, and pray

seriously before the service, we would all experience much more of the Lord's guidance. It is encouraging how much people value periods of silence in worship, and how we are learning to use them instead of being embarrassed by them.

PREPARATION FOR WORSHIP

Worship requires careful preparation — both of the leaders and the individual worshipper (1 Corinthians 11:28). If we leaders do not prepare ourselves in prayer, in confession, or in listening to God, we need hardly be surprised if our worship doesn't speak to us. If most of the congregation is unprepared and unexpectant, not even the magnificent *Alternative Service Book* (ASB) alternative Prayer of Humble Access[6] will rescue us.

> Most merciful Lord, your love compels us to come in.
> Our hands were unclean, our hearts were unprepared; we
> were not fit even to eat the crumbs from under your table.
> But you, Lord, are the God of our salvation,
> and share your bread with sinners.
> So cleanse and feed us
> with the precious body and blood of your Son,
> that he may live in us and we in him;
> and that we, with the whole company of Christ,
> may sit and eat in your kingdom.
> Amen.

Presumption is a very dangerous sin. It is fatally easy to assume that because we are open to God's voice, because we have experienced a greater variety in worship, that God must speak to us on any given occasion. Some people have a desperate psychological need to 'hear' God's voice.

Consequently, they think they 'hear' something — usually for someone else — and then descend upon the victim with a 'word' from the Lord. People I know have been put under pressure to move house, change jobs, get married and so on . . . , all because well-meaning friends have felt they've heard God's voice. I would reiterate[7] there are tests by which such 'guidance' must be checked. It is very embarrassing, and difficult to handle, when things go wrong, and it may be advisable to ask people to share the gist of their message with the leaders before they are allowed to speak in public.

Nevertheless, it is marvellous when God does speak, marvellous when people hear, and most amazing of all when most of a congregation recognises God's voice at the same time and in the same way! Better a few mistakes than no openness.

The late David Watson used to remind people that one meaning of worship is to 'kiss towards'. If we have that attitude to worship, we shall truly come as the bride prepared to meet the bridegroom and to hear His voice.

Notes and references

1 See Chapter 14 of this volume.
2 See Chapter 16 of this volume for part of Bishop Ban It Chiu's own testimony.
3 Kendrick, Graham. *Carol Praise*. No 91. Marshall Pickering.
4 See Chapter 5 of this volume.
5 See Matthew 9:13 and Matthew 12:7.
6 *Alternative Service Book*, London, 1980, p 170.
7 See Chapter 1 of this volume.

7

LISTENING AND THE BODY OF CHRIST

'As you come to him, the living Stone — rejected by men but chosen by God and precious to him — you also, like living stones, are being built into a spiritual house to be a holy priesthood, offering spiritual sacrifices acceptable to God through Jesus Christ (1 Peter 2:4-5).'

LIVING STONES

We, the individual stones, are being built into a spiritual house. We might will it otherwise; we may prefer our own company and want to keep our own counsel (my religion is my own private affair!); we may long for a succession of isolated 'mountain top' experiences — but it isn't usually possible. Jesus intended his sheep to graze together. We cannot spend our lives going off by ourselves and getting lost or ignored.

Imagine a grey, stone Cotswold wall. It is well laid, it needs no mortar, each stone is touched by a number of other ones. That is a picture for each of us. We should be one of those stones; surrounded, supported and supporting other stones. Some are very close, some are more distant. Of course, like any other picture, this has its limitations. In Christian experience, the stones move and relationships change. Nevertheless, God intends each of us to have an inner group of people who are spiritually precious to us.

THE SUPPORTING TIER

Ideally some will be our counsellors, whether in the local church or outside it. They form the row beneath our stone. They are that small group of people whom we can trust with our innermost thoughts, our ultimate hopes, and our spiritual direction. Each of us needs such people — the more responsible our job, spiritually, the more we need them. I have found over the years a number of people to whom I can turn. It may be helpful to mention a few. Canon Keith de Berry, in whose church I first was converted, has been one. A little while ago, when reeling under a severe and unexpected spiritual depression, I visited him. We hadn't met for several years, but he knew enough of me and my situation to listen sensitively and to ask the right questions. As is often the case, time was running out. He stopped and insisted that we prayed together. Already the darkness was lifting. Then he prayed including the lines from a hymn:

Vainly we wait for the harvest time till God gives life to the seed.[1]

He couldn't have known this was a hymn which had spoken to me over many years. Light burst into my depression. Although the circumstances which had caused the depression didn't change for some time, the power of the depression was broken.

Another was Reg East, founder of the Barnabas Fellowship at Whatcombe House. I first met him when I took over as secretary of the Bath and Wells Diocesan Healing Group. Reg was due to speak at a healing conference. In the meantime we became friends. He ministered to a severe problem in the family, and then I had the confidence to ask him to pray through some difficult times in my past.[2]

A third was a bishop. We tend to think that bishops are far too busy for individual problems. One bishop said to me 'Treat me as a friend, if you need me . . .' I faced a big problem. I had had contradictory medical advice over a tiresome condition. Quite suddenly, I felt very depressed and uncertain about my future. A quick phone call to his secretary, who discerned that there was a measure of urgency, led to an appointment within three days, and a most helpful and encouraging hour.

Each of these, together with a number of others, have supported my 'spiritual' stone. They have been good friends, advisers and praying partners. All have had the courage to direct me, challenge me, rebuke me, and to stop me taking myself too seriously. All have pointed me back to God, none has claimed infallibility. None has tried to become my spiritual 'guru'.

THE SECOND TIER

The second tier, the stones at my own level, consists of my closest spiritual friends. These have varied over the years, but include Jane, my wife, staff colleagues, parishioners, godparents of my children and other clergy. There are so many that it is less easy to give examples. Two will suffice.

The times that Jane has prayed for me – occasionally in my sleepless periods, even being woken up in the middle of the night to pray with amazing effect – are without number. Her occasional blunt criticisms, so occasional that they are far more effective, show me the way forward. I remember returning some years ago, full of enthusiasm, from the wedding which inspired this book. I told her all about it. Her quiet comment 'You'd better do a lot more praying' was all too true!

David Prior[3] is another. We don't meet very often, but inevitably such meetings are very positive. I have learnt so much from his preaching, writing, counsel and, above all, his friendship. I believe, too, that I have been able to help him in the area of healing, through one dark pastoral situation, and with the occasional flash of inspiration. Last time we met, after a profitable evening anointing many people with oil at the end of a house party (see James 5:13ff), I suggested to him that he train some leaders and invite his congregation to come forward after morning service. When we last spoke, people were streaming forward to respond! More important, however, their shared ministry has been shared friendship. David and his wife, Rosemary, have been good friends to Jane and me. Although we meet only occasionally, it seems so easy to share our troubles, rejoice in encouragements, to laugh at past events, and to be serious about the dilemmas that trouble us.

Most of the others that I would want to name would be parishioners and it would be invidious to single any out. It is always difficult for a clergyman to have real friends in his own congregation, yet I have gained enormously from those who have crossed that invisible barrier which most congregations erect between themselves and their rector (or is it vice-versa?).

THE TIER ABOVE

The third tier, the stones whom I support, are many and

varied. They range from one-off visitors, usually contacted at healing services, to confirmation candidates, via almost every conceivable sort of parishioner. Again, it is difficult to be specific.

It is an immense privilege to listen to, talk to, and pray for people. To me, it is the best part of my calling. I learn so much from those who come, and am constantly amazed by people's faith, humility and courage. One of the tragedies of the modern clergyman's job is that he is expected to look after so many people, to be part of so many projects, that it is possible to lose touch completely with people.

I include extracts from two letters, because they illustrate the privilege of service: 'You may recall, you first visited me over four years ago, soon after I had returned after eight weeks in hospital following a traumatic cancer operation. Being in constant pain, it came as somewhat of a surprise to find that great relief was felt for up to two hours after your visit. Later visits, which included prayer for healing, did much to help the very pronounced scar tissues fade away. About six months later, I avoided a predicted operation when a swelling, caused by what may have been undissolved stitches, disappeared after more prayer. As you know, I couldn't have made such great strides without the day and night care of my husband and the medical skills of my doctor and the district nurses. But I feel greatly blessed by knowing all my friends in the church and by their prayers.'

Much more typical is a parishioner who writes as follows: 'Guidance has come to me through people. I know that God sent you here three years ago, to rescue my son and myself. At that time I was in deep depression, addicted to tranquillisers, locked in a bad marriage. It's not surprising that I had little or no confidence in myself. I had no job and no faith. (You've certainly earned your money with this lot!) Through you, a colleague, and a lay leader, I have learnt that some men are to be trusted and became my friends. That to me is nothing short of a miracle.

'God is guiding me still and I pray that I will be worthy of all the kindness and help that I have been lucky enough to receive.'

THE STONES MOVE

All models have their limitations and it would be terrible if my stone wall illustration became a rigid rule. Different people's needs are different at different times. Also, in Christ, we are all equal. The bishop who counsels me may need my prayer of healing, my friendship, or my encouragement. The depressed lady, freed from tranquillisers, may give me enormous support and hope. Some whom I have begun by counselling or even leading to Christ have become my closest friends and counsellors. We all have gifts and graces, and we need to learn to depend on each other. I don't always need an 'expert' to sort me out. My wife or some discerning parishioner can do just as well! It is important that we learn to listen, and to try and discover whom God would have us see. Satan, that great author of confusion, will gladly send us scuttling in many directions, wearying good Christian folk with our confused tales of conflicting woes. In Christ, all are one, and although it doesn't always work in practice, there should be a great deal of interchange at all levels. The new disciple, whom I am helping, may have fresh insights, and a simple faith, far deeper than mine. The aged counsellor, to whom I look up, may need my help and encouragement as he faces the problems of illness, bereavement, loneliness and the like. In Christ, good relationships tend towards equality as we all recognise our place at the foot of the cross.

Of course there is a place for spiritual authority and spiritual leadership; scripture and experience make that clear, but the authority is to be exercised with gentleness and the leadership must have the quality of servanthood (see John 13). True authority, it should go without saying, can only be exercised with the willing agreement of those who receive it.

LISTENING THROUGH FRIENDS

Friends can help us to listen and discern the will of God. Think of Barnabas. How he helped Saul of Tarsus. How he took him and presented him to the suspicious and frightened disciples in Jerusalem (Acts 11: 26-28). And before we are too hasty in judging the Jerusalem leadership, spare a thought for our Christian friends in Communist lands, never quite sure if the new converts are genuine or plants by the KGB, or its equivalent. Remember how Barnabas was sent to keep the Church in Antioch on the apostolic rails (Acts 11:19ff). He did a good job, recognised the grace of God, and continued an effective ministry. What does he do? Set himself up as Apostle of Antioch? No, he collects brother Saul and shares the leadership with him.

With friends like Barnabas, listening to God becomes so much easier. By nature I am a solitary person. Leave me alone with a book, a chess set, or alone in the country, and I am blissfully happy. But despite this, and despite what some of my Christian friends still feel, I am so grateful to those who, in good times, in ordinary times, and in hard times, have helped me hear the voice of God.

INDIVIDUAL ACCOUNTABILITY WITHIN THE BODY

However much I may seek other people's prayer and counsel, in the last resort I am accountable to God for whatever I do.

As Jeremiah says in his great prophecy of the New Covenant (Jeremiah 31: 29-34) 'Whoever eats sour grapes — his own teeth will be set on edge.'

Here is a warning story from a mature Christian who has been greatly blessed in various ways by God:

'Guidance is quite a difficult area for me — sometimes I feel I've got it right and have heard God's voice — through the Bible, through prayer, through the work of other people — and these are times when I feel most at peace about the way I should go. All too often, though, I tend to listen, when asking for guidance, only to the directives I want to hear. Recently, after having a baby, I was offered a part-time job. I mentioned it to a few Christians, most of whom surprised me by stressing the value and importance of the family, and the fact that the time for returning to work would, possibly, come later. I heard what they said, but I was listening for other advice. The job demanded more time than I had anticipated. The resulting situation was one of oppression, because the baby's health problems intensified at exactly that time. I was torn between his needs and those of the job. I should, indeed, have waited!

'Looking back, I think that the best, but hardest way of attaining guidance is to pray with an open mind and to look for a sense of peace, which seems to indicate, or accompany the "God given" advice.'

On that occasion, the Body of Christ got it right, and the individual ignored their hesitations. There are other celebrated occasions when individuals have had to back their own convictions that they've heard God correctly. Two notable examples are William Carey's call to missionary work in India.[4] He is alleged to have been told 'When God chooses to convert the heathen, He will do it without your aid or mine!', or the resistance to Jackie Pullinger's call to Hong Kong[5] and her dramatic ministry among the opium addicts inside the Walled City.

In the next chapter we shall explore ways in which each individual can fulfil Jeremiah's great prophecy, ' "They will all know me, from the least of them to the greatest," declares the Lord' (Jeremiah 31:34). As individuals, we need one another, but not to such an extent that there is no freedom to grow or to make our own mistakes. The baby's mother has learnt from her mistake — she, I am sure, will now be able to listen more clearly for God's silent voice.

Notes and references

1 *Hymns Ancient and Modern Revised*. 'God is working His Purpose out', No 271.
2 See Chapter 13 of this volume, the section headed 'The Healing of our Past'.
3 Rector of St Michael's, Chester Square.
4 Finnie, Kellsye M. *William Carey by trade a cobbler*. STL/Kingsway, 1986, p 32.
5 Pullinger, Jackie and Quicke, Andrew. *Chasing the Dragon*. London, Hodder & Stoughton, 1980.

8

PRAYER – GOD'S SILENT VOICE

Christians disagree about many things; but one thing we are all agreed about is the vital importance of our prayer life. We may have very divergent methods, expectations, and experiences; we may learn from many different traditions, teachers, or books; but we are united that prayer is the hidden centre-point of our religion. We are united also in proclaiming the intrinsic difficulty of practising what we preach, or of praying as we know we ought.

It is outside the scope and purpose of this book to look at the content of a normal prayer life.[1] I am concerned to explore whether we can hear God's voice; and, if it is possible to hear God's voice, how do we recognise that it is His voice and not the product of our own imagination or, worse still, the voice of some spiritual enemy?

Each disciple must, I believe, find his own path of prayer. Reluctantly, I shall give examples, suggest principles, offer advice, yet as I write I realise the fearful inadequacy of my own prayer life, and the danger of encouraging mere methods.

The safest place to start, indeed the only safe place, is Scripture. We may learn from the Saints how they did their praying. Then we may read biographies, diaries, books by the great men and women of prayer. But all the time we

read, we should begin to hear the silent voice of God calling
each of us to pray.

CREATING TIME

Prayer demands the best of our time; we cannot give God
second best and expect much by way of communication. I
have an infuriating habit of trying to do two things at
once — up to a point it works; but I cannot listen to my
wife while reading a book. I cannot counsel a parishioner
while answering the telephone, I cannot pray effectively
while washing up, driving a car, and so on. When I was
seeking Jane in marriage, I gave her my total attention; when
I'm praying it should be like that. I may use other times
for prayer (just as I can do mathematics with one ear on
a boring meeting, or talk to my wife while washing up); but
if I pray only in these sorts of circumstances, I can hardly
be surprised if my prayer life seems utterly barren.

  Herein lies the first great battle of the will. 'Thy will be
done' we pray. If we mean it, we will find time to pray. John
Wesley found four hours a day — and disappointed Dr
Johnson[2] by going to bed so early. Wesley clearly rated
listening to God as more important than listening to Dr
Johnson. I wonder whether we make similar decisions?

  I cannot tell you when to pray. I know some who get up
very early, I know some who use their lunch hours, I know
some who get away for special days, I know many who fail.
God understands our difficulty. He knows that there are
times when making space is almost impossible — the young
mother with a demanding toddler, the patient in hospital
in constant pain and surrounded by continuous fuss, or the
self-employed business man who has to work a twelve-hour
day. But, He also knows that each of us needs time, and

He will show us how to find it — if we dare to ask!

Just recently there was a rather nasty case of a medium who was sent to prison for swindling a woman out of a lot of money. The details of the case are unimportant. But the medium said in his defence that he spent one and a half hours each day getting 'psyched up' in occult meditation. What a tragedy that many Christians feel they've done well if they've managed a tenth of that on a regular basis.

FINDING A CREATIVE PLACE

Jesus constantly withdrew into the mountains and hillsides to pray. We need places to withdraw to. It may be in a church — if so, we will need to wrap up against the cold, and to prepare for the distractions of the tourist, the tramp, or other parishioners. It may be in the countryside — if so, we will need to remember we are not on a nature walk. It may be in a quiet room at home — if so, it would be wise to eliminate the telephone and as many other potential distractions as possible.

I like praying in church. It feels right. I know that others have prayed in the same building for hundreds of years. For me, it is best late on a Saturday night or fairly early in the morning. Disturbances must be accepted — the tramp will need a cup of tea, the parishioner will need a prayer or some advice, the tourists are usually quiet and reverent.

I like praying in the countryside. I walk and talk, I walk and listen. God often seems to speak through natural things. I find that matters of parish policy, family worries, sermons, scripts, often become much clearer in the country. One of the frustrations of a weak hip is that prayer is more difficult. Walking is limited by pain, sitting and kneeling likewise. Yet pain is a great reminder of Our Lord — a Man of sorrows, and familiar with suffering (Isaiah 53:3).

I like praying at home – when I'm left in peace! Some years ago my Aunt gave me a beautiful painting. It is a large, romantic Victorian watercolour of a lake surrounded by mountains. One of the best birthday presents I've ever received was when Jane had the picture properly lit. I love to sit on a hard chair, and meditate silently upon the *Waters of Konigsee* – the calm blue water, the towering mountains, the fragile man with his dog, punting a little boat, the Madonna and Child in a lakeside cave.

ARE YOU SITTING COMFORTABLY?

There is a long ascetic tradition in prayer. We may not, nowadays, recommend beds of nails, or other forms of physical punishment; but we have a sort of built-in 'rule' that we should find some suitably uncomfortable pew, floor, kneeler, or what have you. Yet, if we are to pray, and above all, to listen, we must be comfortable.

For me, that means a good hard chair. It usually means a little deep breathing, a releasing of the muscles (especially the neck where so much tension builds up), uncrossing the legs and unclenching the hands.[3] A chair seems a good place in which to try and listen; kneeling seems more appropriate for confession and intercession. Sometimes other physical positions seem appropriate. I was deeply moved by an African praying prostrate on the floor. Occasionally, I find that is the only reverent place as I sense the glory of God in some new way. Sometimes, there is such a sense of exultation that, like the lame man by the Gate Beautiful (Acts 3), I go 'walking, and leaping, and praising God'.[4]

THE SCRIPTURES AND PRAYER

I invariably read the Scriptures before meditation and I usually meditate before using other forms of prayer. Obviously everyone is different. We each need our own prayer pattern – a pattern which will vary, but will probably have a basic discipline so that we don't spend valuable time wondering what to do next.

The importance of Scripture should be obvious. Scripture not only teaches what God is like, but also how ordinary men and women meet God. Scripture also lays down enough basic guidelines to solve many of our problems without recourse to lengthy prayer sessions. Scripture takes us away from ourselves to God. Normally, I follow the set Anglican readings. Their 'given-ness' is immensely helpful and if sometimes they, irritatingly, leave out sections, particularly of the Old Testament, these can always be filled in. Today, away from home, I have read the first two verses of 1 Peter. Aided by what promises to be a superb commentary[5], I have been reminded that Peter was concerned not to give a five-minute testimony on what the Resurrection meant to him, but to offer 'the Lord's interpretation of His own work in the light of His own word.' I needed to hear that, I was already becoming conscious that this book was becoming too much of a personal testimony and too little of what the silent voice of God is saying to His world.

Scripture is often the voice of God directly to us. A great deal depends on attitude and expectation. If Bible reading becomes a mechanical chore it will become dead. Equally, if it is allowed to become irregular, it will soon become sporadic or non-existent.

Sometimes the Bible speaks very directly to our own situation. A series of sermons by David Prior on Jacob spoke to my lameness (as well as to deeper spiritual conflicts); preparing for a series of sermons on the Ten Commandments spoke deeply to me on my attitude to religion, to Sunday, to sex, to money; reading Daniel, in the Anglican cycle, challenged me about standing fast on matters of principle. The Bible has an amazing power to speak. It needs to be read prayerfully, it needs to be read sensibly, it needs to be read responsively. Above all it needs to be read.

AIDS TO PRAYER

Music can be a tremendous help. Recently, listening to an organ recital, I found its varied themes a tremendous incentive to pray. Sometimes tapes of Christian worship can lift me into a prayerful mood – especially on a long car journey.

I ended one adult confirmation class with a time of silent meditation. We sat in near darkness, surrounded by the light of candles. We took the theme of 'Christ, the Light of the world'. One young mother, who previously couldn't bear to look directly at light, was deeply moved and, perhaps, even experienced a real measure of physical healing. Everyone else responded positively to what, for them, was a new experience. A vase of flowers, a church banner, a cross, all of these and many others have helped me from time to time. Sometimes harsh objects, such as a lump of wood, a barbed wire fence, a pile of rubble, can speak equally powerfully. Christians must beware of using only 'pretty' objects on which to meditate. The true cross was anything but pretty. Something harsh or untidy focuses our thoughts on the sufferings of the world and may lead us into God-directed action. Corrie Ten Boom[6] shows us how a plague of fleas brought peace and prayer and how her dying sister had visions for the future, surrounded by death, torture and squalor.

A PRAYER DIARY

Prayer diaries (usually called journals) are in fashion. Partly, I fear, for man-centred reasons; mainly, I hope, through a desire for us to remember what God has done for us and spoken to us. I write mine about once a month. Stretching back over fifteen years, it is a record of good times and bad, of people for whom I was praying, of situations which seemed so important then, of forgotten disasters, of joy, of humour and of hope.

It acts as a useful corrective both to spiritual pride and its close companion, spiritual despair. It is a wonderful reminder of how God spoke – occasionally 'prophetically' before the event, sometimes during some great spiritual crisis, often afterwards, looking back with thanksgiving and relief. It is a sober reminder of times of darkness, of disobedience, of despair, and even of demonic powers. It is a happy record of people. Some, whom I've been privileged to help; others with whom I've apparently failed. Prayers answered and prayers not answered – at least in the way I'd hoped! Sometimes the references are too coded for me now to understand, sometimes they are too personal ever to share. Writing seems to bring me close to God. I often sense His presence and direction. If the prayer diary helps anyone know God better, then it is an important journal; if it is written with an eye for future publication, it would be better burnt.

The Psalms, particularly those that may reasonably be attributed to David, are a remarkable prayer diary. We need to recover their use in our worship. They cover such a wonderful variety of needs and themes; they speak so amazingly to our attitudes and concerns today.

The key to prayer is silence. Our natural instinct is to talk. Of course, there needs to be talk — adoration, thanksgiving, confession, intercession — but, above all, there needs to be silence. Not just a negative silence which might lay one open to all manner of 'spiritual' experience; but a positive Holy Silence when the disciple comes into the presence of the Father.

'Do not be quick with your mouth, do not be hasty in your heart to utter anything before God. God is in heaven and you are on earth, so let your words be few.' (Ecclesiastes 5:2)

> Oh, the love of the Lord is the
>   essence
> Of all that I love here on earth.
> All the beauty I see,
> He has given to me,
> And His giving is gentle as silence.[7]

This sort of silence is amazingly refreshing. Frequently I've got up on a Sunday and been faced with many services, a somewhat unfinished sermon, calls from family and parish. The temptation, particularly with the sermon, is a rapid rewrite. Rapid rewrites usually make matters worse! Gradually I've learned the wisdom of a quiet half hour. On Sunday, having already prepared and studied the day's readings, my Scripture reading will be much briefer. On Sunday I need silence. In that silence comes spiritual refreshment. From the refreshment sometimes comes inspiration. From the inspiration can come response . . .

But what if God does speak? Perhaps there is some point to be added to an address, perhaps there will be some special word to the congregation. I must remember! I can only remember if I write it down. I find it essential, if I experience God's prompting, to write down what it is — it may be a note added to a sermon, it may be a diary reminder of a letter to write or it may be someone to see.

Having listened, having heard, I must obey. After a day of retreat, I found myself having to share some awkward convictions with Jane. Things that I would have preferred to have ignored or left buried, but I knew no peace until I had spoken to her. Effective prayer invariably leads to effective action. As far as I can see, every recorded prayer session in the Bible had a purpose — Nehemiah to prepare for his return to Jerusalem; Jesus to discern the Father's will in various uncertain situations; the Early Church to procure Peter's release. Our praying is not for some personal spiritual glory trip, but to learn to co-operate with God in the work of the Kingdom.

SPECIAL WAYS OF PRAYER

All that I've written so far, while primarily concerned with the individual at prayer, also applies to pairs of pray-ers, or prayer groups. Praying with one other person is a very special experience.

'Do two walk together unless they have agreed to do so?' (Amos 3:3).

'Again, I tell you that if two of you on earth agree about anything you ask for, it will be done for you by my Father in heaven' (Matthew 18:19). Brother Ramon[8] has proposed what he calls an 'Emmaus Walk'. The essential ingredients are time (about two hours), preparation (prayer, Scripture reading, commentary on it, silence), a prepared walk (the outward half discussing the Scripture, the commentary, and anything else that the Spirit leads to), a silent return journey, and a brief time for recollection, silence and prayer. This can be a deeply moving experience. Its artificial construction can help a pair − for instance, a husband and wife − who don't find it naturally easy to talk and share at any spiritual depth to become more open with one another.

Ordinary walks can become spiritually enriched conversations. These sort of encounters, offered verbally or silently to God, can be amazing times of communication. Two such walks stand out in my memory. Strangely, both followed similar routes.[9] One was with my Parish Secretary. The time had come to look to the future. She knew it was time to give up. I had some vague plan for her to become Parish Visitor. We needed to talk and pray through this. Joyce was very uncertain. She loved the office and felt that giving up would create a yawning void in her life. In the event, the walk prepared the way. The change of direction was traumatic, but the ultimate rightness of the decision became clear to everyone.

More normally, two meet for prayer together in a home. It may be husband and wife, spiritual colleagues or prayer partners. I am thinking, particularly, of situations where there is a deep spiritual 'agreement' in the Lord, which makes such prayers so potentially effective. Curiously, after times of disagreement followed by confession and rebuilding, such prayer seems even more effective!

RETREATS

Retreats are part of many spiritual disciplines. They may be brief, perhaps just part of a day, or a weekend; they may be much longer. Their purpose is quite simple, to follow Jesus' example of withdrawing to a quiet place (Luke 9:10 for instance). Recently I attended one led by a very elderly clergyman. In the course of the day we had three short talks, celebrated the Eucharist, ate a silent lunch, and, in quiet, prayed, read or walked. The talks were so simple, yet so direct and practical. I immediately felt challenged to sort out a huge block in my thinking about the future. The Lord, through His servant and the silence, pointed out some very poor thinking about finance, about the future, and past mistakes in the home. The sense of relief, and release, was tremendous. My fellow clergy, who like me can be pretty cynical about such events, were equally moved.

A friend of mine was in considerable physical pain. We prayed, we talked, we explored the reasons – stress from a demanding job, deep pain from past hurts, various practical needs – but there was no release. Then she went on an individually guided Ignatian retreat. Her account is as follows:

The individually guided Ignatian retreat is based on the simple truth that everyone is at a different stage in their relationship with God and thus each has different needs. There is no syllabus to be got through but a journey is made according to the guidance of the Spirit. Each retreatant has their own director who helps them to recognise, during a daily interview, what God is doing in their lives and how they are responding. Apart from the daily interview lasting approximately forty-five minutes and two periods of corporate worship, the rest of the time was spent in silence.

How did I spend the silence? Initially two one-hour periods of prayer had to be built into the day, and even though this increased into three hours after the first couple of days, there was still plenty of time to walk, swim, or just sit and be.

I had wondered what it would be like with only the Bible to read and a notebook to record my responses to my prayers which were based on passages of Scripture selected for me by my director.

The pattern was something like this:

(1) Five minutes preparation for prayer.
(2) Forty-five minutes of prayer based on the selected Bible passages and noting down the thoughts and feelings that occurred.
(3) Ten minutes reflection and, if necessary, amendment of notes before listing the most relevant points either to discuss with my director or reconsider in the next prayer time.

My journey took me into:

(1) New experiences of the love of God for me:
    'It was you who created my inmost self, and put me together in my mother's womb; for all these mysteries I thank you: for the wonder of myself, for the wonder of your works' (Psalm 139: 13-14 JB).
(2) Reflections on busy-ness and how I balance the sitting and listening against the fretting about all the tasks that need to be done. (Martha and Mary: Luke 10: 38-42)
(3) Acknowledging the danger of trusting in my own strength or thinking I might be important!

'Beware of saying in your heart "My own strength and the might of my own hand won this power for me." Remember Yahweh your god: it was He who gave you this strength and won you this power.' (Deuteronomy 8: 17-18 JB)

'In the light of the grace I have received I want to urge each one among you not to exaggerate his real importance.' (Romans 12:3 JB)

'There must be no competition among you, no conceit; but everybody is to be self-effacing. Always consider the other person to be better than yourself, so that nobody thinks of his own interests first, but everybody thinks of other people's interests instead.' (Philippians 2: 3-4 JB)

(4) Meditating on Chapters 18 and 19 of St John's Gospel, I found the scene before Pilate was particularly challenging: would I have been one of Pilate's staff, part of the crowd shouting for the crucifixion of Jesus, or one of the silent onlookers?

It was obviously impossible to move from the Passion direct to the Resurrection – the crucifixion had to be faced. Powerful woodcarvings showing Christ being nailed to the cross and John, with the women, standing near the cross, underlined both the agony and desolation our Lord must have experienced. But even in His pain He remembered the needs of His mother and entrusted her into the care of John.

The climax of the retreat was experiencing anew the triumph of the Resurrection, in particular our Lord's appearance to the disciples, and to note His greeting 'Peace be with you' – how easy it would have been for Him to say 'Where were you on Friday?' Of discovering how easy it is to be like Thomas and want proof despite the evidence of so many, but also realising that the ultimate happiness is being able to say 'My Lord and My God' (John 20: 19-29).

The result was amazing! When we next met, she seemed transformed. Although the pain remained, the stress was gone, and many other changes were obvious. Not least, that she was counselling me!

THE PRAYER GROUP

The ability to take right decisions seems to depend very largely on the willingness of groups to pray. Latterly, our Finance and General Purposes (F & GP) committee – a very down to earth bunch – has included some members with a very special commitment to prayer. One consequence of this appears to have been an increasing generosity to overseas missions. This decision, taken in theory, led to some extra money being available. We felt that it should remain unallocated. Unbeknown to the committee, a young member of the church felt that God was calling her to work overseas for a while with TEAR Fund. This involved her in considerable expense. The F & GP's nest egg very quickly found its right niche!

Prayer groups are very rewarding, but are never easy to lead or to be part of. Nevertheless, whatever spiritual gains I have seen in any school or parish with which I've been involved, I would unhesitatingly put them down in great measure to the quality of the prayer group. Many big decisions become so much clearer when a prayer group first hears, then prays, then goes away and listens, and then returns to share their feelings.

It is sad how scared people are of prayer groups, and how difficult it is to help people pray aloud and feel part of such groups. Within such a group, the quality of worship and the silences will probably determine the 'prophetic' nature of the group. Intercession is important, but, again, listening is especially vital. I realise that I, for one, have not yet learnt how to help groups to listen.

Nevertheless, I've frequently felt spiritually enriched and refreshed by such groups and on notable occasions have felt a wonderful sense of God's guidance.

CONCLUSION

In summary, I would say that listening to God in prayer is one of the greatest of all spiritual activities. As we begin to listen (and we will make mistakes, but far fewer than if we don't try to hear), so our whole lives will be transformed. We shall learn to think, naturally, in a Christian way and to hear God's voice in the market place as well as on the hillside.

'Therefore, I urge you, brothers, in view of God's mercy, to offer your bodies as living sacrifices, holy and pleasing to God – this is your spiritual act of worship. Do not conform any longer to the pattern of this world, but be transformed by the renewing of your mind. Then you will be able to test and approve what God's will is – His good, pleasing and perfect will. For by the grace given me I say to every one of you: Do not think of yourself more highly than you ought, but rather think of yourself with sober judgment, in accordance with the measure of faith God has given you.' (Romans 12: 1-3)

Living sacrifice includes living prayer. Living prayer means living God's way. It's as simple and as profound as that.

Notes and references

1 Hanes, David (ed). *My path of prayer: personal glimpses of the glory and the majesty of God revealed through experiences of prayer*. Henry Walter, 1983.
2 Lean, Garth. *John Wesley — Anglican*. Blandford Paperbacks, p 13.
3 East, Reg. Tape *Relaxing into Prayer* available from Shepherd's Cottage, Whatcombe, Dorset. Reg East is a former Warden of Whatcombe House. See also Chapter 13, section 'The Healing of Our Past'.
4 Mission Praise. 'Silver and Gold', No 199. Marshall Pickering, 1983.
5 Clowney, Edward P. *Message of 1 Peter*. The Bible Speaks Today series. Leicester, IVP, 1988.
6 Ten Boom, Corrie. *The Hiding Place*. London, Hodder & Stoughton, 1976, p 197.
7 St Aldgate's Songbook. 'The love of the Lord is the essence', No 134.
8 Ramon, Brother S S F. *A Hidden Fire: exploring the deeper reaches of prayer*. Marshall, Morgan and Scott, 1985, p 99ff.
9 For the other see Chapter 13 of this volume.

CREATION SPEAKS

The glory of the Creation is another great theme of the Psalms. Haydn wrote a glorious aria based on Psalm 19 (from The Creation). Great music, great poetry and profound theology continue to lift even the most staid worshipper a little closer to Heaven. The wonder and mystery of Creation bring many people closer to hearing the Silent Voice of God. Addison puts it well:

> What though in solemn silence all
> Move round the dark terrestrial ball;
> What though nor real voice nor sound
> Amid their radiant orbs be found;
>   In reason's ear they all rejoice,
>   And utter forth a glorious voice,
> For ever singing as they shine,
> 'The hand that made us is Divine'.[1]

Addison was writing at a time when Christianity was at a very low ebb. The early eighteenth century Deists could just about hold on to a belief in a God of Creation, but the personal faith in Jesus and the leading of the Spirit, were virtually unknown to them.[2]

Today, many great scientists seem to have little difficulty in seeing the hand of a personal Creator behind the wonder of the universe.[3] We may all agree with Paul, who when preaching at Lystra, said (in an effort to put the miracle of the healing of a lame man into perspective) 'Men, why are you doing this? We too are only men, human like you. We are bringing you good news, telling you to turn from these worthless things to the living God, who made heaven and earth and sea and everything in them. In the past, He let all nations go their own way. Yet He has not left Himself without testimony. He has shown kindness by giving you rain from heaven and crops in their seasons; He provides you with plenty of food and fills your hearts with joy ' (Acts 14: 15-17). And again, at the beginning of his greatest doctrinal epistle he wrote 'For since the creation of the world, God's invisible qualities – His eternal power and divine nature – have been clearly seen, being understood from what has been made, so that men are without excuse ' (Romans 1:20).

Nevertheless, creation also presents us with a deep mystery, a shadow side, a searing wound. Paul, too, recognises this. 'I consider that our present sufferings are not worth comparing with the glory that will be revealed in us. The creation waits in eager expectation for the sons of God to be revealed. For the creation was subjected to frustration, not by its own choice, but by the will of the one who subjected it, in hope that the creation itself will be liberated from its bondage to decay and brought into the glorious freedom of the children of God' (Romans 8: 18-21). We may very properly look at the majesty and the beauty of Creation, but we may not forget the wilderness and the violence. God may well speak to us very clearly through the glory of nature; but He will also want to challenge us through its shadow side. To accept one and to ignore the other is as unrealistic, and as erroneous, as preaching of the Resurrection and ignoring the cross.

CREATION SPEAKS

Some are moved by the wonder of the stars, some by the grandeur of the trees, some by the brilliance and creativity of the animal kingdom, many by the amazing variety of the birds and flowers. For me, it is the butterfly who silently speaks deepest to my soul.

I don't know why. It is as foolish to wonder why as to try and rationalise one's favourite artists, writers, or composers. But God brought butterflies into my life at a time of great darkness. My mother was very ill, soon to die, after what would now be a routine heart operation. My teaching career was about to be sacrificed on, for me, the unwilling altar of ordination. My deepest love was showing clear signs of disappearing to the other side of the world.

At that time, I had the dubious honour of being in charge of the school's junior-junior cricket game. The absolute bottom rung of a non-existent ladder. Then one afternoon, circumstances (or was it the Lord?) provided a means of escape. The Natural History Society needed a driver to help with an expedition to the New Forest. Someone else, a very distinguished cricketer, took over my game for the afternoon. I joined a group of enthusiasts wandering around some gorse bushes on the edge of the Forest. I waved a tattered school butterfly net. A small green insect made a temporary halt! 'A green hairstreak,' pronounced the voice of authority. It was dazzlingly beautiful, so small, so brilliant, yet its emerald green perfectly camouflaged when released on to the gorse.

In the next few months, as I faced my mother's death, a false start at a theological college, my father's depression and death, there was great solace from the world of the butterfly. Each new discovery seemed like a personal gift from God. I remember a bush on the edge of the school nature reserve which seemed to explode with scarlet. Moses-like, I watched with amazement as tiger moth after tiger moth emerged, opened its wings, and sped across the water meadows. I remember the first sight of courting white admirals dancing high in the sky in an intricate marital flight, I remember the wonder of the large dark insect on a woodland path that flew away transformed in a blaze of royal blue/purple as its iridescent wings caught the light of the sun. Gradually the message grew more profound − it wasn't just the gratuitous glory of creation − the silent voice of the Creator also provided parables for those who had eyes to see.

PARABLES

There is good scriptural precedent for allowing nature to speak to us. The writer of Proverbs enjoyed watching ants;[4] Jesus drew attention to the flowers and the birds of the air;[5] Peter likened the Devil to a raging lion.[6]

Consider the life cycle of a butterfly. The egg is laid, eventually the tiny caterpillar hatches. It is often wonderfully camouflaged, defenceless, concerned only with food and survival. Its life is confined to a very small territory − possibly even to just one nettle or branch of a tree. It is utterly selfish; so selfish that some species will eat smaller brethren in order to protect their own food supply. It lives a virtually two dimensional life − eating well and growing inexorably. Then there is the first great change. It has sloughed its skin before, but now it hangs upside down (or folds itself in leaves, or wanders off and attaches itself to an alien stem or whatever). For several days it hangs virtually motionless, taking in no food, and even more vulnerable than in its caterpillar state. Eventually the skin bursts open, somehow the soft chrysalis attaches itself to the silken pad that the caterpillar has already prepared. The chrysalis hardens, changes colour, and lies dormant. If touched it will react violently, but it has no means of escape. Eventually, the chrysalis changes again. Brilliant colours appear in the miniature wing cases; suddenly the case cracks, and a tiny ragged insect emerges. Its body is full size, its miniature wings about a quarter size. Desperately it pumps its life blood into them, the wings expand, the butterfly stays still – preparing, perhaps, for the first flight some hours later.

That cycle speaks to me of so many aspects of our faith. The first is *conversion*. The selfish and destructive caterpillar becomes the brilliant and beautiful butterfly which enriches our lives, does no harm, even achieves a measure of pollination, and whose main concern is propagation of the species (evangelism!). But it is not only a metaphor of sudden conversion. There is a point of emergence, but there is also the whole gradual process of change throughout the life cycle. The tiniest caterpillar has 'wings', and the dormant chrysalis clearly has 'wings'. The potential for flight is there. Provided that the butterfly emerges safely, flight is certain.

Many Christians dislike the 'new birth' metaphor;[7] reacting against what can seem like jargon and insensitive brashness. Yet the emergence of the new-born butterfly is a perfect illustration of our helplessness.

'Like newborn babies, crave pure spiritual milk, so that by it you may grow up in your salvation' (1 Peter 2:2).

There was a time when we were all spiritually helpless. If you have ever had the privilege and joy of leading someone to Christ, in a real prayer of penitence and faith, you will have been struck by their complete dependence. I tremble, and wonder if they'll ever fly. Yet, amazingly, they do. I described the results of Tim's conversion earlier.[8] How well I remember his uncertain profession of faith. How well I remember getting up from an attack of 'flu to go into a cold church to pray with him. How well I remember the uncertainty in both of us as he left the church. But the Holy Spirit had come, inexorably, new life appeared, eventually the spiritual butterfly flew.

The butterfly life cycle also speaks to me of *renewal*. So often one can see the potential within people, and yet they seem stuck, almost immovable and apparently unchanging. Denis and Elizabeth were one such couple. Surrounded by a young family, Denis already high up in the administration of the Health Service, Elizabeth teaching music and physically unwell through a severe water-retention problem, they were trapped in an increasing merry-go-round of business. They provided the music for our family service, but apart from that their spiritual potential was unfulfilled. It was obvious that God could take them much further. They were like chrysalids. The wing colours could be seen, but would the butterflies ever escape? On a parish holiday, they asked to speak to me. They spent a whole day talking with Jane and me. It was one of those rare occasions when there was time! Next evening, they joined others in coming forward for prayer.[9]

The results were extraordinary — both immediate and long term. Elizabeth experienced a spiritual release which immediately caused her to pray in tongues, a physical release that reduced her weight by some seven stones over the next few months, a musical release which caused her to compose songs — one of which if she'd been more concerned about copyright would have been in her name in *Mission Praise* — and lead the worship for the whole of St Aldate's.

Denis, outwardly, experienced nothing. Inwardly, he had

the certainty of a call to ordination. A call which he quickly obeyed, and which has now led him into the leadership of a church in a difficult part of Reading. Elizabeth, too, is an ordained deacon. Their children, now virtually grown up, show encouraging signs of Christian maturity.

The life cycle must also speak of *resurrection*. Michael Green puts this so clearly in *What is Christianity?*[10] Some chrysalids look utterly dead. The brown hairstreak pupa is just like a dull dark lozenge. There is virtually no sign of wing pattern, no movement when touched, just utter drabness. But the emerged butterfly is quite striking. I remember walking down a forest patch in Bernwood, Oxfordshire, in early August. The path was lined with tall hogweed plants with their brilliant white flowers. From fully thirty metres away, a flash of bright colour caught my expectant eye. I approached cautiously. A tiny brown hairstreak, its wings just twenty millimetres long, was walking around the flower, feeding. The brilliant colour was dazzlingly wonderful as the sun lit up the wings into a fiery golden orange. Somewhere in the undergrowth of a nearby sloe bush lay the empty pupa case – the discarded grave clothes – no longer important, except as evidence of the transformation! Long ago St John wrote of a far greater resurrection in these words:

So Peter and the other disciple started for the tomb. Both were running, but the other disciple outran Peter and reached the tomb first. He bent over and looked in at the strips of linen lying there but did not go in. Then Simon Peter, who was behind him, arrived and went into the tomb. He saw the strips of linen lying there, as well as the burial cloth that had been around Jesus' head. The cloth was folded up by itself, separate from the linen. Finally the other disciple, who had reached the tomb first, also went inside. He saw and believed (John 20: 3-8).

The folded graveclothes remind me of the empty case; the head cloth lying separate, and the buterfly having departed.

Finally, the life cycle speaks to me of *faith*. Once we were staying in an attractive camp site near Uzès in Southern France. Our car and tent were in a rectangle surrounded by privet hedges and mulberry trees. A red admiral attached itself to us. Each evening it would come and sit on the roof rack of our car to the huge delight of Rachel, then aged two. One day we were picnicking in the edge of a wood. It was very hot, the wood blissfully cool. Suddenly I was aware of butterflies flapping around. They were flying uncertainly, as though newly emerged from the chrysalis. I looked up and saw one sitting with its wings open high up on the trunk of a tree. As I watched a hornet descended upon it, sat astride it, and devoured it. Four fragile large tortoiseshell wings, pierced with holes from the hornet's feet, fluttered to my feet.

The drama wasn't quite over. Looking up again, I saw to my horror, another tortoiseshell sitting inches away from the hornet on the same tree. Jane and I threw earth, sticks and stones at the tree. Eventually, Jane landed a stone just below the insects. Hornet and butterfly flew off in opposite directions.

That night on our campsite, we witnessed the flight of faith. A hornet buzzed slowly across our rectangle. The red admiral rose from the roof rack, flew around the hornet, and escorted it out of its territory. It returned in triumph to its perch.

'Your enemy the devil prowls around like a roaring lion looking for someone to devour. Resist him, standing firm in the faith . . .' (1 Peter 5: 8^b-9^a).

The tortoiseshell we saved reminds one of the text from Jude 23[a] '. . .snatch others from the fire and save them . . .' Part of our Christian task is to help rescue those in real danger of being devoured. Drugs, drink, occultism are certainly among the many dangers that can kill and certainly prevent even apparently new-born Christians from any flight of faith. Firm, decisive action is often required. The parable of the butterflies is a constant warning to be vigilant. And if I ever get complacent, I remember my innate fear of wasps and hornets and the words of St Paul: 'Therefore let anyone who thinks that he stands take heed lest he fall' (1 Corinthians 10:12 RSV).

GUIDANCE

On a number of occasions, God has spoken to me, and helped me see the way forward, when I've been observing nature. Once I was sitting alone in a large field set aside for camping in Austria. I was praying about a future mission in the school where I taught. I looked up and saw a cornfield full of newly made corn stooks. There was a group of about thirty in the bottom of the field, and a steady trickle on the right hand edge of the field disappearing over the crest of a small hill. The Lord seemed to say 'These represent those who will become Christians next term, and those on the edge of the field represent the ongoing work in the future.' I was amazed, and encouraged. The fulfilment was almost exact. Some thirty-five boys genuinely professed faith and many are Christians today, some fourteen years on. The work continued, and grew, long after I had left. Then, sadly, it seemed to dry up and finish. I never walked over the crest of the hill.

On another occasion, I was staying at Old Alresford

Place — the Winchester Diocesan Retreat House. I was praying about, and concerned about, the healing ministry in St Aldate's Church. I was still a very new member of staff, and there was a lot of justifiable hesitation about the public healing ministry in such a church. I was walking in the garden, admiring the great beech trees which were about to spring into life. Then at the foot of one, I noticed a great cluster of crocuses. The words of Isaiah came to mind.

> 'The desert and the parched land will be glad; the wilderness will rejoice and blossom. Like the crocus it will burst into bloom . . . Then will the eyes of the blind be opened and the ears of the deaf unstopped. Then will the lame leap up like a deer, and the mute tongue shout for joy' (Isaiah 35: 1, 5-6).

Surely God had spoken? Wasn't this the confirmation that I needed? So it proved. The next Parish Church Council (PCC) meeting unanimously agreed a way forward and the ministry of healing became a recognised part of the ministry offered in that church.[11]

A third occasion was much more surprising and shows how God can use simple events in surprising ways. I was walking on the banks of the River Gard, near Uzès, thinking and praying about my future. Big decisions lay ahead. I was also keeping an eye out for any passing lepidoptera. Suddenly, resting in the sand, I noticed a huge black butterfly with golden edges to its wings. For a while I thought, 'At last, a Camberwell beauty', the most elusive (to me) of all the great European butterflies! Jane rushed for a camera, the butterfly took off. I pursued it down the banks of the river, shouting at an astonished fisherman, as I waved my net, *'Non pour le pêche, pour le papillon'*. The butterfly alighted with its wings closed. It was huge, but it certainly wasn't a Camberwell beauty.

It became a sort of *idée fixe*. I knew it couldn't be a Camberwell beauty, but there was nothing else it could be . . .

Eventually I tracked it down in my book of European butterflies. In English it was called 'the two-tailed Pasha', an African species which has colonised a tiny bit of Southern France and the coastline of other South European countries. It was too rare to merit more than a picture of its underside.

Six months later, David Prior came over from Africa to visit St Aldate's. Michael Green, the rector, wanted the parish to appoint a vicar, so that he would be freer to exercise a wider ministry of writing, evangelism, and leading teams out from the parish.

As a team, we decided to ask David to consider the job. He was, to say the least, uncertain. He was very happy in South Africa, running a very responsible multi-racial parish. However, Michael, and those consulted in Oxford, were very keen for David to come. As we met to pray, I kept on seeing a picture of a two-tailed Pasha. I thought it was a nice distraction, but it wouldn't fly away. Then an interpretation came to mind.

I had failed to recognise the butterfly — very unusually for me — mistaking it for something else. I had had an *idée fixe*, although it didn't really look right. I, and more importantly, others, had been the same about the appointment. God had a different plan! David, from Africa like the butterfly, was God's choice.

Feeling foolish, I shared my picture with David, to whom I'd never even spoken. He came to St Aldate's for many other good reasons, and complemented Michael's ministry in a truly remarkable way.

Years later, when I had completely forgotten the prayer

time — but not the butterfly — he told me how important
it was and how it had helped him decide.

Recently, David himself gave me a powerful testimony
of how nature spoke to him and to others.

In September 1987, Rosemary and I spent three days in
the Yosemite National Park in California, one of the most
remarkable scenic areas of the United States. One of its
unique phenomena is the giant sequoia tree. These trees
grow to an immense height, often have a girth wide
enough for a car to be driven through a hole carved
through their trunk, and are many centuries old. The
oldest tree in the Park is reckoned to be 3,000 years.

As we walked through this massive forest early one
morning, with hardly a soul around, I had an almost
tangible sense of peace . . . and of quiet reprimand.
These trees had spent hundreds of years quietly getting
on with being what God intended them to be — no
rushing around, no mass of meetings or goals to achieve,
no frantic anxieties or fears. They have stayed there
faithfully saving themselves and speaking to people like
us.

Names have been coined for the more striking trees in
the forest — for example, the Three Graces (speaking
of co-operation, not competition); the Faithful Couple
(2,000 years together and still going strong); the Telescope
Tree (you can walk inside and look up to heaven); the
Shelter Tree (where fifteen horses once sheltered in a
storm); the Fallen Giant (eloquent of the tree on which
the Son of God was killed). To walk through the sequoias
is to feel the steady majesty and eternal faithfulness of
the Creator. To walk through the sequoias with a lively
imagination focused on Jesus is to experience new dimen-
sions of the salvation He achieved.

When we returned to Britain, back into the busy schedule of the parish, one of my first speaking engagements was an evening gathering in rural Hampshire in an old granary set amidst trees. I started to talk about the sequoia trees of Yosemite. There was an uncanny grip that evening, as though the theme had an extraordinary relevance. The meeting closed about 10.00 p.m. and I was driven to the local station to catch a train back to London. That night the famous October hurricane struck the Home Counties. Along with so many areas, the woods around the old granary were devastated. Everyone present will remember that night and that talk.

LIVING WITH QUESTIONS

Not all parables, or visions, from nature are pleasant. Many biblical ones were profoundly disturbing – Joseph's dreams, Jeremiah's boiling pot. Let me take you back to butterflies. Come to the Westbury White Horse. Nearby you will find an unspoilt Roman *vallum*. It is full of rare flowers – bee orchids, horseshoe vetch . . . and so on. Butterflies abound, including many of the rarest in Britain. We watch a female marsh fritillary carefully laying her eggs on the underside of her caterpillar's feed plant. Meticulously, she lays a cluster of, say, 200 eggs. Elsewhere she will repeat the operation. Eventually these 200 eggs hatch, the caterpillars are decimated by beetles, spiders, birds, and the dreaded ichneumon wasp. A handful survive to become chrysalids the following spring. Wandering predators devour most of them. One fine May day, one butterfly emerges – all that is left of one half of the parent butterfly's egg batch. What waste, what devastation. And yet, of course, without it the population would become a swarm, and there wouldn't be enough greenery to eat!

I have no neat answer to this. I don't even want to blame it on the Fall. Obviously, St Paul is right when he talks of 'creation groaning', but he also says[12] 'For the creation was subjected to frustration, not by its own choice, but by the will of the One who subjected it.'

In other words — Paul acknowledged 'the shadow side' of God. Throughout creation, throughout mankind, there runs this dark, shadow side. We cannot escape from it. For us the selfishness of our nature, the frailty of our flesh, the destruction of our environment, and the death of our bodies, represent the most painful parts of this darkness. In creation, leaving aside earthquakes, hurricanes, environmental disasters, the shadow side is seen as clearly as anywhere in the ichneumon wasp forcing a living caterpillar to play host to its deadly offspring.

Suffering and glory are inextricably linked in Scripture. Suffering and glory are seen also to be part of the total experience of nature.

More recently a different parable spoke powerfully to me, and I believe to others. Searching for a Harvest Festival theme which might at least make a comprehensive school think, I noticed two sorts of wood in our garden. One was a living tree, grown almost accidentally from a cutting put in a jam jar to feed some caterpillars which needed to be taken indoors to protect them from our miserable summer; the other a log awaiting its inevitable fate on the fire.

I was able to speak of trees and their vital importance in the world; of the floods in Bangladesh, partly caused by the cutting down of Himalayan forests in another country; of the terrible African droughts, partly caused by the demolition of rainforests for firewood; of the ease with which trees can be grown if we set our minds to it; of my mother-in-law at the age of over sixty, working in Africa on a development project where all the mature trees are disappearing while she tries to protect a new tree nursery from locusts, caterpillars and the like; of the sacrifice and danger of working overseas. It's not been easy for my mother-in-law to cut herself off from her family for several years. The poignancy of the theme of danger was greatly enhanced by the recent death of the husband of a member of the school staff.

The dead log, so necessary to the African for desperately needed firewood, symbolises our destruction of nature. The two trees speak urgently to a world which is devastating God's creation. The parable of the trees offers despair or hope. Despair if we assume that mankind must inexorably destroy all that is good and necessary; hope if we believe that there can be a way forward if we heed the message and take it seriously.

The dead log, theologically, is the cross. The living tree is the Resurrection. As the Alternative Service Book puts it:[13]

'The tree of shame was made the tree of glory.'

For me, too, there is hope in the children's response. A Christian group are planting a tree in the school grounds, and raising money to help support an ex-pupil who is going to Tanzania to work for TEAR Fund.

The trees give me hope — and urgency. If I wasn't fully convinced that God has called me to my present job, they would draw me out of pastoring into the vital world of the environment. We cannot sit back and do nothing.

'Now if we are children, then we are heirs — heirs of God and co-heirs with Christ, if indeed we share in his sufferings in order that we may also share in his glory'.[14]

The New Testament sees Christ as the Creator.

'For by Him all things were created.'[15]

If we are co-heirs, then we have a tremendous responsibility for the state of His Creation. We may not understand the shadow side, we may enjoy the beauty, but we must protect what we have been given. The message of the first chapters of Genesis is of responsibility, care and justice. 'Non-violent dominion'[16] to quote a former Bishop of Winchester.

The heavens do indeed declare the glory of God. We, too, must do the same on earth.

> O Lord, our Lord, how majestic is your name in all the
>   earth!
> You have set your glory above the heavens.
> From the lips of children and infants you have ordained
>   praise because of your enemies, to silence the foe and
>   the avenger.
> When I consider your heavens, the work of your fingers
>   the moon and the stars, which you have set in place,
>   what is man that you are mindful of him,
>   the son of man that you care for him?
> You made him a little lower than the heavenly beings
>   and crowned him with glory and honour.
> You made him ruler over the works of your hands;
>   you put everything under his feet:
> all flocks and herds, and the beasts of the field,
> the birds of the air, and the fish of the sea,
>   all that swim the paths of the seas.
> O Lord, our Lord, how majestic is your name in all the
> earth! (Psalm 8)

Unfortunately, many Christians of our generation, like Hezekiah in 2 Kings 20:18, don't seem to mind that trouble may be in store for our descendants. The voice of wounded

Creation is crying out to us, the needs are obvious, the situation is urgent, yet the voice of Christians is so often silent. We need not a voice crying in the wilderness, but a prophetic voice warning us of the wilderness that we are all responsible for creating.

Notes and references

1 Hymns Ancient and Modern Revised. 'The spacious firmament on high', No 170.

2 Butler, Joseph. *The analogy of religion, natural and revealed, to the constitution and course of nature*. Glasgow, Collins, 1824.

3 Polkinghorne, J C. *The Way the World is: Christian perspective of a scientist*. London, Triangle, 1983. Hawking, Stephen W. *A brief history of time: from the big bang to black holes*. London, Bantam Books, 1989. This book poses many theological as well as scientific questions.

4 Proverbs 6:6ff.

5 Matthew 6:25ff.

6 1 Peter 5:8ff.

7 See John 3:3ff and 1 Peter 1:3, 23.

8 See Chapter 6 of this volume.

9 See Chapter 5 of this volume.

10 Green, Michael. *What is Christianity?* Tring, Lion Publishing, 1981, pp 52-59, photographs showing the contrasting stages of the caterpillar through chrysalis to butterfly.

11 For many years, prayer for healing had been offered effectively but privately. What I was concerned with was the question of whether it could be offered publicly after the main service.

12 See Chapter 10 of this volume and Romans 8: 18-22.

13 *Alternative Service Book*, London, 1980, p 155 – Proper Preface – The cross.

14 Romans 8:17.

15 See Colossians 1:16.

16 Taylor, John V. *Enough is Enough*. London, SCM Press, 1975, p 50.

10

CIRCUMSTANCES GUIDE

There is a delightful cartoon which some kind parishioner left in one of my prayer books. It shows a rather puny Christian standing before a fierce looking judge. The caption at the bottom says 'If you were accused of being a Christian would there be enough evidence to convict you?'

Many Christians, myself included, tend to assume that the evidence required will be of dramatic signs and wonders – conversions, healings, prophecy or neon light flashes of guidance. Yet, actually, the evidence required is much simpler, much more commonplace. How do we react in normal circumstances? Do we think/act Christianly in a minor crisis? Does God play a part in our everyday decision-making? Do we subconsciously act in a Christian way? Does our conversation edify or destroy? Do our actions, in the market place, classroom or home, uplift or deny Christ?

The Lord showed me this recently in a very simple experience. One afternoon, during the first phase of writing this book, I walked in Bernwood Forest. I was relaxing after a hard morning and particularly hoped to see a brown hair-streak butterfly. They are elusive, even in places like Bernwood where they are known to live. I walked into a quiet corner of the wood where I was confident of a sighting. It was a beautiful afternoon in late August; prime viewing time! I surveyed the hogweed, the bramble flowers, the sloe bushes, with increasing impatience and frustration. Surely, Lord, you could meet this small need of mine! After all, I am spending most of the day writing a book for you. Other butterflies flitted by, I ignored them. Deer wandered lazily across the path, I just noticed them. I knew I must go soon. Then I saw it! Not the beautiful insect I described in Chapter 9, but an old, tattered, worn-out butterfly with as much beauty as a disgruntled ninety-year-old on a bad day. On the way back to Stanton House, I walked up a rough track. It was carpeted with wild flowers. Peacock butterflies were everywhere. They looked so fresh, so beautiful. Their great 'eyes' staring at me with a marvellous kaleidoscope of colour — purple, brown, black, gold and blue. Peacock butterflies are common; brown hairstreaks are rare. The silent voice spoke 'Despise not the common things'.

I realise I make the mistake of looking for the spectacular. I look for the great miracles of healing and ignore the masses of smaller wonderful signs that God is doing all around me. I look for the dramatic conversions and ignore the more normal spiritual growth there is happening all around me. I rejoice in the occasional dramatic freeing of someone from evil powers, and ignore the release from the 'demonic' powers of money, sex, ill temper and despair. I fail to notice God's grace and guidance in life of the normal, quiet Christian, and look for something startling.

The peacock butterfly is far more beautiful than almost any other butterfly in the world! It can be seen most of the year, most of the time (even fast asleep during sermons in churches in winter!). I hope you understand what the Lord was teaching me! Because, as we continue to think about His guidance and the everyday ways in which He speaks, it is a lesson that we all need to learn!

THE SCRIPTURES AND CIRCUMSTANCES

But, says an insidious inner voice, is it scriptural? Isn't most of the Bible full of amazing stories of dramatic guidance? Doesn't God intend us to know His will in this sort of way in each situation?

Of course, it is true that the Bible has many wonderful stories of guidance. But it is equally true that on many occasions 'circumstances' dictated how people acted. It is not for nothing that Jesus has often been called 'the Master of circumstances'. He lived so completely at one with the Father that He, instinctively, acted correctly. We will take many more right decisions if we have the right foundations in our Christian life. If our life is based on Scripture, prayer and worship then we will often be in the right place at the right time. When our spiritual discipline slips, so will our faith, and we will find the exact opposite – endless frustration and inevitably getting things wrong.

William Temple once said 'When I pray coincidences seem to happen . . .'

Without going into detail, I would like to sketch a number of incidents in the Bible where circumstances played a major part in decisions which affected many lives. Return to the woman at the well (John 4:4ff).[1] Forget about 'words of knowledge', evangelism, and fields ripe for harvest; just consider the circumstances. Jesus arrived tired, and presumably hot and thirsty. The Samaritan woman arrived going about her 'daily round and common task'. Jesus spoke to her. All that followed for her, her town, and perhaps even for Samaria (see Acts 8) is well known. At a human level, Jesus spoke to her because he had a need. He didn't manufacture it as an excuse for talking to her (Vicar, could you just drop in casually. You see, my daughter has this problem . . .). He had a need which was the only realistic way of breaking down a racial barrier.

We have already noted[2] how the Apostolic church solved its first major social problem. We've seen how circumstances, in this case a sharp bout of persecution, steered the Jerusalem church into evangelism in Antioch and other cities. Carefully study Acts and you will find a remarkable number of times when circumstances, usually persecution, forced Paul to move on.[3] The celebrated row between Barnabas and Paul (Acts 15:36ff) led to the evangelisation of Cyprus which presumably wouldn't have happened otherwise. Paul's nephew was in the right place at the right time (Acts 23:16) to thwart a plot to kill him. Paul's amazing ministry in Malta (Acts 28:1ff) couldn't have happened without the storm at sea.

Some people hold a determinist view of circumstances and life. In that case, it is all inevitable, pre-planned, and unremarkable. I don't believe that that is the teaching of the Bible; although I do think that we can be held in bondage by 'fate'. The scriptural view seems to allow man a great deal of freedom — to be led by the Spirit, or to fall victim to the pull of the flesh (see Galatians 5:16ff). The Scriptures do also teach us, very clearly, of the sovereignty of God. We may not understand God's election or choice (see Ephesians 1: 3-14 and John 15:16); we will certainly not understand God's ultimate purpose for our world. What we can understand is that the Father-son relationship with Him is the jewel in the crown of any scriptural experience of God. It cannot be a coincidence that Paul reaches this theological height at the midpoint of Romans 8: 12-17. For the first seven chapters, he has given us his most thorough account of Christian doctrine, he scales the greatest heights in the eighth chapter, and then continues with theological and practical teaching for the rest of the book. If we truly believe that God is our Father, then we shall be able to accept His choice of circumstances, career and friends. But that doesn't allow us to sit back lazily and leave choices to chance!

CIRCUMSTANCES CAN CREATE WRONG DECISIONS

One evening, King David was lying on his bed (2 Samuel 11:2ff). For whatever reason, he got up and strolled around the palace roof. From this viewpoint, he observed a woman bathing on a nearby rooftop. The consequences of this simple act are well known and tragic. Tragic for Uriah, the woman's husband, tragic for Bathsheba, tragic for David, for his family, and for the Kingdom of Israel. The murder of a loyal army officer, the death of a baby, grotesque unhappiness in David's family, terrible wars between Israel and Judah, and even the disasters for both states in future centuries, to some extent sprang from David's unfortunate temptation.

Chauvinists might say that it was the woman's fault for bathing publicly on her balcony; opportunists might say that the end (Solomon) might justify the means. But the plain facts were that David, one of the greatest men of God that has ever lived, didn't know how to cope with a straightforward circumstantial temptation.

He didn't need to find out about her, he didn't need to send for her . . .

The Scriptures give us a few clues as to why such a great man failed. David was at the height of his secular power. He had won battle after battle. The frailties of Israel were secure. He hadn't bothered to go to war, uncharacteristically he'd sent Joab instead. His family life was already uncomfortable (see 2 Samuel 6:20ff). Perhaps the deepest problem lay in the Lord's refusal to let David build the Temple (2 Samuel 7).

Earlier, when in deep trouble, David had written Psalm 34. There he had expressed confidence in God to protect him. He had experienced the goodness of the Lord. Now life was easier, his spiritual guard was down; it was too easy.

Circumstances can similarly trap believers today. Over-tiredness, lack of prayer and relaxation, frequently lead us to take bad decisions. Here is a simple illustration.

A few weeks ago I was tired and very busy. I was in the midst of some unusually complicated pastoral problems, none of which were of my creation but all of which I felt I had been led into. I returned home late, nearly six o'clock, with an evening meeting ahead. Jane and the children were entertaining a 'Frenchman' with an unusual hard luck story. They were anxious to help him. I felt trapped into action, and too tired to think straight. His story seemed plausible, but a bit unlikely, his prayers in English and French a little too fluent. He asked me to make a reservation in a Youth Hostel in Bath. He asked for money to get there, and rather more to cover his expenses for a few days. As I gave him the money, the 'silent voice' warned me . . . But I was too tired . . . I didn't think of asking a simple question 'Please show me your passport/documents'. After all, he was a 'Christian'. I ought to have remembered that 'born-again' strangers are very common at Vicarage doors!

Of course, he didn't turn up in Bath; of course, I should have known better. Far worse decisions than losing money can be made in such situations. Circumstances can drive people to wrong, and sometimes disastrous, decisions. Frequently one mistake leads to another. At no point is God's guidance sought.

For example – a Christian girl finds that she is pregnant, this leads to an unhappy marriage with the boyfriend. Things slide from bad to worse. A family mismanages their finances. The wife, for the wrong reasons, is forced to work. The pressures on the family intensify. The extra money solves one problem and creates several others. A Christian is unemployed. The temptation is to moan, blame God, and drift around in everyone's way. The opportunity to take time, to learn about the faith, to give basic service to the community, to help the local church is missed.

'We live by faith, not by sight' (2 Corinthians 5:7) might be paraphrased 'we walk by faith, not by circumstances'. How easy these words are to write, or to preach about, how hard they are to live by.[4] Circumstances dominate our thinking. We react to them. Part of the answer is to seek God — especially when we know we've made a mistake. Part of the answer is to learn to discipline our life so that we have space to react wisely, whatever the circumstance.

CIRCUMSTANCES AND TIME

Most Christians complain that they are too busy. Yet few of us have learned to manage time. If we're honest many 'inspirational' actions later proved ill thought out and ill founded. Of course, we do receive guidance to call on people on some occasions, but quite often our schedule lacks an overall plan and thus becomes time-wasting.

God has priorities for each day. If we are organised, doing the unpalatable urgent tasks first, we shall have space for the sudden crisis or inspiration. If we are free from anxiety, we won't waste time on things that don't matter.

Let me illustrate — the other day, on a Friday, a parishioner reminded me that I hadn't returned some notes he'd lent me for this book. He wasn't worried, but I was. I couldn't find them! Intuitively, I sensed that I had put them with some other material which I had returned to someone else. Two phone calls established that this material was locked in an office out of Shepton. There was nothing that I could do that night. I had a choice — to accept the circumstantial guidance and forget it for the weekend — or to continue to search frenetically.

What did I do? I searched, wildly. I made a thorough nuisance of myself. All to no avail. The problem wasn't urgent, and, of course, it was solved when the notes turned up in my other friend's office on Monday.

CIRCUMSTANCES AND LIFE STYLE

Christians shouldn't need 'guidance' to realise the dangers in obvious things like excess food and/or drink; driving too fast; 'innocent' sexual stimulation; books that feed our imagination in the wrong way; dependence on cigarettes or coffee, let alone drugs!

But perhaps the Spirit is speaking to us in more subtle ways. Is our diet wrong? Is our life style too stressful? Do we have the wrong priorities? When we entertain has it got to be an elaborate nightmare?

Often the simplest advice is the best. Once, one of our children was very unhappy at school, especially in the lunch hour. After prayer, we realised that there was a very simple solution — she could come home for lunch! On another occasion, my sister-in-law recommended me, to help my hip, to wear 'trainers' — shoes with a spongy sole. I have always despised such things; now I have to admit that, suitably 'blacked' out and clerical, they have helped enormously!

'Do not grieve the Holy Spirit' (Ephesians 4:30) says St Paul in the midst of some very practical teaching about Christian behaviour which should be better known. How often does our 'life style' grieve the Spirit and prevent us really hearing the voice of God?

CIRCUMSTANCES AND OPPORTUNITIES

I've just heard a lovely story. A student who had recently become a committed Christian, bent down to check her shopping bag. As she glanced up, she saw a man nearby. She gave him a lovely smile and greeting. He said it had made his day. As she looked fully at him, she saw how terribly deformed he was from plastic surgery. She reflected afterwards; what if she'd seen him full face at first? She might have instinctively turned away. I believe that because she is walking with the Lord, she had the grace to act rightly and make someone else happy.

Each encounter is an opportunity for good or evil. Each conversation, each phone call, can help or hinder the Kingdom. Sometimes we seem to have just one opportunity to form a relationship, or to take an existing one deeper. I never cease to wonder when a relationship which has been superficial for years suddenly becomes deep and profound. God's guidance – when to speak and to be silent, when to talk and when to question, when to open oneself, and when to listen – is so crucial.

I saw Jane, my wife, in the distance at Lee Abbey. In the week, circumstances gave me just one opportunity to talk to her. If I hadn't taken it, it is doubtful that we would ever have met again.

CIRCUMSTANTIAL GUIDANCE

We all have to take a small number of really significant

decisions. Should I marry X? Which is the right job? Where should I be living? Likewise in churches we have a small number of vital decisions to make. Should we have a mission? What sort of person do we want as our next vicar? What sort of services should we have?

What do we do when there seems to be no clear external guidance? Let me give a few examples. After ordination, when I returned to Winchester to continue teaching mathematics and to help the chaplains, the headmaster made it clear that he felt this should be a temporary return. A few years later, he repeated this and I started to look for a curacy. I hadn't the faintest idea how to go about it; nobody had told me! In desperation, I wrote to the two Theological College principals who knew me. One was now a bishop, the other still in office. I presumed that they knew something about placing curates! The bishop wrote a long and helpful letter with various suggestions, including the line 'You could try a place like St Aldate's, Oxford.' The Principal, Michael Green, Rector designate of St Aldate's, tentatively suggested that I followed him there.

It all seemed too good to be true. With hindsight, I know that Michael's offer was more tentative than I realised. I snapped it up without much thought. He was struck down with a severe attack of meningitis and consequently was glad to have one less decision to take. I can't claim any very clear guidance, but it certainly turned out, from my point of view anyway, to be an excellent decision.

After I had been in Oxford two years, another opening appeared. St Matthew's Church, in South Oxford, had been built ninety years earlier by Canon Christopher, St Aldate's great Victorian Rector. After many years of independence, a dwindling congregation, a crumbling building, and a firm bishop armed with the *Sheffield Report*,[5] combined to bring St Matthew's to its knees. A returning missionary,

Brian Ringrose, was given just three years to lead the church out of the wilderness and then it had to choose — to join one of the three neighbouring parishes.

Faced with three unpalatable choices, the PCC opted narrowly for reunion with St Aldate's. We actually lived in the parish, and it was painfully obvious that we ought to move or to offer ourselves for the somewhat daunting prospect of St Matthew's. Once again, there was no clear guidance, just a sense of co-operating with what God was calling us to do.

A number of factors made the decision easier — there was no obvious alternative either for me or for St Matthew's; a number of young families who lived in the area were committed to staying and helping to rebuild the church; the support of the team at St Aldate's made the job far less isolated and, away on retreat, I received a word based on Deuteronomy 4 'possess the land which I have given thee'.

It turned out to be a very happy decision for Jane and me — and, hopefully, for St Matthew's. Certainly the current strength of the church (two incumbents later), far greater than in my time, would have been undreamt of by the faithful few who prayed, in the desolation of earlier years, for the Lord to revive their church.

Soon after arriving in Shepton where, as recorded in Chapter 5, the guidance was a good deal clearer, I was faced with a tricky decision on a matter about which I knew less than nothing. The heating system was plainly inadequate. A complicated, and expensive, report had recommended drastic changes. An enthusiastic member of the PCC recommended under-pew heating. This system, far from universally applauded in other churches, would be very complicated, but might at least force the congregation to sit closer together and further forward (we couldn't afford to do the whole church!). A third option was to build an

internal porch to keep out the draughts which made life
misery for everyone whenever anyone entered the church
in winter. I had told the PCC that I didn't believe in 'votes'
and that we should be virtually unanimous before any
decision was taken. In the end, it was clearly a question of
under-pew heating or the porch. We would do one first, and
then the other when we could afford it. We had to take a
decision! I was a lukewarm supporter of the pew-heating
scheme. My churchwardens were adamant that they wanted
a porch. We had to vote! I think there was a one vote
majority for the porch. It proved such a success that the
church started to feel quite warm, even in the depths of
winter, and the under-pew heating was quietly forgotten.
Thank you, Lord!

Now I include three examples of guidance concerning
matters of housing, career, and safety.

In each case circumstances, common sense, and an
awareness of God combined to take what seems to have been
a wise decision.

WHICH WAY?

After several months of enthusiastic, though unsuccessful, house hunting, the initial excitement waned and
the situation was becoming tense and frustrating, when
one day I found my perfect house, the sort of place I had
longed to live in, but my husband didn't like it. That is
not quite true, he liked the house, but not the situation!
It was on a busy B-road, particularly in the summer when
it was a tourist route, and fields belonging to this property
were on both sides of this road. As we have sheep, dogs
and cats he felt it would be both dangerous and noisy.
During the next two weeks our relationship suffered. I

was furious, frustrated and disappointed, and the whole business of buying (and selling) houses was beginning to get me down. Throughout the period I had been praying for guidance, particularly as we were moving after eighteen years in one much-loved house. After church on Sunday I asked two friends to pray for me, briefly explaining the situation and stressing that I particularly wanted prayers for my relationship with my husband. During the prayers, one friend, for some reason, prayed that 'we would find a house away from a road'. Some weeks later, we went to an auction for another house, but were unsuccessful and, strangely, not overly disappointed. The next day we heard of a house with land that was going on the market the following week. We rushed to see it that same day, it was up a long drive and about a third of a mile from the nearest lane. The house left a lot to be desired, but the whole family felt we could live there and the outstanding sense was of peace. From then on all the technicalities of moving house went smoothly, extensive alterations to the house were amazingly well done and, eleven months later, our nineteen year old daughter was baptised, again, something I had longed and prayed about for several years.

After spending some time abroad, I came home without any job to go to, so I asked for guidance as to what I should do next. I asked the Lord to open the right doors and to close the wrong ones.

While I was looking for jobs I tried to spend regular times each day in prayer and Bible reading. These times became very precious to me, as the words in the Bible came alive to me in a way I had not known before, and it became a great joy just to spend time with the Lord.

After six weeks, during which time several doors had remained firmly closed, I was reading job adverts in a paper when I suddenly thought that I would like to do a particular kind of job. As this work had not previously appealed to me, I had not applied for any jobs in this field.

Later that day I received a phone call asking me to make an appointment to see someone, and at the interview a few days later I was offered a job in the same area of work that I had noticed in the paper.

I had known when I received the phone call that this was the open door I had asked God to show me, so I had several days to come to terms with the new idea. I was able to accept the job in peace, knowing that the Lord had opened the way for me, that He would guide and help me with the work too.

CIRCUMSTANCE AND COMMON SENSE

It was on April 19th 1941. We had been fire-watching the night before and we were very tired. It was a noisy night with gunfire all around, but we decided it was time for bed. Helen wanted to finish a chapter in her book and I said 'If you want to stay up any longer, we will wear our tin hats'. Helen laughed at sitting indoors wearing tin hats, but I felt compelled to get them. A few minutes later a 1,000 lb bomb landed in the back garden, the point of impact being only eight yards from where we were sitting. Our bedroom was at the back, and the back of the house was completely demolished. Helen's tin hat had a deep crease in the front made by shrapnel, and she would have been killed had she not been wearing it. We were both taken to hospital, but were able to leave about two weeks later. It could only have been divine intervention that made me get the tin hats.

At this stage, many people will object. Circumstances can also lead to disaster. To take a simple example — a clergyman gives a lift home to a member of a youth group. On the way home, he has a serious accident. What are we to say?

Scott Peck[6] discusses this sort of question in a chapter called 'The Miracle of Serendipity'. He marvels at the implausible frequency with which people walk out of terrible situations alive. His 'unscientific' impression is that the frequency of 'statistically improbable occurrences that are clearly beneficial is far greater than that in which the result seems detrimental.'

Jesus faced the question with characteristic forthrightness — 'Or those eighteen who died when the tower in Siloam fell on them — do you think they were more guilty than all the others living in Jerusalem? I tell you, no! But unless you repent, you too will all perish.' (Luke 13: 4-5). In the end it is a matter of faith. Christians cannot expect to be protected from unpleasant circumstances, but they can continue to trust God in spite of them, and to continue to seek His guidance.

We can never know why God allows such things to happen, but we can move with the first disciples from the blackness of the first Easter Eve into the light of the Resurrection.

'We live by faith, not by sight'. With these words written deep in our hearts, we should all have a little more confidence when we sing 'Thy hand, O God, has guided thy flock from age to age.'

Notes and references

1 See Chapter 4 of this volume.
2 See Chapter 5 of this volume.
3 See Acts 14:5ff; Acts 16:40; Acts 20:3ff.
4 See Chapter 13 of this volume (especially p 221ff).
5 *The Sheffield Report* was an attempt to reduce the number of separate parishes in many dioceses.
6 Peck, M Scott. *The Road Less Travelled*. London, Hutchinson, 1983, p 255.

11

GUIDANCE IN RELATIONSHIPS

First, I must admit that one short chapter on guidance in
relationships in one short book seems almost trivial. Many
of the issues which I am going to touch on would merit a
book in themselves. That said, it seems inescapable that we
consider the issue. We spend all our life forming
relationships, and most of the joys and heartbreaks of life
concern relationships. The Scriptures are full of stories of
relationships – good, indifferent and disastrous. Church
history likewise. Our local church will probably be judged
more by its quality of relationships than for anything else.
Here, more frequently than anywhere else, people seek
guidance.

'See how these Christians love one another'[1] wrote one
ancient author. Christians talk a great deal about love. Some
Christians exhibit an amazing selfless love; many Christian
marriages shine as beacons of hope in a shifting world of
scandal, marital break up and divorce; Christian friendships
can be deep and profound, cutting across natural barriers
of race, class, politics. Yet, despite all these signs of hope,
we have to admit relationships in Christ can be very hard,
and sometimes appear less successful and harmonious than
their normal secular equivalents.

Why should this be so? There are, I think, a number of
reasons. First, the very ideal can seem so high as to be

dauntingly unattainable.

'Dear friends, let us love one another, for love comes from God' (1 John 4:7). That leaves little room for failure! Yet as the average Christian surveys his local church, he knows that both he and it fall well short of the ideal. When he looks around, he finds it hard to love the apparently diffident and unapproachable vicar; the choir which doesn't like his sort of music, the woman who preaches a sermon when she is meant to be leading the intercessions; the noisy baby; the member of the ministry team who fixes him with a loving stare and offers to pray about his problems, and so on.

And when he gets home his wife upbraids him for spending too much time on 'church' matters; his children misbehave and he doesn't know how to control them 'lovingly'; and his young cousin wants to be ordained, but has a steady homosexual relationship.

A second problem is that many Christians find it very difficult to express their feelings accurately.[2] The vicar is aware that X and Y who are members of the church don't get on. Most of the rest of the church is aware. If he wasn't a Christian, he could cheerfully ignore their problem − adopting the popular maxim 'I never interfere − I never do anyone any harm.' But now he feels he ought to help. He feels led to tell Y, gently, to stop gossiping, to accept X and his position in the church, to forgive and forget. But somehow it comes out all wrong, and now he's got nearly as big a problem with Y as Y has with X.

A third difficulty for Christians is that they underestimate the undermining work of the powers of darkness.

' "In your anger, do not sin. Do not let the sun go down while you are still angry, and do not give the devil a foothold' " (Ephesians 4: 26,27). Bad relationships give the devil a foothold in fellowship. Bad relationships in marriage open couples up to Satan's attack, and stifle a Christian's prayer life (1 Corinthians 7:5 and 1 Peter 3:7). If Satan asks to sift the believer as wheat (see Luke 22:31), if Satan stands as the accuser of the brethren (Revelation 12:10), if Satan prowls about as a roaring lion (1 Peter 5:8), then it stands to reason that Satan will attack Christian friendships, Christian marriages, and Christian families. 'We are not ignorant of his devices' says St Paul (2 Corinthians 2:11 AV). Sadly, most Christians are! They don't understand the danger of unconfessed anger, unforgiveness, and letting the sun go down on their wrath. It isn't always practical, or wise, to pick up the phone to try and mend a quarrel late at night, but a Christian couple can surely learn to forgive and forget as they make their way to bed.

A fourth, and in my view, the most serious difficulty, is that Christians ignore, and sometimes defy, the biblical teaching on relationships. The first four chapters of Genesis give us some models of bad relationships; sadly, this continues throughout much of the Old Testament. Things are somewhat better in the New Testament where much teaching is given on relationships between man and wife; parent and child; and on being members of the Body of Christ. Nevertheless, even the Apostolic Church is beset by quarrels (see Acts 15:2; Acts 15:37; 1 Corinthians 9:5; Galatians 2:11; and those unfortunate women in Philippians 4:2 who are remembered for nothing except their disagreement). Time and time again, modern Christians think they know better than the Bible, ignore its teaching and, scarcely surprisingly, are unable to hear 'the silent voice' if and when they turn to God for help.

Now I must be specific, hoping that these pen portraits from Scripture will help each of us seek God's guidance in our very varied situations.

A DISAPPOINTING MARRIAGE (Genesis 24ff)

It would be hard to imagine a more perfect beginning. Abraham's godly servant fulfilled his role in a truly wonderful manner. Isaac was out in the fields meditating (Genesis 24:63) when he first saw Rebekah. He loved her, she apparently loved him. Yet within a few years, this marriage, apparently arranged by God, had become a disaster.

'Isaac, who had a taste for wild game, loved Esau, but Rebekah loved Jacob' (Genesis 25:28).

It looks as if the original spiritual unity of the marriage has completely disappeared. Esau and Isaac have made food a priority (Genesis 25:30ff); Rebekah schemes to outwit her husband and achieve the patriarchal blessing for her favourite son. Jacob connives with opportunism and deceit, and finally has to disappear fast! What a family.

There is only one recorded agreement between Isaac and Rebekah – they both disliked Esau's Hittite wives (Genesis 26:35)!

At one level, the source of the trouble was the birth of the twins. Rebekah went to 'inquire of the Lord' and discovered that the Lord's primary purposes were to be fulfilled in the younger son. From then on, Rebekah set about to scheme what the Lord had planned.

It cannot have been God's plan to achieve His purposes by such scheming and trickery.

With this example as a solemn warning, I want to look at some of the principles for guidance in the marriage relationship. Richard Foster[3] describes the gentle oversight of some prospective marriages. Some disasters could be averted, and many marriages strengthened, by a realistic discussion with the leaders of the church before the relationship goes too far. Christians are remarkably adept at spiritual blackmail. The fact that 'I fell in love' when I first saw Jane, the fact that the Lord gave me a word of comfort on the night of my mother's funeral, the fact that circumstances pointed to a lonely ordinand, suddenly bereaved of both parents, put an appalling strain on her. Actually, I had to lose her, and find her returning of her own free will before our relationship could be on a right footing. But nobody taught me any of these things when I was a young Christian; consequently, I blundered from one mistake to another, leaving a trail of unhappiness for myself and other people. Christians are unusually inept in these situations. We don't want to hurt other people, so we hurt them far more by our inability to express our feelings, or lack of them. Jane's lack of certainty in the early years of our friendship was openly and lovingly expressed, and a model for anyone who sees amber lights flashing when their prospective partner sees multiple green.

I would also sound a word of caution about apparent 'coincidences'. David Prior[4] tells a sad, but profound story of his first engagement which culminated in the 'sign' of driving through a dozen green traffic lights. That 'sign' could have formed the basis of a wrong marriage.

Ideally, each prospective partner should be able to look up to the other spiritually, have enough interests in common to sustain a relationship over the breakfast table when the children have grown up, a deep sacrificial love, and a clear sense of God's calling both to marriage and to an effective place in His Body.

Marriages which grow in love, understanding, sacrifice, are wonderfully healing. The ability, and the will, to pray together are vital (1 Peter 3:7). Curiously, even committed Christian couples find this difficult. It is partly a difficulty with time (prayer together cannot be a substitute for prayer alone), but it is also a difficulty of the 'will'.

The modern practice of 'marriage encounter' weekends has much to commend in it, and any wanting to explore a very profound understanding of love should read *The Road Less Travelled*.[5]

Obviously, the marriage relationship changes with time. The arrival of children, serious illness, new spiritual insights, change of house, and a host of smaller things, can cause a relationship to mature or to founder. I believe that God is concerned with every part of our relationship − physical, emotional, material, spiritual − and that His Voice and His Word can guide us in each and every situation. The real problem with Isaac and Rebekah seems to have been that they each had different priorities − food and a favourite son − and that neither priority was God-given!

MARRIAGES WITHOUT A CHRISTIAN CENTRE

St Paul and St Peter both faced this issue.[6] In Apostolic days, it normally occurred when one partner was converted subsequent to marriage. Marriages between believers and unbelievers were discouraged − probably forbidden.

'Do not be yoked together with unbelievers' (2 Corinthians 6:14) which, although it doesn't directly refer to marriage, must include the marriage relationship. 1 Corinthians 7:39 is even clearer!

These are hard sayings − particularly in church situations where the number of unmarried women usually outnumbers the number of unmarried men very considerably − but if the Christian faith makes all the difference, and claims that it should, then a divide at this point brings a disastrous flaw into the marriage. Essentially, either the Christian partner will find their ability to be involved in the Body of Christ limited, perhaps severely limited, or their partner will resent their many absences from home and may be unhappy about some of the spiritual relationships formed.

St Peter (1 Peter 3: 1-7) has some wise words for partners who find themselves in this situation. But, presumably, he is thinking of the case where neither partner is a believer when married, and one partner is subsequently converted (see 1 Corinthians 7: 12-16 for some very helpful teaching about divorce in that situation). I have often felt uneasy when one partner has professed faith, and wish that I had been bolder and tackled the other partner at the same time. It seems to me that people who find themselves in this spiritually one-sided marriage need an exceptional amount of love, comfort and understanding. Their time for service is limited; and their unbelieving partner needs much love, care and consideration. I only wish some Christians in this situation would make it clear how deeply they are concerned about this divide, and I wish that others would learn to shut up and stop trying to badger their partner into the Kingdom. Peter encourages wives (and, presumably, husbands) to win their partners over without words by their submissive, pure, and reverent behaviour! I don't believe a Christian partner in these situations should accept a position of responsibility (let alone ministry) in a local church without clearly talking it through with their partner.

What I have said above also applies to those who disobeyed Scripture, either deliberately or through ignorance, followed their own love and married a non-believer. God doesn't want to leave you in a state of condemnation. Confess your sin (yes, it was a sin), seek God's forgiveness, and pray that you, too, may see your partner won for the Lord.

Much responsibility rests with Christian youth leaders to have the courage to teach biblical principles clearly. Often, young people are much more open to God's guidance; if they are first taught the principles, they may well hear the Lord's voice when decisions have to be made.

MARITAL DISHARMONY AND BREAK UP

People in glass houses shouldn't throw stones. It is with a profound sense of the graciousness of God to my own marriage, and with a deep awareness that I don't begin to understand the pain of most situations, that I write this paragraph.

Jesus taught that marriage is indissoluble (Matthew 19:6). He, also, was pastorally understanding to those whose marriages had failed. This comes across both in Matthew 19:9, in His pastoral attitude to the woman at the well (John 4), to the woman taken in adultery (John 8), and to the woman who interrupted Simon the Pharisee's dinner party (Luke 7:36ff).

What does one say to a Christian who is married to someone who regularly beats her up?

What does one say to a Christian whose husband/wife is continually unfaithful?

What does one say to a Christian whose partner wants a divorce?

What does one say to a couple who are clearly incompatible, and whose children are suffering because of their appalling rows?

Scripture always offers hope of change (1 Corinthians 6:11), but that change may only be possible, if there is separation. While separation is usually seen as the beginning of the end, it could be the means of one or both parties having the space and time to seek counselling. Not even the marriage bond requires a woman to stay in a home which is dangerous for her and her children.

Guidance is hard in these situations. Not least, because only one partner is usually prepared to seek it.

GUIDANCE AND THE UNMARRIED

The disciples received Jesus' teaching (Matthew 19:1-9) with the comment 'If this is the situation between husband and wife, it is better not to marry.'

Jesus replied, 'Not everyone can accept this word, but only those to whom it has been given. For some are eunuchs because they were born that way; others were made that way by men; and others have renounced marriage because of the kingdom of heaven. The one who can accept this should accept it.' Leaving aside what Jesus meant when He said 'some are born eunuchs'; leaving aside the now unusual state of 'being made that way by men'; we shall concentrate on the last saying: 'others have renounced marriage because of the kingdom of heaven. The one who can accept this should accept it.' The emphasis here is quite clearly on the high calling of celibacy. Jesus was celibate, and for many years the Church emphasised this as an ideal. Inevitably, some took it too far, and forgetting that Peter and many of the other apostles were married (Mark 1:30, 1 Corinthians 9:5), and ignoring Paul's warning against extreme teaching (2 Timothy 4:3), they proclaimed celibacy as essential for the highest service of God. Nevertheless, the Protestant reaction against this teaching has surely gone too far. Jesus clearly regarded celibacy as a high calling, so did Paul in the often misunderstood and misquoted 1 Corinthians 7.

Many of the finest Christians today are celibate. Sometimes they belong to monastic orders, sometimes they have taken a private vow of celibacy, sometimes they are celibate because they haven't found the right marriage partner, sometimes they are celibate because they recognise that their sexual orientation makes it unwise for them to seek marriage. Christianity calls us to make many sacrifices. Many celibate Christians have discovered the truth of 1 Corinthians 7:32 and 35 and have been able to devote themselves to the Lord in a remarkable way. His service is perfect freedom.

My Aunt lived a happy, fulfilled, celibate Christian life. In her case, many potential husbands, and perhaps her true love, lay buried in the mud of the Somme or some other First World War battlefield. She enjoyed a rewarding old age, free at least from the sorrow of widowhood!

How does a Christian hear God's voice in these matters? In many cases it shouldn't be necessary to hear anything, the matter should be settled by the Scriptures and the teaching of the church. However, there are obvious cases where people will need 'guidance'. Before making a definite vow of chastity, I would need to be very sure of God's calling. Some do make this and discover their mistake. Many others make it and discover perfect freedom.

It is extremely difficult for the single person, who feels a real need of marriage, when no one turns up! I had to face this question, very seriously, when single, a priest, and over thirty. I know many others who have found this a real struggle.

Many older single people can find the church 'family' very frustrating. Others, having accepted God's call to singleness, are wonderfully fulfilled and enjoy contact with young children and families.

One way we have felt guided to include unmarried people in our family is in the choice of godparents for our children.

GUIDANCE FOR PARENTS

Scripture stresses the importance of being good parents (Colossians 3:21; Ephesians 6:4; Titus 1:6). Scripture also gives plenty of warnings of what can happen when family relationships go wrong.

Nevertheless, contrary to popular opinion, very many Christian parents, notably in my experience, some clergy families, have seen all their children growing up to salvation. In our age of ever-increasing family chaos, it is certain that God wants His people to raise up righteous families — brought up 'in the fear and nurture of the Lord'.

Psalm 103:17 contains a great promise, as does the end of Peter's Pentecost Sermon (Acts 2:39). Parents could use these texts as a basis for praying not only for their children, but for the future generations as well.

Francis MacNutt[7] stresses the importance of parents praying for their unborn children. John the Baptist was filled with the Holy Spirit from his birth (Luke 1:15) and Elizabeth his mother, likewise, when the baby leapt in her womb (Luke 1:41). Do we believe enough for our children?

Parents need also to pray for and with their children on a regular basis. They are our most important, sacred charge. We will need God's guidance about schools, hobbies, books, TV, friends, holidays and a whole host of practical matters.

We've discovered that Christian-orientated holidays (not run by Daddy!) are a great way of helping them discover their own faith. They are encouraged by meeting other similarly thinking children, and by, for once, being in a situation where they are not part of a small minority who go to church or Sunday school.

Of course, Christian households must be fun! Endless prohibitions, religious exercises, best behaviour, will cause them and their faith to develop (if it does) in a negative, defensive way. I remember reading the diary of a Victorian clergyman who, among other delights, made his family, as a Sabbath task, write epitaphs for a deceased brother!

We have found our children respond to prayer for healing, and have learned to pray simply in a wide variety of ways. They each have their problems, questions, difficulties at school, relationship problems; like the young adults they are, they can display a very mature faith which can put me to shame!

We've had some very direct answers to our prayers for our children. We've wrestled with problems of schools, discipline and illness, and we've rejoiced at some marvellous times of love, joy, self-control, though seldom, it must be admitted, of peace!

I must add that I am deeply impressed by households that I've met amid the Restoration churches. There seems to be a maturity of faith, a politeness, a simplicity which is most engaging.

Christian parents must learn to release their children. They may hope, believe, and pray that they will grow up in certain ways. But in the end, the children are free to choose. They may reject the Christian way. Often such rejection, very painful to the parents, is only temporary. In times of spiritual decline, the succession of faith seems particularly erratic. Michael Wilcock[8] makes this point very clearly when discussing the faith or lack of it in successive Old Testament Kings.

Perhaps one of the greatest failures of Christian parents is in the area of evangelism. We assume that our children are believers, when many need to take a clear step of commitment to Christ. One friend, recently bereaved, writes movingly of his daughter's trust in Jesus two days before her fourth birthday. This profession of faith, backed up by ample evidence over the next fourteen years, helped him through the sorrow of her tragic death.

Christian grandparents find guidance in such matters particularly hard. They long to see the faith take root in the later generations.

One miracle of guidance occurred for an old lady of eighty. She became a Christian at this advanced age. She said to the man who helped her to faith 'I've wasted so much of my life — what can I do with the rest of it?' He replied 'Pray, especially for those members of your family whom God particularly lays on your heart.' She prayed for two of her grandchildren. One quickly became a Christian and is a clergyman's wife. She is now mother to a large professing Christian family. The other, a student drop-out, had a dramatic conversion. The last thing his grandmother was able to do before she died was to attend his ordination! He has been given a tremendous gift of evangelism — not least among his extensive family.

Sadly, many grandparents don't experience this sort of joy. In the end, they can only pray, and give suitable gifts such as Bibles and Christian books — in moderation.

GUIDANCE AND CONTROVERSY – REMARRIAGE AFTER DIVORCE

Sooner or later, every church leader will face this issue.[9] It is a very complex one, but the most common pastoral situations, for the Christian, are those where a Christian man or woman has been left by his or her first partner and the situation where, after the failure of a first marriage, a man or woman is genuinely converted and now wants to marry someone else.

In the first situation, depending on the circumstances, 1 Corinthians 7:15 may offer freedom to remarry. I have certainly taken a marriage service in such circumstances (see the end of Chapter 15 — Guidance in the Mud and the Mire).

In the second situation, many questions about the past could, and perhaps should, be asked. Nevertheless, in a real sense, he/she is now a new creation, the past is forgiven and set behind them (2 Corinthians 5:17ff) and I think in some circumstances they could remarry. We know that Jesus upheld, totally, the sacredness of marriage, but did He intend to lock people into past situations that are now legally finished? He declined to answer the Sadducee's conundrum on marriage (Luke 20:27) and in practice offered forgiveness and hope to adulterers and people who had clearly failed in this area (Luke 7:36ff and John 8:2ff).

I have seen some wonderful signs of conversion as people approached a second marriage, as well as some already converted Christians making a wonderful new beginning in a second marriage.

Such a situation cannot be God's ideal — but can it be God's best plan in a given situation, at a given time?

GUIDANCE AND CONTROVERSY — HOMOSEXUALITY
AND LESBIANISM

Homosexual relationships are even more emotive. We all have our prejudices. It seems to me that the Scriptures are painfully clear. Homosexual physical relationships are wrong (Romans 1: 24-27). The Gospel offers a number of ways forward. Some through conversion and/or prayer, can put their homosexual practices behind them. I have known that happen. One current Christian leader gives a moving testimony of his own conversion and deliverance from active homosexuality. Others can take Jesus' teaching in Matthew

19:12 and become, or remain, celibate.

I don't see any reason why men and women of the same sex should not live together as friends. It used to happen, frequently, and only recently have such friendships been assumed to have a 'sexual' dimension.

But what of the man who genuinely feels that he cannot renounce or control his homosexual feelings? The man who feels that God, in whose image he is made, gave him such a nature? I have known a number of such people. One such, married and, thanks to the exceptional love of his wife, had a happy, stable marriage. He never, I think, was able to renounce his homosexuality. It must have caused his wife great grief. It held him back for a long time from commitment to Christ. It ruined his career, and ultimately caused a final depression which led to his death. God understands his suffering and his sin. I don't, but I cannot judge.

'Will not the Judge of all the earth do right?'[10] Before we leave this whole difficult subject, we had better all read Matthew 5: 27-28. 'You have heard that it was said "Do not commit adultery". But I tell you that anyone who looks at a woman lustfully has already committed adultery with her in his heart.'

Faced with these words, we all can put away our stones.

GUIDANCE FOR LEADERS

The difficulty is that those of us in leadership have, in a real sense, to advise. We have to guide, we have to shepherd, we cannot just turn our faces to the wall and say 'It's your problem . . .' That is why, in the end, Christian leaders must be seen to be above reproach. We will fail, and when we fail, we may fall a long way, and in the mercy of God be restored. But we cannot deliberately set out with questionable relationships (adulterous or homosexual) and expect the respect of the people of God. Paul, as so often, sums it up clearly in 1 Timothy 3: 8-13:

> Deacons, likewise, are to be men worthy of respect, sincere, not indulging in much wine, and not pursuing dishonest gain. They must keep hold of the deep truths of the faith with a clear conscience. They must first be tested; and then if there is nothing against them, let them serve as deacons. In the same way, their wives are to be women worthy of repect, not malicious talkers but temperate and trustworthy in everything.
>
> A deacon must be the husband of but one wife and must manage his children and his household well. Those who have served well gain an excellent standing and great assurance in their faith in Christ Jesus.

RELATIONSHIPS IN THE BODY

'A new command I give you: Love one another. As I have loved you, so you must love one another. By this all men will know that you are my disciples, if you love one another' (John 13: 34-35).

By this shall men know that you are my disciples! Is it possible? Jesus demonstrated it, taught it, expected it!

But, 'Are we meant to like everyone? Surely that's impossible,' says a mature older Christian. 'I can try to love them; but how can I like them?' I don't know! And therein lies the root of the sort of petty relationship difficulties which I sketched at the beginning of the chapter, and which mar so much that passes for Christian fellowship. I believe that we can love everyone, certainly every Christian. I believe we can like every Christian. They all have something of Jesus; we must be able to like that! Obviously, I shall like some more easily than others. Curiously, it's those that exasperate me the most! I suppose that I expect more because I like them more, and that I'm disappointed when they prove as unreliable — as me.

I believe we should train ourselves to see the good in people and get their motes firmly in perspective. Prayer will often show how to improve relationships. Expressions of appreciation, not useless insincere gushing, can work wonders. Encouraging faith enables timid people to grow and mature. An occasional well-merited rebuke is the deepest sign of love. (Think how often Jesus rebuked the twelve!)

But, sometimes, a fellowship or church is beset with bad relationships. What can we do? Prayer, plus action according to the Scriptures, and in accordance with whatever special guidance is received, is the only way forward. Key passages are Matthew 18: 15-17, Matthew 18: 21-35, and Matthew 5: 21-26.

The parable of the unforgiving servant (along with many others of Jesus' sayings, notably Mark 11:25, Matthew 6:12 and Matthew 6: 14-15) simply leaves us no option. We must forgive!

Of course, the church isn't perfect, and forgiveness is hard. Think of the case of Paul and Barnabas. Barnabas had persuaded the apostles (Acts 9:27) not to reject Paul after his conversion. Later, Barnabas had found him in Tarsus (Acts 11:25) and brought him to help lead the church at Antioch. Barnabas led him off on the first missionary journey. Not for nothing was he nicknamed 'Son of Encouragement'. But twice Barnabas and Paul fell out.

The first time (Galatians 2:13) was serious. The second (Acts 15:36) was disastrous. On each occasion, relationships were the problem. In Antioch, Barnabas deferred to Peter's (wrong) judgment on an early church controversy. Just before the start of the second missionary journey, again in Antioch, fresh from the triumph of the Council of Jerusalem, Paul and Barnabas were having great encouragement (Acts 15:35). Then they quarrelled. This time it was over Mark. Paul didn't want to take an unreliable young man on another journey; Barnabas wanted to give him a second chance.

On this occasion, it is not even clear who was right and who was wrong. At least, Barnabas stood by his young cousin and thereby, perhaps, paved the way for the writing of the oldest gospel! On the other hand, Paul got on with the job and the two evangelistic missions took place.

But the end doesn't justify the means. It is clear from Colossians 4:10 that there was reconciliation all round. It would be good to know how it happened!

Once I was at a church where the Scriptures were used to heal a potentially serious rift. During the previous week, there had been a lot of misunderstandings among one group in the church. On Sunday, all those involved came to church to discover that the Gospel for the day was Matthew 5: 21-26. The sermon was partly about releasing anger and receiving forgiveness. The minister encouraged the congregation to use the Peace to obey Matthew 5: 23-24, and to be reconciled before receiving communion. A number of people did just that. Peace broke out! That is one of the many right uses of 'the Peace' in the midst of the Eucharist.

Mark you, I don't know how I would have coped with the man who was reported to have said 'Vicar, if you introduce the Peace, war will break out!'

I will discuss[11] the real problem of forgiving the unforgivable, the pain of abused children, unwanted babies, rejected children, rape victims. But many of us don't face these sort of problems. It's the 'normal' problems of a

Martha who might feel put out that a Mary is commended
(*viz*. Luke 10:38ff); or a Simon the Pharisee who might feel
resentful at Jesus' acceptance of the woman who interrupted
his dinner party (Luke 7:36ff); or the fellow citizens of
Zacchaeus who feel that his repentance is hollow and his
forgiveness too cheap (Luke 19:1ff); or to move from
imagination to fact, the ten disciples furious with James and
John for trying to pinch the best seats in heaven (Mark
10:35ff).

Matthew 18: 15-17 is important. There is a time and a
place for confrontation. Two things are vital — it must be
done for your mutual good, for the good of the Body of
Christ, and not to score points! It must also be done at the
right time. If the erring brother (or husband, or pastor . . .)
is tired, depressed, and generally overwrought, it is probably
not the right time. Immediately after a service is not the
moment to blast the Vicar for a poor sermon, bad preparation, terrible hymns or ill-behaved children. Criticism may
be made, but always put yourself in the other person's shoes.
How would you receive it? Why did they act like that? So
often people do and say stupid things because they're
embarrassed, rushed, or burdened with their own or
someone else's problems. Jesus always showed compassion;
dare we do less?

Not all relationships were sorted out even in the early
church. John, the Apostle of Love, couldn't cope with
Diotrephes (3 John:9). Sadly, sometimes Christian leaders
become like that. At that stage, something must be done.
Either Diotrephes is allowed to ruin a church, or he must
be disciplined. A failure to act promptly can only lead to
worse trouble later.

Guidance in such matters is never easy; St John must have
found it especially difficult.

A much better example of good relationships is the friendship of Paul and Timothy. Paul gave Timothy a wonderful example by encouragement, by gentle rebuke, and by teaching.

He also gave Timothy a model for all shared leadership. 'And the things you have heard me say in the presence of many witnesses entrust to reliable men who will also be qualified to teach others.' (2 Timothy 2:2)

Good relationships, good leadership, will extend the Kingdom. Good relationships flow out of love. Good leadership flows from good relationships. Spectacular guidance is seldom necessary, the plain teaching of Scripture, lovingly given and received, should be sufficient.

Notes and references

1 Chadwick, Henry. *The Early Church*. Pelican History of the Church. London, Penguin Books, 1968, p 56. Tertullian quoting a remark made by a pagan.

2 Plass, Adrian. *The Sacred Diary of Adrian Plass (aged thirty-seven and three-quarters)*. Basingstoke, Marshall Pickering, 1987. An hilarious account of this sort of thing is given in this book.

3 Foster, Richard J. *Celebration of Discipline: the path to spiritual growth*. London, Hodder & Stoughton, 1984, p 155ff.

4 Prior, David. *Living by faith: Abraham's example for today*. London, Hodder & Stoughton, 1986, p 36.

5 Peck, M Scott. *The Road Less Travelled*. London, Hutchinson, 1983, Section II.

6 See 1 Corinthians 7: 12-16; 1 Peter 3: 1-7.

7 MacNutt, Francis. *The prayer that heals, praying for healing in the family*. London, Hodder & Stoughton, 1982.

8 Wilcock, Michael. *The Bible Speaks Today: The message of Chronicles — one church, one faith, one Lord*. Leicester, IVP, 1987.

9 Green, Michael. *Matthew for Today*. London, Hodder & Stoughton, 1988 for much fuller discussion.

10 Genesis 18:25.

11 See Chapter 13 of this volume.

12

GUIDANCE AND HEALING

We live in an age where healing has become an urgent question. Advances in medicine have increased our expected life span, reduced infant mortality, and eliminated many diseases. All these good things have heightened the disparities of life and not always improved its quality.

In this chapter, we shall explore the Church's varied teaching on the healing ministry, we shall consider how to hear God's voice, we shall open up the question of God's call to us to be involved, and finally to touch the much wider question of healing in society.

AN UNCERTAIN TRUMPET?

Broadly speaking, if you seek help from the church you will be offered three tracks. The first will point you to a growing number of churches which are following Jesus' example and teaching, and are expecting 'signs and miracles' to follow the preaching of the Kingdom of God (Acts 8: 4-13) by the apostles and their successors. Such believers will point you to Early Church testimonies such as those of Irenaeus of Lyons (c. AD 170) who clearly experienced miracles in his own time.[1] They will supply testimonies from their experience today, and will generally encourage all of us to seek God's healing as part of 'our experience of the Kingdom'. Such teaching is often accompanied by rhetorical questions such as 'Do you really believe that God, our loving Father, wants any Christian to remain sick?'

The second will also point you to a growing number of churches holding healing services and will encourage you to a quieter, more sacramental, ministry. The laying on of hands, anointing with oil, the spiritual discipline of quiet, confession, fasting and so on will often be encouraged. There will seem to be fewer miracles, but perhaps fewer bewildered people who have not been healed when they expected to be.

The third will reject the healing ministry and, even more vigorously, associated ministries of 'inner healing', 'deliverance', 'the healing of the family tree' on one of two grounds. Either that, in their view, 'God doesn't work in that sort of way (today)'; 'He doesn't select some for healing and ignore others'; or quite simply 'healing, and other gifts of the Spirit, ceased in the days of the Apostles'. The first set of objectors will see healing as a dangerous and unacceptable example of God's selectivity – they will quote sad letters, like the one I read in a Healing journal, which told of a father, who had recently experienced the death of a young child, attending a healing service and being very put off by hearing a testimony of the healing of the preacher's small daughter from some minor stomach ailment. They will also doubt whether God does heal, or guide, in any direct way. The second set of objectors will quote 1 Corinthians 13:8, and other arguments about the special ministry of the apostles and the warnings against false miracles (2 Thessalonians 2:9), to nullify any examples of healing in today's church.

A SIGN OF THE KINGDOM

Jesus sent His disciples out and expected them, among other things, to heal the sick. He saw the healing ministry as an important sign of the Kingdom of God. The apostles, likewise, looked to God to heal in response to their preaching 'your word with great boldness' (Acts 4:29). St Paul, too, experienced miracles, including healing, as a part of his church planting strategy. See, for instance, Galatians 3:5 where he is clearly upbraiding the Galatian church for reverting to a safe, legalistic form of Christianity. We find healing, together with the related gifts of knowledge, miraculous powers, and distinguishing between spirits, clearly listed in the 'gifts' of the Spirit in 1 Corinthians 12: 4-11. We also have the classic text in James 5:13ff where a Christian sick person is instructed to call the elders of the church 'to pray over him and anoint him with oil'.

It seems clear to me that the New Testament writers expected the post-Apostolic church to continue praying for the sick, to continue to seek the gifts of the Holy Spirit for healing and to recognise the sovereignty of God in these matters. Nevertheless, it is also clear that even in New Testament times, Christian leaders became ill! The illnesses of Epaphroditus (Philippians 2:26) and Trophimus (2 Timothy 4:20) caused Paul difficulty and anxiety. His own illness (Galatians 4:13), possibly the thorn of 2 Corinthians 12, actually brought blessing to the Galatian Church! This remarkable story tells how Paul's illness was both a great burden and a great blessing to the Galatian church. It ought to preserve us from a simplistic theology of healing and make us realise that in each and every situation we need to seek to listen to God's voice.

In today's church much the same is beginning to happen. In many parts of the world there are regular reports of healing miracles which are seen as signs of God's Kingdom. (Luke 9:1ff) Even in Britain, where Christianity could hardly be said to be advancing, there is an increased awareness of God's power to heal. This is shown by the number of healing services taking place, by books which are being written, conferences held and, most importantly of all, by the testimony of those who have been healed! The people of God are increasingly listening to God's voice in this wide area.

QUESTIONS THAT NEED AN ANSWER

The fact that some people are healed, apparently in direct answer to prayer, raises acutely the question of why others aren't. Every group that prays for the sick will sooner or later experience the apparent failure of praying for people who either get no better or die.

Fred Smith[2] often made a provocative comment. 'If I go to a place and pray for ten blind people and one receives his sight, this is an encouragement to the others.' Many of us find it hard to see things that way! Yet we have to face this apparent selectivity even in Jesus' ministry. When He went to the pool of Bethesda (John 5:1ff), He only healed one man. What did all the others think?

Yet the problems faced here by the healing ministry are exactly paralleled by the situation in evangelism. When Jesus went to Jericho, His visit apparently led to the salvation of only Zacchaeus and his household.

We are face to face with one of the deepest mysteries. Later we shall explore particular ways in which we can hear God's voice and how this relates to individual situations; for the moment, we need to accept 'Now we see through a glass darkly . . .' (1 Corinthians 13:12 AV). What seems a failure to us, may not be to God! A person's early death, which seems a travesty to an unbelieving world, may be God's Will for the situation. As we shall see in Chapter 14, God often speaks most clearly to the dying.

OUTSIDE GOD'S BOUNDARIES

Something which the Scriptures are very clear about is to warn us against any occult involvement. Warnings in the Old Testament, for instance, Deuteronomy 18:9ff, Isaiah 47:12ff, are reinforced by the salutary stories of Simon Magus (Acts 8:9ff), the slave girl in Philippi (Acts 16:16ff), and the somewhat hilarious episode of the sons of Sceva (Acts 19:13ff), which had the deadly serious consequence of the Ephesian bonfire of magic scrolls. These stories, together with many Old Testament warnings and the authoritative ministry of Jesus, should warn all Christians off anything remotely pertaining to spiritism and the occult.

It is a sad reflection on the lack of faith and adventure in today's church that so many church-goers, let alone the millions outside the church, seek healing from dangerous spiritual sources. I shall say more about this important area in the next chapter.

'Faith healing' often seems to work. It is often practised by well-meaning people (although it can be a financial racket); but, whatever the physical results, seeking help in this area brings us into direct disobedience to God's word.

HEARING GOD'S VOICE – HIS TIMING

'The power of the Lord was present for Him to heal the sick' (Luke 5:17). This often overlooked verse is, I believe, a key to beginning to understand God's timing. All of us who have been privileged to see God heal, have experienced special times of God's anointing (see 1 John 2:20, 27). There are times when we sense — or others sense God's presence in a special way.

To give another example, I quote from a letter I received recently. 'I can never remember not believing in God, but I acknowledge that before my cancer scare it was somewhat shallow. I really needed Him as I approached my operation, and I felt He was indeed with me. As you know, I wrote to you at that time, and you arrived here even before I had time to post it. I was so sure God had sent you that day. Once you arrived as I was actually praying for God's help. Do you remember that day? I was getting desperate because that morning the Breast Care sister from the Royal Victoria Hospital, Bath, had telephoned me to see how things were. She warned me that if I didn't persevere and force my arm, however painful, into its proper functional state, I would be left with a permanent disability. I am so grateful to her for spurring me on, although at the time I really felt sorry for myself; I thought I would never succeed! Later that day, you called and we prayed together. It is difficult to describe how wonderful I felt, but I really knew God was answering these prayers. Within two hours, all the tightened tendons had been released, and my arm was fully functional again. I wanted to go out and shout to the world, to tell of the real power of prayer, for that day God showed me, through prayer, my very own personal miracle that He loved me.'

The writer testifies to her cancer operation having brought her to a spiritual crossroads which led to release from guilt, a new relationship with her mother, an ability to pray aloud, and a real desire for God's way in her whole family.

To complete the sense of God's timing, the letter came when I was feeling in a trough — burdened not least by the daunting task of writing this chapter!

HEARING GOD'S VOICE – HIS WAYS

There are many ways in which healing is received. The most obvious, and frequent, is through medicine and surgery. Reading ancient novels, the shadow of the wasting disease (tuberculosis) is seldom far away – it would seem a complete miracle to a previous generation if they knew that 'the killing disease' had been eliminated. Conventional medicine is often God's means of healing, often prayer supports and seems to speed up the effect of medicine/surgery. It is profoundly dangerous to set up the healing ministry of the church in opposition to such normal channels.

I remember receiving a phone call one lunch hour. The caller, whom I knew a little, sounded urgent. He wanted to see me immediately. I sensed that it was one of those rare occasions when I must drop everything and meet him. He was a leader in a small Free Church. He'd heard a talk I'd given on healing and, as a result, asked his elders to anoint him with oil for the healing of his diabetes. They had all 'believed' for healing. He had stopped taking his insulin. I asked how he felt. 'Awful', he replied. I asked him to start taking his insulin immediately, and to stop putting God to the test. 'If you're healed you will know it, and blood tests will make it clear.' In fact, he wasn't healed, but his sugar readings stabilised and he was able to live with the illness much more easily.

Healing is also received through 'alternative' methods. I feel it would be wrong to discuss these in this short chapter. Guidance as to which of these approaches, if any, are appropriate must be sought and tested along the lines outlined at the end of the first chapter. As a family, we have benefited from 'alternative' as well as 'conventional' medicine.

Healing is received quietly in the home. The letter quoted in the previous section is a fairly typical example. Here is an example:

My two-month-old daughter was in hospital, assumed to be dying and weighing only four pounds, although her birth weight had seemed to be normal. The hospital had just phoned asking permission to have her baptised by the visiting priest, as her condition was now critical. Memories of Sunday School prayers caused me to kneel down and pray from the heart, but nothing happened. I got up feeling empty and vaguely let down.

I switched on the radio, listened without hearing, went shopping and returned to hear a man's voice in the room. I thought someone had broken in until I realised I had left the radio on. The voice was that of a minister who was explaining the crucifixion. He said that Good Friday's cloud was rimmed with the silver lining of the Resurrection, and that out of grief, joy would come. It dawned on me that this message was the answer to my prayer, but I was not moved − after all, I had been a lapsed Christian for a very long time.

However, I walked across to the bookcase. I don't know why. I wasn't in the mood for reading. It was an involuntary action. As I opened the glass doors, a book fell out. It shouldn't have done! It was a thick book called *Bible Stories for Children* and ought to have remained in its position, but there it lay, spreadeagled on the carpet. As I lifted it up, I found myself reading the miracle of Jairus' daughter. Well! If that wasn't an answer to prayer, what was?

My depression melted away. I felt a tingling happiness I'd never before experienced. My husband returned from work expecting to find me in tears instead of broad smiles. But the good news he had to tell me overcame his surprise.

'The hospital phoned me at the works,' he said. 'They have finally discovered what treatment to give the baby and she's going to be all right.' 'I know,' I said, joyfully, thereby mystifying him even further.

Interestingly enough, that baby's subsequent Christian commitment and another dramatic healing, helped both parents to real Christian conversion some forty years later!

Healing is often received at public services. These have great advantages and some disadvantages. There is usually a high level of faith, the prayers are usually tuned in to listening to God's voice, the very act of coming to such a service is often a remarkable venture of faith; on the other hand, such services attract the curious and sensation-seekers; and, more seriously, the time available to pray with people is brief. In the home, or the study, I may be able to spend an hour with people; in church, it will be five minutes or less, because of the pressure of numbers. However, the level of faith of the worshippers often lifts the praying team in a remarkable way.

Recently, I took a team from our parish to lead a weekend in a town parish in the Midlands. The visit lasted three days, beginning with a dinner for eighty on the Friday evening, continuing with teaching on the Saturday, and concluding with a healing service on the Sunday evening. By the Sunday night, I felt very tired. Then we had a great service of praise led by the local church. At least twenty people indicated they wanted prayer and those ministering were hard at work in different corners of the church for over an hour. One woman came up for prayer with three children. The youngest, a girl of about five, had been substantially deaf for over a year — possibly due to the stress of the break-up of her parents' marriage. She sat on the knees of one of my team and we prayed for her and her brother. I don't remember anything except a great sense of peace, and a slight surprise when she seemed to be able to respond when I whispered to her. Two days later, the vicar reported to me that her hearing was now considered normal.

This 'sign' was a great encouragment to me, and a constant reminder that we are to speak the word, and leave God to perform the signs and wonders through the name of Jesus (see Acts 4: 29-30).

Our diocesan healing group sometimes organises public healing services, and teaching, at Wells Cathedral. Two unusual healings occurred in connection with the last one:

Two days before the service, a man came to see me about a spiritual problem. Years earlier he had been involved in occult activities and experimented in various other ways at University. Subsequently, he had married, settled down to a good job, become a Christian, suffered a severe break-down, been substantially cured, moved south to a new job, home and church. All was fairly well, but he couldn't share his faith with his wife — not surprisingly, she'd had plenty to put up with! — and he felt that he was a disturbing influence in Christian groups.

I enjoyed meeting him, but felt a real sense of his spiritual disturbance. We went to the church to pray, but as I couldn't find a suitable prayer partner (Jesus sent His disciples out in pairs — and that is a sound guideline for all of us), I prayed a holding prayer, like an old fashioned dentist's temporary dressing. I asked him to come to our Cathedral Day of Healing two days later. I planned to pray for him there, in the greater atmosphere of faith, and to ask him to be anointed with oil after we had cut off any evil powers that were troubling him. I was unusually confident that God would set him free.

During the service, in the afternoon, I was greatly occupied in prayer. My contact arrived – looking different. 'What's happened to you?', I asked. 'Whatever it was left me last night,' he replied. I met his wife on the Cathedral steps after the service. She looked a bit shattered when I tried to explain what had happened and how important her own commitment to Christ would be. A short time later, she turned to the Lord, and the family was able to experience God's healing power in a fresh way! For me, the wonderful thing was that God brought about the healing without any direct ministry.

HEARING GOD'S VOICE – WHICH WAY, LORD?

People are often confused as to how to seek healing. Christians[3] are commanded to seek the ministry of the elders of the church![4] We miss much blessing by ignoring this teaching. I can think of so many examples of migraines, sleeplessness, bad backs and allergies, which have been healed as a direct answer to prayer. I can think of a few people who expected surgery whose condition was healed. I can also think of scores of people who have needed and benefited from conventional medicine and surgery. Here are three contrasting examples which illustrate something of the dilemma, and some of the ways in which God acts:

Jane used to have a terrible back problem. It was caused by a riding accident, but in her first pregnancy, and for at least a year afterwards, the pain and disability were acute. My prayers had little effect! One afternoon, Fred Smith was teaching a group of us, and he started to pray for Jane. 'You will have no more back problems, and no more problems bearing children,' he said. She felt an instant release, and was soon out of pain. Three more children were born, with no back pain. Although she has to be careful, her back has essentially been healed. Fred was given the gift of faith for that situation.

Meanwhile, I have faced a steadily deteriorating arthritic hip. First diagnosed as serious in 1975, many people's prayers have kept the pain at bay. Recently, however, it has become worse, and I very easily put my back out. This invariably responds to prayer. Recently, I lay on the floor for about twenty minutes on a Saturday evening while Bishop Ban It Chiu ministered to a bout of sciatica which eventually left. I felt very fit on the Sunday. But despite much prayer from a caring parish, an improvement due to different shoes, most of my praying friends seem to think God intends me to have an operation. I'd be delighted if they were all wrong! Often healing is through meditation and prayer. Here is the testimony of a parishioner:

On January 28th, I had a hip replacement operation at St Charles Hospital in London. My recovery was very slow; we were having regular visits from a Sister of Divinity who, one day, sat on my bed and asked how I was getting on. I replied 'A little depressed, Sister.' 'Oh, and why is that?' 'Now look, Sister, you see this man walking down the ward with just one walking stick?' 'Yes.' 'Well, he had the same operation as myself the day after me, and is now walking with a stick, and I can't even walk with the help of a frame.'

Sister then said 'Let's have a little prayer, shall we?' She then took something from her handbag and slowly massaged my leg, while we both prayed. She then said, 'Mr Hill, you will be much better tomorrow.' I said, 'I hope you are right, Sister.' The morning came, my condition had not changed. Midday, I was visited by a lady therapist. She said, 'Now, Mr Hill, are you going to walk for me today?' I said, 'I will certainly try.' I took the frame and walked across the ward and back. She gasped 'Marvellous! A miracle has surely happened.' I then told her the story of the prayers the day before. She replied, 'Are you a religious man, Mr Hill?' I said 'I am not a religious fanatic, but a great believer.' She paused, then said, 'You will soon recover.' Within a week, I was home, walking with the aid of sticks. A miracle indeed. Thanks be to God.

Sometimes, as I've indicated in earlier stories, there is a complete and wonderful healing. Usually this seems to correspond to a situation where someone has an unusual level of faith. I remember a very distressed girl coming for prayer at one of our recent healing services. She was in a lot of pain, with a poor prognosis, and yet had a real measure of 'faith'. My praying partner and I both felt elated as we prayed, and I wasn't surprised to hear a few weeks later that, after a night of intense pain, the situation changed and the girl was pronounced clear of her very serious illness.

HEARING GOD'S VOICE – THE RESULTS OF PRAYER

There are a number of realistic possibilities – each, I believe, will help us to understand what God is saying to the individual. In the end, that is what matters. If healing prayer helps someone to find a new or closer relationship with God it is wonderful. If it is an end in itself, it is of little value.

People get either worse, no better, somewhat better, or completely healed after prayer.

Occasionally people get markedly worse. This may be because it is God's time for them to die. Indeed, healing prayer may appear to accelerate death by bringing enough peace to someone to help them release their fight to stay alive.

Otherwise, if people get worse, I believe it indicates severe spiritual disturbance, or else an alternative solution. A headache which becomes a vicious migraine is likely to be a sign that the migraine is caused by some occult involvement of the person, or their ancestors — more of this in the next chapter. One lady's piles got much worse. She was enabled to have a much needed operation and her 'healing' took place far quicker!

Frequently, people don't improve physically. This can happen for many reasons. Sometimes God intends them to use normal medical means. Sometimes they are not spiritually open (they don't want the cost of real Christian commitment, they don't want to forgive, they don't want to confess some buried sin . . .), sometimes there isn't any real faith for improvement. Lack of faith is a great block to those of us who pray for the sick; it can also be a block among those who are prayed for. Graciously, God frequently overrrules our lack of faith, or most of us would never get anywhere!

And, of course, as indicated earlier in this chapter, and by countless testimonies from all over the world, there are many remarkable improvements and complete healings. It is a most wonderful experience to be with someone when they are healed, and to give thanks to God for the healing power of Christ.

HEARING GOD'S VOICE — HIS CALL TO MINISTER

A question frequently asked at healing services and seminars is 'how do I know if I've got a gift of healing?' Like other calls, it will be felt inwardly, and confirmed outwardly.

To me, the call came gradually. It began through reading about healings in the church in different parts of the world; it was strengthened by attending a service in Winchester Cathedral where the preacher, Dr Kenneth McAll[5] testified to some remarkable healings of physical and psychiatric illnesses, it was further strengthened by attending a house meeting where Ian Andrews[6] prayed for people and I saw several people visibly healed before my doubting eyes, and it was confirmed when the church I was serving recognised that I had a call in this area and a few people started to receive clear physical benefit from prayer.

It has never been the main part of my ministry, but has always been a way in which God has graciously shown the reality of His presence to a sceptical world. I have also felt called to encourage many lay people in my congregation to pray for the sick. Some people have a definite 'gift', others pray because they are part of the leadership team and are open to being used in this way.

A fairly typical testimony from someone involved in the healing ministry runs as follows:

> When I attended my first seminars on healing and laid hands on someone, I experienced a strong power and violent shaking of the hands. After a time I began to get a word from the Lord 'Go and heal the sick in my name.' This became so persistent that, after some months, I told John and he felt this to be a clear indication that I should join our healing group, and I now take part regularly in the healing ministry of our church.

What are we to make of this sort of thing? Is it the guidance of God, or is it some dubious psychic phenomenon? I believe that, provided the person is a baptised Christian believer, we should, in general, accept the 'phenomena' that may accompany their ministry.

Jesus used strange things — spittle (Mark 8:22ff) for instance — and was also aware of a release of power (see Mark 5:30). I believe, however, that these phenomena are usually only allowed to help our rather feeble faith. When I feel, as I often do, a sharp transference of pain from a migraine, or a cancer, or a bad back, it helps to raise my faith and enables me to pray for longer and with, I think, greater effect.

Nevertheless, I believe that the simpler our ministry, the better it will be. We live in an age which wants to see strange exhibitions. The signs of the Kingdom, of which healing is one, should be clear, efficacious, and decisive.

In order for this to happen, we need to be equipped with more of the gifts of the Holy Spirit. Without these gifts we will often listen and labour in vain. With them, mountains can be levelled with astonishing frequency!

THE GIFT OF FAITH

Miracles do happen! I have prayed for many cancer patients. Some have received remissions, some have experienced a measure of healing, some have experienced spiritual renewal without any physical improvement (apart from the considerable benefits of modern medicine which has so transformed people's attitude to a once unmentionable disease), a few have felt dramatically better, and one whom I wrote about in *Growing up to Salvation* (p 48) was amazingly healed. She is still alive and well ten years later.

There seem to be different levels of faith. Paul talks about faith as a spiritual gift (1 Corinthians 12:9). I believe this means that there are some occasions when we will be given an overwhelming certainty that God will heal.

Some of us seem privileged to experience these levels of faith occasionally. A few seem to have 'the gift of faith' as a clear feature of their whole life ministry. Once such, I believe, was Fred Smith of Abingdon, who died recently. He was a good friend to me and his New Testament Fellowship used the Anglican church of which I was priest-in-charge in Oxford. He used to tell how when he stopped to have a Thermos of tea on a hill overlooking Bath, the Lord gave him the gift of faith at a completely new level. His amazingly humble book *God's Gift of Healing*[7] ought to be more widely read. I well remember him telling our church of the healing of Ken, who was a recent convert to Christianity. Ken was covered in lumps from a form of lymphoma, which although non-malignant, left him with little real hope of living long. Ken came to a healing service that Fred was taking and, among many others, was prayed for. Fred, like his Master, never spent long with individuals. The next morning, Fred was rung up by an excited vicar to say that all Ken's lumps had disappeared. Two months later, Ken received hospital confirmation that he was completely clear. A little while later, Fred was being interviewed on Radio Oxford. A resourceful producer tracked down Ken, in another part of England, and got him to testify to the genuineness of his healing.

Fred was a very humble man, much given to prayer, and someone whom God seemed to be able to use in unusual ways. I remember the occasion when a world famous evangelist came to Oxford. The evangelist had suffered a severe physical injury which was threatening to curtail his programme. I was involved on the fringes of the organisation, and persuaded everyone to allow me to ring up Fred.

I told him the situation. 'That's funny,' he said, 'when I was down the garden this morning the Lord said to me

"You will be praying for — today!" I couldn't really believe it . . .'

It would be nice to recall that the sequel was a dramatic healing. We were summoned to an Oxford hotel, talked with the great man and we were allowed to pray for him. He wasn't physically healed, but certainly completed his programme with good grace, less pain, and considerable effect.

THE GIFTS OF KNOWLEDGE AND DISCERNMENT

It is possible to waste a phenomenal amount of time in the healing ministry. There are just as many blocks to receiving God's healing as there are to guidance! (Read Chapter 2 again, and you will see what I mean.) Two gifts that I long for, and occasionally receive, are 'knowledge' and 'discernment' (1 Corinthians 12: 8 and 10).

Jesus gives examples of each. He completely discerned the woman at the well (John 4:17) with his blunt statement 'You are right when you say you have no husband. The fact is, you have had five husbands, and the man you now have is not your husband. What you have just said is quite true.'

Jesus' supernatural knowledge of the woman's true marital state led to her conversion, and witness to the whole town.

Don Latham, leading a healing service, gave a powerful example. He was about to pray, when the Lord told him that there was someone, whose big toe was very painful, in the congregation. Don felt pretty stupid sharing this knowledge, but an enormous Christian Marine hobbled up for prayer. His military career was being ruined by the physical condition of his toe — and he badly wanted it healed. This clear healing led to the far deeper work in the lives of others who witnessed the healing and were converted, and Don learned another lesson in trusting the Lord.

One word of caution. It has become fashionable at large healing services for people to exercise these gifts. It seems to me that too little effort is made to correlate the 'words' with actual 'needs'. Either the Holy Spirit has spoken, or He hasn't, and we need to know! It is also not clear to me[8] that this is what the Scriptures mean by the use of knowledge. In Scripture, there is a clear one-to-one correlation with word and situation. See the salutary case of Ananias and Sapphira (Acts 5), and the more cheerful case of Paul who knew that the cripple at Lystra (Acts 14:9) had the faith to be healed.[9]

Discernment usually refers to guidance as to whether or not we are dealing with demonic powers. If someone is demonised, no amount of psychiatry, pills, or healing prayer will do much good. Jesus recognised demons – or to be more accurate, the demons recognised Him! Jesus' exorcism commands were sharp, quick, and to the point. I believe that, if we are given the right diagnosis, God will enable us to release people who are demonised very easily, and with minimal fuss. Trouble sets in when the person concerned wants to hold on to occult things, when our diagnosis is incorrect, or when our own faith and spiritual state are at a particularly low ebb.

Books like Michael Green's *I believe in Satan's downfall* give detailed signs of how to recognise such a problem. We should never get involved in this ministry alone, nor without some experienced pray-ers. False discernment in this area causes great embarrassment and can do enormous harm. Many people think they are demonised when they are not. It is, after all, much easier to think that 'my bad temper is caused by an evil spirit'. Then it ceases to be my fault. I needn't exercise 'self-control' until someone else has exorcised my temper!

None of us likes ministering in this field. We feel foolish, vulnerable, and under spiritual attack. Yet I have to testify that, as with the story quoted earlier in this chapter, when people are set free it is a truly wonderful experience.

HEALING IN SOCIETY – GOD'S VOICE TO TODAY'S CHURCH

We have seen how God is healing individuals. However mysterious the reasons, the results are undeniable. But why is the Spirit being poured out in this way? Some see this as a sign of the last times, others as God's answer to the sceptical 'Death of God' theology in particular, and the secular world in general. What is God saying to us?

Could it be that He is calling us to engage in healing at a far deeper level? Our world is deeply divided – between East and West; between North and South. What is the healing that God is really looking for? The words of Isaiah come to mind:

Is not this the kind of fasting I have chosen: to loose the chains of injustice and untie the cords of the yoke, to set the oppressed free and break every yoke?
Is it not to share your food with the hungry and to provide the poor wanderer with shelter – when you see the naked, to clothe him, and not to turn away from your own flesh and blood?
Then your light will break forth like the dawn, and your healing will quickly appear; then your righteousness will go before you, and the glory of the Lord will be your rear guard. (Isaiah 58: 6-8)

Just as listening to God in nature leads me to listen to God about nature and the environment, so listening to God in the healing ministry, leads me to listen to God about injustice and oppression. These are great issues, too great for this little book. But it is God's purpose that 'The earth shall be filled with the glory of God as the waters cover the sea', and that can happen only as the signs of the Kingdom of evangelism and healing incorporate the third sign of social justice. It is much more comfortable to remain at the level of God's voice to the individual; in many ways it seems much more rewarding. But what is God's voice to the church really saying? Perhaps if a Diocesan Healing Service is the visible tip of an iceberg as far as the healing and caring of the church within a given area is concerned, then the Church Urban Fund is the visible tip of another much greater iceberg as far as the social responsibility of the Church within a nation is concerned.

Notes and references

1 Gardener, Rex. *Healing Miracles*. Darton, Longman and Todd, 1986, p 134.
2 Smith, Fred and Saunders, Hilary. *God's Gift of Healing*. Chichester, New Wine Press, 1986.
3 See James 5:13ff.
4 Non-Christians are also often healed through prayer. This is a sign of God's kingdom and an opportunity for them, which may never easily recur, to discover the Lord for themselves. It obviously requires great discernment to know when it is appropriate to encourage such people to come for prayer.
5 McAll, Kenneth. *Healing the Family Tree*. London, Sheldon Press, 1986.
6 Andrew, Ian and Wraight, Pat. *God can do it for you*. Basingstoke, Marshall Pickering, 1982.
7 Smith, Fred and Saunders, Hilary. *Op Cit*. pp 110-111.
8 Wright, Nigel. Article in: *Renewal*, January 8th 1989.
9 See also Elizabeth Riley's testimony in Chapter 5 of this volume.

13

GUIDANCE AND THE QUEST
FOR HOLINESS

Wholeness is one of today's 'in' words. We live in an age
of wholefoods, holistic medicine, whole people . . . In the
Christian healing ministry, the question of physical healing
is often replaced by a search for wholeness which may
involve all manner of counselling techniques as well as prayer
and the laying on of hands. The biblical word is not wholeness, but holiness.

'Make every effort to live in peace with all men and to
be holy; without holiness no one will see the Lord.' (Hebrews
12:14)

'But now that you have been set free from sin and have
become slaves to God, the benefit you reap leads to holiness,
and the result is eternal life.' (Romans 6:22)

The writers of both epistles set before us a goal of
holiness. Holiness which leads us to God; holiness which
makes the whole question of hearing His voice so different.
The truly holy person will instinctively act correctly in many
situations – he knows His Master's Voice – he will only
occasionally need direct guidance or counselling.

A friend[1] told me recently that he is extremely reluctant
to give direct counsel. He prefers to listen and direct people
to appropriate Scriptures to listen to God's voice. We live
in the age of the expert, the theological guru, the wise

counsellor, the gifted retreat leader, the anointed charismatic leader, the expert on inner healing and so on . . . ; we need to learn to hear God's voice for ourselves!

As Jesus taught, 'I am the good shepherd; I know my sheep, and they know me'. 'When he (the watchman) has brought out all his own, he goes on ahead of them, and his sheep follow him because they know his voice.' (John 10: 14 and 4)

Now, obviously, many do need counsellors, and all of us need the friendship and love of the Body of Christ; but at all stages of our spiritual journey, we need to reaffirm the principle of seeking to hear God's voice through the silent, but living pages of Scripture.

Why then do so many Christians find their lives in such a tangle that they apparently need a great deal of counselling, inner healing, deliverance . . . ? St Paul sets out the ideal very clearly.

> 'If we have been united with him like this in his death, we shall certainly also be united with him in his resurrection. For we know that our old self was crucified with him so that the body of sin might be done away with, and that we should no longer be slaves to sin — because anyone who has died has been freed from sin' (Romans 6: 5-7).

and he continues a few verses later:

> 'In the same way, count yourselves dead to sin, but alive to God in Christ Jesus' (Romans 6:11).

Quite simply, the quest for holiness, and with it the inner certainty that solves most problems of guidance, is found in a conversion experience which sees the past 'buried with him in baptism' (Colossians 2:12) and the present under the guiding control of the indwelling Holy Spirit.

'So I say, live by the Spirit, and you will not gratify the desires of the sinful nature' (Galatians 5:16).

But for most of us, the problem is not as simple as that! We may long to be holy, we may desire to be whole, we may long for freedom, and yet the past clings on to us ever more tenaciously. Interestingly, this struggle is clearly understood by the writers in the very areas of Scripture in which we have been looking!

Turn on from Romans 6 to 7, and you will discover St Paul writing 'For I have the desire to do what is good, but I cannot carry it out' (Romans 7:18). Read on a few verses in Galatians 5 and you will hear 'For the sinful nature desires what is contrary to the Spirit, and the Spirit what is contrary to the sinful nature. They are in conflict with each other, so that you do not do what you want' (Galatians 5:17).

Most significant of all, our opening quotation from Hebrews is followed by this warning:

'See to it that no one misses the grace of God and that no bitter root grows up to cause trouble and defile many' (Hebrews 12:15).

I want, at this stage, to identify three types of spiritual block which, if present, will certainly block our growth in holiness, and will make it difficult for us to hear God's voice. I have called them — the need for healing of our past, the need for healing of our family tree, and the need to be cut off from any occult links.

These are all areas where sensitive spiritual help is needed, and where the gifts and insights of the Holy Spirit are needed if such ministry is to be effective. I certainly don't believe that all, or even most, Christians need ministry in these areas; but that some of us need to be set free, partly so that we can grow in holiness, partly so that we can begin to hear

God's voice clearly, and partly so that we can serve others more effectively.

Unfortunately, because of what is happening in our society, an ever increasing number of people seem to come to faith in Christ bringing a trail of harmful experiences with them, and no matter how much they truly seek freedom, the ivy of the past clings ever tighter around their spiritual sapling as it seeks to grow.

THE HEALING OF OUR PAST

A few years ago, as a Lenten discipline, I started to listen each day to Reg East's tape on contemplative prayer.[2] This tape, which lasts about twenty minutes, takes you through a simple spiritual pilgrimage — sitting still and relaxed, relaxing the mind, expressing our love to Jesus, inviting the Holy Spirit to heal our thoughts, guide our present, and heal our past. I found it then, and still do, very refreshing.

I started listening on Ash Wednesday, by the end of the week I realised that a problem of sleeplessness had returned with a vengeance. For many years, probably all my adult life, I had been a bad sleeper, but this had been masked by sleepless nights caused by a succession of wakeful children! Recently, however, the problem had gone. The youngest child was now two, and sleeping well, and I felt that people's prayers had been answered. But Lent '86 was grim! I was trying to write a thesis for an important course on which I was going, trying to lead our increasingly busy parish, trying to relate to a growing family . . . and now sleep had disappeared.

Reluctantly, I returned to sleeping pills, and sought guidance. Because of the pressure of normal parish life, it was easy to attribute my sleeplessness to overwork; yet, somehow, that didn't seem right. I continued to listen to the tape, gained strength and consolation from the period of disciplined quiet which supplemented normal prayer and Bible reading, and tried to listen.

Then, at last, God made the connection for me. Sleeplessness had returned on the very day that I had set aside special time for meditation and listening! Satan's counter-attack? No! God's inner voice? Yes! The latter part of the tape was about the healing of past hurts. Eventually I went to see Reg, and we discussed and prayed through a number of real difficulties surrounding my birth and childhood. Suffice it to say that a difficult wartime marriage, a first few months which I only just survived, the pressure of being an only child . . . had left an imprint of restlessness which needed healing.

I felt a new peace. I had learned something which I could sometimes share with others. I was grateful to God for at last allowing me to face up to the disturbances of my early life. And my sleep? That didn't return until a year later. For several months, two parishioners gave themselves to prayer for me in this matter, and quite suddenly I started to sleep. I've taken about four sleeping pills in the last eighteen months.

Esau, to whom the writer of Hebrews refers in 12:16, had a traumatic family life which certainly affected his later spiritual development. He seemed to develop a 'bitter root'; many of us have that potential. Ideally, the past will be healed when we are converted; ideally, the waters of baptism will cover that past; but in practice many of us may find that God has a deep healing work to do − for the sake of our families, our friends, and our ministry in the Body of Christ.

I have chosen to write about myself in this context, because of the sensitive pastoral nature of such ministry.

Such ministry usually takes us into deeply clouded waters
– the all too frequent experiences of childhood rejection,
sexual abuse, violence and insensitivity. Most of it is too
painful to be written about, except in the most general terms.

An elderly woman remembers being shut in with her
mother in a closed four poster bed, and not being allowed
to get out when she felt claustrophobic; people constantly
feel unclean because of past sexual abuse; grown men are
still in bondage because of savage discipline from parents;
people have no self worth because they have been constantly
told by parents that they are failures (or not as good as their
brother); twins can have a special problem (Esau and Jacob
for example!). This sort of past often leads to a difficult
present. It is hard to believe that God loves us; it is hard
to receive help (much easier to exhaust ourselves by continually trying to give); it is too difficult to feel of any value;
it can be hard to show physical affection to spouse, children
or friends ('Greet one another with a holy kiss' [2
Corinthians 13:12] is quite the last thing we want to do!);
it can make us irrationally critical of others, and lead us,
wilfully, to wreck group meetings.

Perhaps most difficult of all, it leaves many people with
a real problem about forgiveness. The biblical teaching
(Matthew 6: 14-15; Mark 11: 25-36; Matthew 18: 21-35) is
painfully clear. They know full well what Christ has done
for them, but they feel so hurt, so damaged, so unclean,
that forgiveness seems too painful to contemplate. This can
occur with both the living and the dead. There must be a
way forward, otherwise there is a terrible block to hearing
God's voice in other matters. The way is often slow and
painful.

First, we have to realise that we have a problem. Then
we need to identify whom it is that we need to forgive. Then,
perhaps, we can only pray 'Lord I can't forgive X, but please

make me willing to do so.' With God's grace amazing things can happen. One friend could only forgive her father when he was helpless and dying. The forgiveness brought a tremendous measure of inner peace; then, at last, after years of inner turmoil, the forgiver began to find true wholeness.

HOW DO WE RECOGNISE THAT WE HAVE A PROBLEM?

The last thing that I want to do is to cause a great rush of people to seek counselling! Far too much time is spent in some Christian churches in ministering to the past. Our God is calling us to hear His voice in the present, and go out and serve in this needy world. Nevertheless, if we have a problem, it is important that it is sorted out in God's time and in God's way.

St Paul says, as we have already quoted, 'we should no longer be slaves to sin'. Jesus says 'If the Son sets you free, you will be free indeed'. (John 8:36). If we find we are in bondage to certain habits, moods, depression, or that we cannot exercise self-control in certain recurring situations, or that we are a spiritual iceberg seemingly untouchable by the loving warmth of God, we may well need 'the healing of our past'. Such ministry need not be long and complicated. Frequently God will guide counsellors, perhaps using the spiritual gifts of knowledge and discernment, into the key areas in which prayer is needed.

If we had a stronger doctrine of conversion, if we understood more clearly what St Paul meant when he wrote:

> Having been buried with Him in baptism and raised with Him through your faith in the power of God, . . . set your hearts on things above .. . . For you died, and your life is now hidden with Christ in God . . . Put to death,

therefore, whatever belongs to your earthly nature . . . Therefore, as God's chosen people, holy and dearly loved, clothe yourselves with compassion, kindness, humility, gentleness and patience. Bear with each other and forgive whatever grievances you may have against one another. Forgive as the Lord forgave you. And over all these virtues put on love, which binds them all together in perfect unity (from Colossians 2:12 − 3:14).

then we would have no need of such ministry. But Paul understood the struggle (*viz.* Romans 7: 14-20), and I believe the Scriptures present us with this tension. God's ideal is that the past is buried − lock, stock, and barrel − our reality may be rather different.

THE HEALING OF THE FAMILY TREE

You shall not make for yourself an idol in the form of anything in heaven above or on the earth beneath or in the waters below. You shall not bow down to them or worship them; for I, the Lord your God, am a jealous God, punishing the children for the sin of the fathers to the third and fourth generation of those who hate me, but showing love to a thousand generations of those who love me and keep my commandments. (Exodus 20: 4-6)

The full text of the third commandment, supported by Exodus 34:7, Numbers 14:18, and Jeremiah 32:18, is largely ignored today. The idea of the judgment of God is unfashionable enough, without adding to it the seemingly unfair punishments to later generations. Yet, in our heart of hearts, we know that it is true! We know that the character failings of our ancestors work out in our own lives and in the lives of our children. But there is a deeper problem than that: serious spiritual disobedience (which is what the third commandment is about) can lead to serious spiritual problems in later generations.

Before going too far down a negative track, it is important to remember Psalm 103:17 (part of the Anglican funeral service) which reads 'But from everlasting to everlasting the Lord's love is with those who fear Him, and His righteousness with their children's children.' God wants righteous families; God has raised up righteous families in which generation after generation have served the Lord. I hope the New International Version (NIV) is right to insert the word 'generations' in the positive promise at the end of the third commandment!

To revert to the family tree: pastoral experience seems to show that the warning of the third commandment affects people today in a number of ways. If it were just a matter of inherited tendencies to sin, we could seek release from them along the lines of the Scriptures quoted at the beginning of the chapter; but, when it comes to past occult links, non-Christian religions, pseudo-religions, past spiritual disobedience like suicide or abortion, then there seems to be a deeper problem. Dr Kenneth McAll has written extensively about this in his book *Healing the Family Tree*.[3] I have personally found his ministry inspiring, and his counsel helpful. Theologically, evangelicals might question some of his approaches; but I believe that using the third commandment as our starting point, there is a sound biblical basis for such ministry.

Again it is difficult because of the sensitive pastoral nature of such ministry to give many examples. But I have seen such prayer to be effective in a number of cases . . . A mother with a seriously ill daughter which led to an immediate release, although the daughter knew nothing of the prayer; a depression substantially broken when prayer was made to release the effects of suicide on the family tree; a man's migraines healed when we recognised the effect of his mother's spiritual disobedience at the time of his birth; a young woman released from the effects of a suicide pact with a fiancé, which she had broken, but which he had fulfilled and consequently died.

Here is a more detailed example. A fairly recently converted Christian businessman came to see me, seeking prayer for healing from a persistent stomach disorder. He shared with me a tremendous bondage to superstition which he felt affected his business and family life before he became a Christian. For example:

'Decision-making depended upon the omens being right — one magpie seen on the road spelt bad luck, fingers had to be crossed the right number of times, wood had to be touched and so on. Failure to apply these rituals in the right way generated great fear of the consequences.'

After his conversion intellectually he had accepted Christian teaching on superstition and the occult. He renounced the rituals and accepted instead the protection given to every Christian. Nevertheless, a deep-seated fear invariably surfaced whenever one of these rituals was broken.

At a distance, it all sounds quite trivial, but that wasn't how it felt as, on a hot July afternoon, we went for a walk to discuss the problem. It quickly became clear to me that it was substantially an ancestor problem. He had been brought up in a notoriously haunted pub, and claimed to have tape-recorded the resident ghost when a teenager. He had traced a history of 'white magic' back on his grandmother's side of the family tree. As we walked, I came to a fork in the path. To the left I saw a man with a net, evidently taking his bees. Intrigued, despite my unnatural fear of bees and wasps, I suggested we went left. The hives were about twenty metres off the path, but the bees were in great quantity around the bramble blossoms. We hastened by, and my companion was stung twice on the ear. I was very embarrassed! When we were safely in the next field, I put my hand on his ear and prayed with minimal faith for his healing. To my intense surprise and his relief, the pain instantly went.

'They swarmed around me like bees, but they died out as quickly as burning thorns; in the name of the Lord I cut them off' (Psalm 118:12) seemed an appropriate commentary on our experience. It also helped to confirm to me that God did want me to pray to cut off his problems which had arisen from the white magic and other spiritual disobedience in his family tree. I made it clear, as I always do, that we are not judging the ancestors. Their spiritual state is between them and God. But we are, in the name of the Lord, cutting off any negative spiritual influence which they have left behind.

We held a simple Communion Service in the village church near the family pub. I prayed for the complete release for him and his family, and future generations, from any such spiritual bondage. There was a great sense of peace, and a general sense of God's love. The man testifies that, when he awoke on the morning after the service, he felt as if a physical burden had been lifted from his shoulders, as well as a dark cloud lifted from his mind. He has also received a great measure of healing from his stomach disorder.

I mention in passing, that there was a brief negative reaction in one of his children which was speedily dealt with.

But again, I would say, this is not a pathway down which many need to travel. Before rushing to seek help, first quietly seek the Lord and see if, by His Spirit, He makes it clear that such ministry is necessary.

HOW DO WE KNOW IF WE NEED HELP?

Again, I would emphasise that this is not a road which many
need to travel. Furthermore, such ministry need not be long
or complicated. In most cases it seems quite sufficient to
recognise the problem and then lay it to rest − most
effectively in silent prayer in the context of a communion
service.

Not all of us know much about our ancestors. Family
skeletons can lie carefully hidden. Nevertheless, if there is
a problem, the Holy Spirit will show us. Either by the simple
facts of our known family history, or by the 'chance'
discovery of some unknown piece of information, or by
inward witness, invariably confirmed by others.

If the family tree contains evidence of suicide, abortion,
or spiritism, then there is a potential problem. Such
influence, like the bees, needs to be cut off in the name of
the Lord. We are not judging our ancestors (many Christians
were and are ignorant or disobedient in these areas); we are
releasing our generation, and our children and grandchildren, from their effect. As to what exactly is happening
I prefer to remain reverently agnostic; as to its effect, I must
bear witness to the cleansing power of the Risen Lord.

Other Christians have testified to me of release from
bondage through less obvious disobedience − other
religions,[4] Christian Science, Freemasonry and so on. One
of the most difficult things is that the ancestors may have
been greatly revered people, but that doesn't mean that all
that they did was right in the eyes of the Lord! One of the
saddest stories in the Old Testament is of the godly
Hezekiah's miraculous recovery (2 Kings:20). It is sad
because of the disastrous way he used his extra years. He
celebrates his healing by showing off his treasures to the
envoys of the King of Babylon. In consequence, Isaiah

pronounces judgment on Hezekiah's descendants (2 Kings 20:18). Hezekiah's reply – instead of repenting and seeking to reverse this judgment – is a model of complacency:

' "The word of the Lord you have spoken is good," Hezekiah replied. For he thought, "Will there not be peace and security in my lifetime?" '

If Hezekiah, one of the few godly Kings in the old Testament, could bring judgment on his descendants, how much more may our ancestors, or we ourselves, do the same?

THE CUTTING OF OCCULT LINKS

Contact with the occult (via ouija boards, tarot cards, fortune-telling or similar things) distorts our spiritual vision and hearing. Many of today's Christians were yesterday open to occult ways. Such experiences may seem harmless, but they invariably distort and mar attempts at discipleship.

Sadly, it is all too common to seek 'guidance' by such means. Here are a couple of examples:

Recently, after a parish dinner at the beginning of a weekend of teaching about the healing ministry, I prayed with a young woman who had just married a divorcee. They were both Christians, but she was challenged by a talk that I gave which included reference to the dangers of this sort of thing. She had had readings from both a fortune-teller and tarot cards. The significant thing was that she had been told she would be involved with one child which was not her own, and have another which would die. Her husband had a child by a previous marriage, and she had had a miscarriage.

She had a strange spiritual experience as we prayed. I wanted to pray to cut off the effects of their predictions, but she was unable to look into my eyes — complaining that she could see nothing but brightness.

As she explained afterwards, she felt all right with me until I called her husband over to join in the prayer. As I looked into her eyes, all she could see was my eyes — no face, no lips, just an absolute nothingness. She began to feel very frightened, she felt that I was a fake, and longed to get away.

I have encountered this sort of thing before, and was anxious to avoid any sort of spiritual battle. We were in a public meeting, and in my limited experience, the enemy likes nothing better than long drawn out exhausting battles. I felt it right to turn away; I then asked her to pray aloud, renouncing her involvement with these occult things, and to join us in saying the Lord's prayer. When we had finished, I turned back, looked her in the eyes, and all was well.

My praying partner (and how essential it is to have the support and insight of others on these sort of occasions) then pointed out to me that she would now begin to feel grief and guilt about the miscarriage. So it proved, and the next thirty-six hours were times of much weeping and darkness. Thanks to my partner's discernment, we were able to handle this, and the darkness passed. When I last saw them, she and her husband looked radiant, their marriage set free from all Satan's potential cobwebs.

In a subsequent letter, she described how the whole incident had brought a new awareness of the Lord, and the spiritual battle, into her life, and how at times she and her husband feel overwhelmed by God's love.

On another occasion, a parishioner told me this story. It shows the depth of knowledge available to those who practise occult things and, more importantly, helps to explain why this man, an innocent victim of the prediction, didn't really turn to the Lord for over fifty years.

'Over fifty years ago, my mother was visiting an aunt who occasionally took in paying guests. It was late evening, when there was a knock at the door. It transpired that two people, a Madam Zelda and her husband, unable to find accommodation anywhere, had been directed by the police to my aunt's house. She was unable to help, and feeling sorry for them, my mother offered to put them up for the three days required. Madam Zelda was a professional palmist and was resting between appointments. During her stay, two friends of my sister called. Madam Zelda agreed to read their palms. During one reading, she suddenly turned very pale and almost fainted. We rushed around getting smelling salts and a glass of water. Having recovered somewhat, she said to the girl whose hand she had been reading 'Go straight home, my dear, it is important.' After the two girls left, Madam Zelda said 'That girl's sister has just met with an accident near here. I am afraid it is serious.' It transpired that the sister was on her way to our house when she was knocked down by an ambulance and was found to be dead on reaching hospital.

On her last day, Madam Zelda read my mother's hand. As she was leaving, she gave my sister an envelope with instructions not to tell my mother its contents, but to read the note and act accordingly. The note stated that on a certain day, in the distant future, my mother would meet with an accident, connected with a piece of rope, or a dog lead, and that on that day my sister and I should be on our guard. My sister put the note away and, in due course, we forgot it. About two years later, I returned from work to find the house in darkness. My mother was lying on her bed where she had been all day. She told me she had gone to my room to change the bed linen, when she tripped over the earth lead of my radio set, attached to a low water pipe. She had hurt her ankle. It had taken her nearly two hours to reach her room, and she was exhausted. We summoned the doctor, who discovered she had broken her ankle. Because of a heart condition, he decided that she go at once to hospital. The following day she was given an anaesthetic, and the ankle was set. The operation was unsuccessful, and during the second attempt to set the ankle, she died under the anaesthetic.

After the funeral, my sister remembered Madam Zelda's prediction. I asked her where the envelope was. After a considerable search we found it. The date on the note was the day on which the accident occurred.'

How such predictions work, I have no idea. That they have a very negative spiritual effect is certain. During adult confirmation classes, after quite a spiritual struggle, my friend came to faith. He then told me this story! We had to pray to cut off its effect from him, and to set him free to worship the Lord for the remaining years of his life.

Today, such 'guidance' is commonplace. One of the largest Oxford bookshops has an enormous occult department, and openly advertises the sale of tarot cards. As I write today in Glastonbury, I would only have to walk through the Abbey grounds into the High Street to find shop after shop stocking occult books and numerous aids to 'divination'.

Much that is sought in these ways is extremely expensive, some of it is nonsense (as when my Uncle, in the 1930s, who was part of the fashionable rebellion against King and Country, was told at a séance that the medium could see a Union Jack floating above him), some of it is dangerously self-fulfilling (as when a man was told he would marry twice, which became a source of potential disaster as his first marriage entered a difficult period), some of it causes deep fear and distress (as when a schoolgirl can't sleep properly for a year after being involved with ouija boards), some of it is potentially true and downright dangerous.

I don't believe that Madam Zelda's prediction caused the death of my friend's mother, I do believe that all the family would have been a great deal better off without her ministrations.

HOW ARE WE SET FREE FROM SUCH PROBLEMS?

As with other spiritual difficulties, once the problem is diagnosed, progress should be rapid and complete. A few bishops offer such ministry at confirmation services. Certainly, baptism and confirmation are wonderful opportunities to renounce the Devil and all his works. 'Do you renounce evil?' is the third question asked of all candidates. It gives a splendid opportunity publicly to seek freedom for ourselves and our families. Such renunciation should be specific and unequivocal. People have a strange fascination with such things and an unwillingness to join the Ephesians in their celebrated bonfire of all occult paraphernalia. (Acts 19:19)

Occasionally, deeper ministry is required,[5] but the guidance I have received is always to do the minimum necessary. If the Devil knows that his influence on a family is to be broken, he will fight to make the whole thing messy and unpleasant.

'But thanks be to God! He gives us the victory through our Lord Jesus Christ' (1 Corinthians 15:57).

Personally, I seem to have heard God's silent voice more clearly in this area than in many others — frequently through surprising biblical texts which have helped those ministering to discover the root of the problem. The end of such ministry seems to be attended by a wonderful sense of the presence of the Risen Lord.

Long my imprisoned spirit lay, fast bound in sin and
  Nature's night;
My eye diffused a quickening ray – I woke, the
  dungeon flamed with light.
My chains fell off, my heart was free, I rose, went forth
  and followed Thee!

Charles Wesley's experience at his conversion, is echoed by
multitudes of people set free from Satan's occult brand of
bondage.

JESUS SPELLS FREEDOM

You, dear children, are from God and have overcome
them, because the one who is in you is greater than the
one who is in the world (1 John 4:4).

We have seen how Jesus can set us free from various types
of bondage in the past and the present. When we are free,
we have a wonderful new opportunity to go on with the
Lord, learning to pray, to listen, and to minister to others,
in a new way.

Jesus may well use any experience we have of the healing
of the past, to teach us how to help others; He may use any
release of our family tree, or from the occult, as a warning,
a signpost to others.

But it is important to remember that the First Epistle of
John which gives us wonderful texts like 'The reason the
Son of God appeared was to destroy the devil's work' (1
John 3:8) ends with the apparent anticlimax, 'Dear children,
keep yourselves from idols' (1 John 5:21). If we are seeking
guidance about the road to holiness, these are key words.
Of course, most of the idols that would deflect us from the

pursuit of holiness are far subtler — the cares of the world, career, money, even family — but the quest for holiness will require some hard decisions. We shall touch some of these in Chapter 15, as we consider the mystery of guidance which does not always take us straight into the promised land.

Notes and references

1 Prior, David. *Living by Faith: Abraham's example for today*. London, Hodder & Stoughton, 1986 and *The Message of 1 Corinthians*, London, Hodder & Stoughton, 1985. David Prior is vicar of St Michael's Chester Square.
2 East, Reg. Tape *Relaxing into Prayer*, available from Shepherd's Cottage, Whatcombe, Dorset. Mr East was a Warden of Whatcombe House.
3 McAll, Kenneth. *Healing the Family Tree*. London, Sheldon Press, 1986.
4 Song, Jimmy. Article in: *Renewal* May 1989.
5 Green, Michael. *I believe in Satan's downfall*. London, Hodder & Stoughton, 2nd edn, 1988.

14

GUIDANCE AND THE APPROACH OF DEATH

'Good night, good night! Parting is such sweet sorrow
That I shall say good night till it be morrow.'
(*Romeo and Juliet*, Act 2, Scene 2)

Juliet's romantic parting from her lover has a poignant, prophetic touch. Within a few brief hours, tragedy has struck. Each lover thinks the other dead, and the sweet sorrow becomes so bitter that each must kill themselves to be with the other.

Tragedy of that sort may make good theatre, but we face news of death every day. Unless we insulate ourselves from news and neighbours, we will daily hear of violent death, multiple tragedies, neighbours bereaved or friends dying.

John Donne speaks for us all: 'No man is an island entire of itself . . . any man's death diminishes me, because I am involved in mankind.' Christians, like anyone else, are profoundly affected by the tragedy of death. No matter how strong our faith, no matter how Christian the one who died, we shall need to express our grief, and perhaps, even our anger and doubts.

Sometimes, the direct guidance of God seems to lead to death. In the early Church, the very gifts that Stephen was given (Acts 6:8) provoked the hostility that led to his early death.

Countless examples could be given from the mission field. One particularly poignant example was the death of Freda, the sister of Frank Houghton, former leader of the China Inland Mission. He had put out an appeal in 1931 for 200 new missionaries to China. Freda was one of the first to respond, yet she died within a year of her arrival. Frank could have asked the question 'Why?'; instead he chose to express his faith as follows:[1]

On Freda's Death

We do not ask Thee to explain
Why Thou has acted thus, nor how
Such seeming loss is turned to gain,
Eternal gain — but even now
Acknowledging that all Thy ways
Are right, we offer Thee our praise.

Others may count Thy dealings strange,
That, with her service scarce begun,
Thy Voice should call her to exchange
Great tasks for heaven's greater one,
But good is all that Thou hast planned
We do not seek to understand.

We do not ask Thee to explain,
We do not seek to understand,
We know He needed her again
Who gave her, and at His right Hand
She shares His joy for evermore
Whom we in steadfast faith adore.

Intellectually, we want to ask 'How could God have guided a young woman to her early death on a foreign mission field? What good did it do the cause?' Surely the potential converts must have said, 'Where is now thy God?'; surely the missionaries must have been discouraged.

The China Inland Mission, and many other missions, were born out of that sort of suffering. Just as the apostles faced great trials, dangers and death (see, for instance, Paul's classic statement in 2 Corinthians 11: 22-29); so Christians are not immune from 'the changes and chances of this fleeting world'. What is different is that the Christian has a real hope beyond death. How we Christians approach our own deaths, how we react to other people's, is a vital part of our witness to the world in which death is largely unmentionable, unacceptable, and profoundly unpleasant.

GUIDANCE TO THE DYING

Most people are aware of impending death. We shall consider later the question of sudden death. Many people don't want to know. Often there is a conspiracy of silence. 'Don't tell him — he couldn't stand it.' 'If he wants to know, he'll ask.' 'Don't visit him, Vicar, he'll think he's dying . . .'

Modern drugs blur the approach of death. The miracle of morphine releases much pain; it takes much of the terror from death, yet it makes the spiritual side of death harder. It is much easier to allow someone to slip away, pain free, without every letting them ask what is happening and where they are going.

The hospice movement treats death rather differently. People I have been privileged to meet in hospices, whether nurses or patients, seem to have a different approach to death. Here are some moving words from a hospice chaplain:[2]

'Dying is a process, not an end (as in the call to both Zacchaeus and the rich young man, the emphasis lies in what came after the call rather than the call itself). Thus the ministry of healing to the dying is a ministry of healing in order that the person may face what comes after death in a whole state.'

There are well mapped stages in reaction to terminal illness, and the healing process is different for each stage.

ANGER

Anger is a natural reaction (Jesus and the Pharisees and the moneychangers). It is also the natural action of a hurt animal. In terminal illness the anger is often directed against God. Sometimes it is hidden, sometimes it lies hidden and festers like a sore. Often the healer's task in cases like this is to draw the anger into the open.

There was a lady whose illness was diagnosed as terminal who was ministered to by a female Christian deacon of her church. The ministry was not going well as the patient remained tight-lipped about anything to do with her illness. The deacon prayed silently to God for help all through the interview, and suddenly began to be aware of the suppressed anger within her friend.

Later, she gathered a prayer group about her who prayed for the healing of this anger. Over the next few weeks the anger erupted every time the deacon visited and silently in Christ's name she received it. Later, in prayer, she handed it over to God.

Eventually, the anger left the patient altogether and she was able to form a relationship with God at a level which she had never dreamed existed. Later she died peacefully and with an inner joy. So she was healed of her anger and prepared to meet her God.

LONELINESS – DEPRESSION

To befriend the lonely and depressed is an act of healing. Often the depression of the dying is a cry to God for help (see the frustration of the men at Siloam who could never get to the water in time to be healed) or the cry 'Son of David, have mercy upon me.' (John 5:7; Mark 10:48)

The healer goes into this friendship with a prayer that he be used as a bridge that the man might find God once more.

GUILT

For many it is only as they approach death that they begin to remember wrongs which have been unforgiven or unrepented of. The healer comes into this situation praying that he might be the catalyst which brings about open repentance. It is never too late, even in unconsciousness to repent.

There was an old lady who had a particular sin lying heavily on her conscience, but could not bring herself to confess it openly. At last she fell into a coma. At her bedside was a nurse, a committed Christian, praying for her. Suddenly that nurse was transported in a vision/dream into the childhood of the patient, to a particular scene and the voice of the patient was heard to say that she was sorry for the act depicted. The chaplain was brought. He prayed with the nurse (who was filled with the patient's remorse) and then blessed and pronounced God's absolution on the patient. The patient (who was still in a coma) then opened her eyes and smiled. She died shortly afterwards, calmly and peacefully.

FEAR

It is there. Many Christians hide it. God can heal fear, but first it has to be faced and then the healer, in prayer lays himself open to God to be used in whatever way He will.

Sometimes the minister is called, literally, to pray peace into the patient. At other times he is called to be a guide.

There was a woman named Irene who was a committed Christian and had been for many years. But she was frightened that upon dying, she would be lost, and wouldn't be able to find her way into the Kingdom.

She lapsed into a coma, but was very restless and obviously troubled. I was by her bedside praying, when suddenly in a vision/dream Irene and I were walking down a dark tunnel towards a distant white light at the end. She was in her hospital clothes and I was holding her hand, guiding her. We came to the end of the tunnel and in the distance, across a white plain was a city set on a hill. I saw myself pointing to it and saying 'There you are, Irene. The heavenly city, new Jerusalem'. Whereupon she set off across the plain.

Suddenly I was back in the room by her bedside. She was still in a coma, but all the restlessness had disappeared. She died later, calmly and peacefully.

In all aspects of the healing of the dying, those who minister are servants, vessels through which the love and redemption of God may pass to those who would be healed. Therefore, an ongoing relationship with God is vital (otherwise we minister *ourselves*, not God).

The healing of the dying is exhausting, spiritually, mentally and physically, and so special times are needed to be alone with God (just as Jesus went away to pray alone before major events).

We go into every situation totally empty, praying only that God will show His servants what to do or say – and He does. We may end up doing anything from 'end time guidance', or giving the laying on of hands, to preparing a 'peace tape' or whatever. The only common factor is that we don't know how God is going to use us beforehand!

Much distress in the dying is as a result of a blocked or failed, or forgotten relationship with God. We offer ourselves as a channel whereby that relationship may be opened.

PRAYING FOR A MIRACLE

To me, what Richard Glover has written above is a miracle. A living testimony to God's grace and presence with the dying. But what of the Gospels? Didn't Jesus raise the dead and heal the dying? Isn't Christian literature full of testimonies from those who, by all reasonable account, should be dead?

Richard Glover, so it happens, is himself, such a living testimony.

'I was in my early thirties with a wife, a three-year-old son and a two-month old baby. I had a pain in my knee and went to the doctor, thinking it to be my old cartilage trouble. He became very serious and booked an appointment with a specialist. It appeared that I had a rare type of arthritis and that the best that I could hope for was that, in the doctor's words "You will be in a wheelchair before you are forty."

'During the next three months, pain spread to every joint in my body, and I was taking the maximum amount of pain-killers allowed. X-rays showed that my joints were crumbling away.

'A friend of mine was taking a healing service sixty miles away and I thought about going, but decided not to on two counts:

(1) The driving would be impossible. (At that stage I could only drive by holding the steering wheel with one hand, and supporting the elbow of that arm with the other.)

(2) I dared not ask for healing, because I didn't feel that I had the faith and didn't think I could live with the disappointment of asking for healing and not receiving it.

'During the week before the healing service, I attended a Eucharist with a few friends who I knew were praying for me. During prayers for the sick, the pain in my elbows disappeared and I could drive.

'So I went to the healing service. I still dared not ask for healing – the best I could manage was to ask for strength to be able to live with being in a wheelchair.

'As hands were placed on me, I was healed completely. I could walk unaided. No more pain. I never took a pain-killer again, and a visit to the specialist showed only that there was no need to see him ever again.

'Subsequently, I have played hard physical contact sports such as American football with no ill effects.'

It seems to me that it is always right to pray for a miracle, as long as we understand that God is sovereign, and that such miracles are rare! The Gospels clearly show us that Jesus raised the dead and healed the dying – but I do not get the impression that this was a frequent occurrence. We are told of multiple healings and exorcisms (Mark 1:34) but only of a few stupendous miracles.

When God does answer such prayer with a miracle, the result seems to be clear and decisive. To persist in praying for physical healing when the patient is manifestly getting worse may hinder their spiritual progress towards death. I have, I'm sure, made mistakes in these matters.

The greatest miracle is the clear sense of God's presence with the dying. Physical healing impresses the world; spiritual wholeness leads people to see God (Hebrews 12:14 for instance).

Here is another testimony about death, to which I would like to add a few words. It is told by his wife.

'On December 4th 1986, Edward went to the doctor with a longstanding cough and cold which he couldn't shake off. In a few minutes the doctor had diagnosed a cancerous growth in the liver region. This news was a great shock to both of us, one has to experience it to know how profoundly stunned the inner self is for a long time afterwards. You either have faith, and hold on to that, or you just go to pieces. In our case, we found greater faith, and a deeper love for each other. Edward didn't go to work, as the specialist predicted he would only have a year at the most, so he wanted to enjoy the short time he had left. We both still had great hopes of a miraculous healing, this positive thinking helped us over the first few months. In the winter, because Edward had lost so much weight, he suffered a great deal from the cold, although the room was warm. In the spring, Edward loved pottering around the garden, sowing seeds, tending young plants and looking after his beloved birds. At last he had time to enjoy life to the full, being free of the pressures of work, meetings, visiting prisoners and hospital patients. In fact, he said the last few months were the best, as he finally had time to ponder and see the beauty around him, as a blind man would rejoice in his newfound sight. In June, he got weaker and weaker. Edward found this very hard to accept and worried about my health, as I had to do everything on my own. But the Lord gave me all the energy I needed. I hardly ever went into the bathroom when Edward was there, for it upset me so much to see his body wasting away. At this stage I could never imagine I would be able to face washing and bathing him myself, be able to dress his bed sores, or massage his back to ease the pain from sitting in one position. With God's help I did, and with devotion.

'How true . . . the things which are impossible with man are possible with God. Not a day passed without Edward thanking God for another day, nor telling me that I was an angel, and "I'll always love you." Through all his suffering, Edward never complained and he worked for his Lord to the very last. The Bible a Month Club was very important to him. It was formed with the hope that everyone would be able to read the Bible in their own language. Edward gained new members daily, including our Rector, Curate, Nurse and any bedside visitor.

'As time went by and Edward became weaker, I had to lift him more, and I just didn't know how much longer I would be able to carry on. Doctors and nurses came regularly and were marvellous. What devoted people they are, I really admire them. The day before Edward died, I rang our Curate, Dale, who came in the evening to give us both Communion. It was a beautiful moment. That very night I had to give Edward a dose of liquid morphine every four hours. As I gave him the last dose at 4.30 a.m. I sat him up, resting his head on my shoulder, and in his right hand he held the Gideon's New Testament (the same one he'd had at his conversion in hospital three years ago). He could still whisper "I love you" and I was able to tell him things he was still able to understand. I was on my own, when the breathing became more difficult, and at 6.00 a.m. Edward died. I sat quietly for a while, said a prayer, then got dressed and rang the doctor at 6.50 a.m. He arrived soon after, as did a good friend. I have lost a wonderful husband and a good friend. Our daughter Esther, who was in London, came immediately, as did my brother from Austria.'

Edward, or Ted, as I knew him, had experienced two great miracles in his life. The first some forty years earlier was in a sanatorium for tuberculosis. He wasn't expected to live. He loved to tell us how a wandering monk came into the sanatorium and looked at him. 'Young man, God will make you better!' He was prayed for, improved rapidly, and was soon discharged.

Despite marrying a Christian wife, Ted remained on the edge of the church until he was taken to hospital for a cancer operation. There, during Billy Graham's visit to Bristol in May 1983, he experienced a clear and remarkable conversion. When he was diagnosed with secondary cancer three years later, many people prayed looking for a second physical miracle. I prayed for him, too, though on this occasion, I didn't feel any surge of faith, rather that I should help to prepare him for death. Shortly before going on holiday in July, I knew that I must write a last letter to him. One night on holiday I woke up. Instead of being distressed (my usual reaction), I remember saying 'Lord why have you woken me up?' 'Pray for Ted' came the reply. Early the next morning, I am virtually certain, was the time of his death.

Shortly before his death, Ted had two great joys. First, he formed a healing prayer group in our church; second, his beloved daughter, Esther, came home from New Zealand and experienced a wonderful and profound conversion. Ted's faith and certainty certainly helped his daughter to open her heart to the Lord. I believe his death was another of God's miracles.

GUIDANCE AND THE TIME OF DEATH

As with my experience with Ted, quite often repeated with others, many people feel guided to be present at the moment of death. Another parishioner writes

'In April 1980, my mother died. She had been a complete invalid for years, unable even to speak. Dad, a saintly man, had done everything for her, but had a break every six months when mother stayed in the Priory Hospital for ten days.

'It was during one such stay, over Easter, that it happened. Martin and I had colds, so had not visited her for a week, but as I took him to school on the first day after the holiday, I had a strong urge to go to the Priory and not straight home. I arrived as they were sorting themselves out, too early for visiting, but was allowed to go into the ward and sit by her bed. Her blue eyes seemed to look right through me as I sat and held her hand. It was difficult to know if she recognised my presence.

'The doctor came on rounds and said it could not be long before she died. There was nothing more they could do to help her. I remember asking ''When?'' and receiving only a shrug. Afterwards I worried at asking such a silly question, and hoped he understood.

'She slept, and gradually I could sense her breathing was changing, so called a nurse, and it was all over. I was so glad to be there – something I never expected to feel.

'I always thought it was just intuition that sent me that morning, but since then have thought more and more that it was a message from the Lord. So many times He has told me when someone is troubled and needs an ''ear''. Many times I have been ''sent'' to get in touch with friends to find they needed someone just to talk to. These are the messages sent from afar, not to the ear, but to the heart. I am more sure of that now, and I hope, more understanding.'

A similar sort of experience encompassing a difficult decision was given to me by another parishioner:

'Many years ago, when my father was in his last illness, I gave up work to nurse him. At the same time I was in process of changing jobs. The new employer was prepared to wait a while till the situation resolved itself.

'After about two weeks, my father became unconscious

and the doctor gave him twenty-four hours to live. The next morning, Dad was sitting up doing a crossword! I had to decide whether to renounce the new job and remain at home indefinitely.

'In the afternoon, I was ironing and praying (rather sadly because it was an interesting job), when the clock struck three, and a voice inside me said very clearly "It is finished", and I said "I'll stop here."

'During the next week my father died, and I eventually took the job after all.'

Many people are depressed that they aren't actually present when their loved ones die. I can only assume that God knows what is best for each of us. While some are definitely guided to be present at the point of death, others are not. It is part of the mystery.

GOD'S VOICE TO THE DYING

As I write, I am thinking of, and praying for, a young woman who is lying in a coma a few miles away. She is surrounded by the love and care of the medical profession, parents, and a close friend. She has suffered from cancer for at least five years, and has lived much longer than the specialists indicated to her father. I have known her as an acquaintance for some time, and as a friend for just a few weeks. In the previous year, knowing that she was seriously ill, I made a number of efforts to contact her, always without success. It seemed that either God was blocking me from seeing her, or that she didn't want to see me.

At the beginning of the year, with some hesitation, I made another attempt. She was in bed, very unwell, but she got up and met me in her kitchen. We had a wonderful talk and prepared ourselves for some prayer sessions which were to include her close friend and a neighbour.

When I returned a few days later, she astonished me by saying that she had been 'born again'! She had visited a local herbalist and told her that when she died she would go into oblivion. The herbalist, a strong Christian, had challenged this. (How many of us would have meekly acquiesced and have been of no spiritual use?) As a result, she had been shown the way to Christ and was amazingly transformed. Our subsequent prayer sessions were deeply moving. I sometimes felt a deep physical pain, my new friend a real measure of peace. One afternoon, I sensed that God was telling me to ask her whether she was at peace about the past. A number of things surfaced which, I believe, she needed to release to God. Knowing how ill she was, yet hopeful of a miracle, I felt that I must trespass on to dangerous ground. Neither of us felt any pain when we prayed, and I left her laughing and happy. Within a day, she had relapsed into a coma that will surely lead to her death.

For a short time, I felt a sense of frustration and failure. Why had God not raised her up? Did I lack faith? But, quickly, I realised, once again, that all of us must accept God's sovereignty in these matters. God's timing is best. He knows what He is doing. He has called her by name. He will, we trust, take her to Himself. (She died as I was writing this.)

SUDDEN DEATH

'From lightning and tempest; from plague, pestilence and famine; from battle and murder, and from sudden death, Good Lord deliver us.'

(The Litany; *Book of Common Prayer*)

Occasionally, Christians produce remarkable testimonies to escape from disasters, guidance to avoid fatal journeys, all of which can leave those who have experienced bereavement from sudden death feeling doubly angry.

Just this Christmas, I received what I thought was a normal Christmas newsletter from a minister whom I hadn't seen for ten years. The newsletter enclosed a photgraph of his teenage daughter, taken the day before her death. She was killed in a motor accident. Faith, confidence, love and gratitude for the girl's life, these were the sentiments which shone through a poignant letter.

It is difficult to react to massive tragedies like earthquakes, plane crashes or floods. We may pray, contribute money, talk about them, admire the rescue work, blame human agencies, question providence . . . then quite suddenly, these tragedies become personal. A name leaps out from the paper − a member of a former youth group was among those killed in the King's Cross Tube disaster.

Some time later, I received a lovely letter from his parents. It showed that they had read my halting words and responded warmly to them. Once again, I thank God for an utter conviction in the safety of the historic evidence of the Resurrection.

I remember Sir Norman Anderson,[3] preaching movingly about his faith in Christ, although he had suffered many tragedies among his young family. Sir Norman had examined the evidence. He was, in a real sense, prepared.

I recall the words of Jesus 'Now there were some present at that time who told Jesus about the Galileans whose blood Pilate had mixed with their sacrifices. Jesus answered, "Do you think that these Galileans were worse sinners than all the other Galileans because they suffered this way? I tell you, no! But unless you repent, you too will all perish. Or those eighteen who died when the tower in Siloam fell on them — do you think they were more guilty than all the others living in Jerusalem? I tell you, no! But unless you repent, you too will all perish" ' (Luke 13: 1-5). Hard words; words which I have felt must be said at some funerals, but words which warn us to have a 'theology of accident' before and not after such events.

I remember many other Christian parents, ministers especially, who have lost children at a young age. I remember their grief, their faith — God's rainbow overarching their tears. I remember especially, my joy at the birth of Timothy, overshadowed by the 'cot' death of a daughter of Christian friends the very next day. I remember their faith. The funeral service was an amazing testimony to the Resurrection. The parents received a vision of their daughter growing into a full spiritual person with the Lord in heaven.

Ken McAll[4] told me an extraordinary story of a woman who visited him from another country. In the course of an uncomfortable first interview, she wandered around his study, picking up books and putting them down. He felt that his visitor was behaving like an aimless teenager. Casually he asked, 'Did you lose a child sixteen years ago?' She snapped back, 'No, I lost twins fourteen years ago.' She marched out of the room, and the interview came to an abrupt end. Some time later, the woman returned. She looked much calmer. 'Do strange things happen here?' 'Sometimes,' Ken replied. 'I've just been walking in your garden. I saw a vision of Jesus — He had two fourteen year olds with Him, and an eight year old girl. I didn't tell you that I had an abortion eight years ago.' Not surprisingly, she received a great measure of healing and forgiveness from this experience.

DEATH THAT SEEMS UNTIMELY

Many people have a happy and holy death. Like ripe apples, ready to fall from a tree, they are quietly released from this world to the next. Ideally, that is how we would all like to die. That is the picture in the Old Testament of Jacob gathered with his family (Genesis 48). That is almost the picture in the New Testament, of the apostle Paul – full of faith, awaiting the end 'For I am already being poured out like a drink offering, and the time has come for my departure. I have fought the good fight, I have finished the race, I have kept the faith. Now there is in store for me the crown of righteousness, which the Lord, the righteous Judge, will award to me on that day – and not only to me, but also to all who have longed for His appearing' (2 Timothy 4: 6-8). I say almost, because the Christian Church found his death untimely, that is, if 1 Clement is a safe guide to their hearts (1 Clement, paragraph 5).

A few years ago, two leading Anglicans faced death from cancer. Their lives and ministries could not have been more different. One a radical scholar, scourge of the simplistic church of the 1960s; the other a charismatic leader, used mightily by God to bring new life and hope to individuals and to churches. Both sought prayer. Both wrote movingly about their impending deaths.[5] Both died confident in the Resurrection faith. In life they had little except Anglicanism in common, in death they were not divided.

In our own church, we have recently faced the death of a much loved churchwarden. Sue had a blunt, down-to-earth faith. During our first meeting, the Curate whispered to me 'By the way, the lady churchwarden has disapproved of everything you've said so far, but keep going . . .' I did! And despite our very different approaches to many things, we became firm friends. Sue had a wonderful gift with people who were in trouble, people who felt unimportant, people whom churches (and rectors) can seem to ignore. She had fought her way off tranquillisers, showed others the way through, and was a tower of strength in our church. Then, quite suddenly, she was diagnosed with cancer, it spread rapidly, and despite many prayers and personal ministry of a kind that she wasn't used to, she died within a few months. I don't find funerals easy. Here at least, I knew the dead person well, but I was also asking questions, and so were many good people. Why? Where was God? What use is a church that believes in healing whose chief officer dies in this way?

I don't really know what I said, but somehow the Holy Spirit lifted our spirits, somehow the truth of the Resurrection and the mystery of God's sovereignty came through, somehow the voice of God was heard.

Before her death, Sue's great desire was that the plaque of the Ten Commandments be cleaned. Dark and dingy they had stood above the chancel arch, unseen for many years. Now, six months on, Moses and Aaron and the Commandments shine down upon the congregation. In a series of sermons, they are speaking. In this and many other ways, Sue's influence lives on.

Fred Smith sums it up well when he writes about his granddaughter's death.[6] His own death, soon after a dramatic healing from a heart attack, came as a great shock to his church. They seemed to feel that such a thing wasn't possible. Fred knew better. He knew that he was mortal, and as his wife Stella said, 'He was beginning to be burdened with arthritis. He'd had a wonderful life. He was ready to go!'

If only we had a proper theology of death, if only we would make preparations (a 'Christian' will, suggestions for the funeral service, and above all, preparation to meet our

God), then death need not seem an enemy. ' "Where, O death, is your victory? Where, O death, is your sting?" The sting of death is sin, and the power of sin is the law. But thanks be to God! He gives us the victory through our Lord Jesus Christ' (1 Corinthians 15: 55-57).

FALSE GUIDANCE AND DEATH

The very title of this section seems harsh. But what are we to say of books, talks, and testimonies which speak of the afterlife in terms of spiritist visions and reincarnation?

I was given one such book to read recently. It purported to tell of a famous medium who had died giving messages to another medium via 'automatic writing'. The essence of the message was that all was well on the other side, the famous were having a splendid time (there was a lot of stuff about the Kennedys and other prominent statesmen), there was a lot of relearning (especially for clergy!), and everyone had the option of rejoining the cycle of life to pay back any 'karma' that needed to be released. The book seemed to have a number of fatal flaws. There was an extraordinary interest in the 'famous'. The medium claimed a previous incarnation as Lazarus' father, and the writer as Lazarus' unnamed (in the Gospels) sister. The cycle of reincarnation was designed to improve people — yet there is no evidence that humanity is spiritually any better than thousands of years earlier. Though 'very religious', and full of quotes from Jesus' teaching, the book totally ignored the central part of Jesus' experience — the cross! It had to, there could be no doctrine of atonement when all were still working at their own situation. There could be no real doctrine of resurrection when each soul was an amalgam of many human lives.

But, what of these all persuasive 'visions' where people are back to previous lifetimes and experience things about which they can have no actual knowledge?

The Christian has, I think, two possible responses. The simplest is in 2 Thessalonians 2:9 'The coming of the lawless one will be in accordance with the work of Satan displayed in all kinds of counterfeit miracles, signs and wonders.' A more complex view may be to see these 'regressions' as experiences similar to some of Dr McAll's patients when he prays for the healing of their family tree. If people can, occasionally, recall the experiences of their ancestors, that would simply explain other 'regression' experiences. We know that butterflies have an inbuilt computer which enables them to retrace the journeys of their ancestors. The monarch butterfly, in America, will hibernate in the same one square kilometre of Mexican mountain despite the fact that those which return the following winter are three or four generations on.

In the end, we need not know. What we must realise is that contacting the dead is explicitly forbidden in the Scriptures.[7] However tempting it is to want to know where our loved ones are, we must wait in faith and in hope for our own time.

THE UNQUIET DEAD

Here again, we face a considerable mystery. A little while ago, I was asked to visit a house because the occupants were being disturbed by tobacco smoke, the sense of a 'presence', and some other phenomena. The owners of the house were ordinary people — neither particularly religious, nor people who dabbled in any sort of spiritism. After some discussion, it emerged that no one in the house smoked, that husband

and wife had independently smelled the tobacco, that one of the children had experienced some curious things in her bedroom, and that a previous owner had committed suicide some years earlier.

A Reader and I said some prayers and the situation first improved, and then normalised. This sort of experience is quite common. I cannot offer any clear explanation, but I can be certain that prayers, offered in the name of Jesus and often a celebration of Holy Communion, are more than adequate to cleanse and release the situation. If there are any 'spirits' present, I tell them to go to Jesus for whatever purpose He may have for them. It seems to me that whatever happens, disobedient or unhappy spirits are better under His authority than continuing to trouble people in their natural life. It may well be that there aren't any 'spirits' present; but that something unpleasant, or at the very least, unquiet, is disturbing the situation.

Reverent agnosticism about the cause of these phenomena seems wiser than speculative theories or dubious investigation.

Some people are much more sensitive in this area, and do have a definite sense of evil. They also seem to be able to sense when the atmosphere is clear. This gift is presumably connected with the 'distinguishing between spirits' mentioned in 1 Corinthians 12:10. Personally, I seem 'tone deaf' in this area, which perhaps makes it easier to pray in faith and relatively free from fear.

THE JOURNEY TO THE CELESTIAL CITY

Bernard Levin wrote in an article in the *Times* that he was deeply impressed by a real believing Christian funeral service. One of the tragedies today is that the majority of services are just formalities. Neither the deceased, nor the mourners, seem to have had much concept of eternity. Not only are hell and the second death (Revelation 20:14) discounted, but there is also little belief in the possibility of heaven. For the Christian, the vision of the Celestial City[8] should be an ever-present reality.

St Paul has some powerful words 'For to me, to live is Christ and to die is gain. If I am to go on living in the body, this will mean fruitful labour for me. Yet what shall I choose? I do not know! I am torn between the two: I desire to depart and be with Christ, which is better by far; but it is more necessary for you that I remain in the body. Convinced of this, I know that I will remain, and I will continue with all of you for your progress and joy in the faith' (Philippians 1: 21-25). Are we torn between life and death? Do we have a vision of departing and being with Christ which is far better than anything on earth? If we do, then notwithstanding the real sorrow of parting, we should be looking forward to our death!

The guidance we receive in this life is an encouragement as to the reality of our faith; the guidance people receive approaching death is a wonderful encouragement to the rest of us who haven't yet been called to the brink of the river.

Notes and references

1 Houghton, Frank. *Faith Triumphant* – an anthology of verse. Overseas Mission, 1973, Poem 39.
2 The Revd Richard Glover, chaplain to St Margaret's Hospice, Taunton and a member of the Bath and Wells Diocesan Healing Group.
3 Anderson, Sir Norman. *A Lawyer among the Theologians*.
4 McAll, Kenneth. *Healing the Family Tree*. London, Sheldon Press, 1986.

5 Robinson, Bishop John. 'God is to be found in the cancer as
  in everything else'. *Guardian*. December 7th 1983, and
  Watson, David. *Fear no evil: a personal struggle with cancer*.
  London, Hodder & Stoughton, 1984.
6 Smith, Fred and Saunders, Hilary. *God's Gift of Healing*.
  Chichester, New Wine Press, 1986, p 138.
7 Deuteronomy 18:11, for instance.
8 Bunyan, John. *The Pilgrim's Progress*. See end section.

15

THE MYSTERY OF GUIDANCE

'For now we see through a glass darkly; but then face
to face: now I know in part: but then I shall know even
as I am known' (1 Corinthians 13:12 AV).

Many Christians drift gently through life. Like a stick
thrown into a stream, they allow themselves to be directed
by the current. Occasionally there are eddies, and
obstructions; sometimes the stream runs fast, sometimes
slow. Eventually, the stick reaches some sort of resting
place – its journey is over.

Such Christians make use of all the great signposts of the
faith – prayer, Bible, sacraments. They usually lead lives
of considerable integrity and are useful and valued members
of their community. Their religion is private, personal, and
secure. But there is little sense of adventure, ecstasy, or
darkness.

Other Christians are tossed about like a boat without a
rudder. They move on the great ocean, wherever the wind
of the Spirit seems to lead. First one fellowship, then
another; first one doctrine, then another; first one calling,
then another.

Such Christians talk much about experience. They have
little time for order, liturgy or contemplative prayer. They
have great commitment to evangelism, to relationships and

to guidance. They lead lives which generate a certain amount of loving chaos. For a while, they are useful and valued members of a community, then they are moved on to new fields and new friends. Their religion is open, alive, and loving. But there is little sense of history or of foundation.

The first group find talk of guidance rather frightening, the second find 'guidance' constantly changing the direction of their lives.

In a sense, we are all really part of both groups. We have, to a greater or lesser extent, to be open to the best of both ways. Once we leave the safe confines of the stream, we become more open to God's call, more open to the Spirit's leading, more open to both the joys and sorrows of spiritual experience.

The biographies of great Christians are full of such experiences. The saints of the Bible are not immune from them. I offer a few such experiences from friends who have been willing to take a risk – not least in describing their experiences in print.

GUIDANCE THAT SEEMED TO GO WRONG

'After returning home from a holiday we felt "restless". For many years we had wanted to live in the country, with a bit of land and try to earn a living in the craft industry. Our children were still young enough to move schools, hopefully without academic problems, and we wondered whether the right time had come.

'As Christians we were concerned that we were doing the right thing and asked church members to pray for us for a definite word of guidance. After studying house prices, Wales seemed to be the most probable place and we made two trips to look at houses. Before our third visit, a church member shared that, while praying for us he saw a picture of a house. It was so clear that he was able to draw it for us. On this third trip we went to see a clergyman in mid-Wales, who told us of a house belonging to a couple in his church who had decided to move. He had only heard of this that very week, and the house hadn't even gone on to the market yet. It was a few miles outside the town. It was the right price, the right size, and the similarity between the house and the drawing was amazing! We felt convinced.

'We sold our house very quickly after that and moved ten weeks later. But within a very short while things began to go wrong.

'Our immediate neighbours in the village refused to speak to us, and when we applied for building permission for a woodworking workshop, they took a petition around the village and many people signed. After meetings, we did get our planning permission, but not before we began to feel most unwelcome. With all the delays, the workshop wasn't completed until fifteen months after we moved. This actually coincided with the Vicar of the village church we had been attending, telling us in a letter that our personalities and spirituality were not compatible with his and it would be better if we worshipped in the nearby town, where we got on with the parish priest! This was absolutely devastating, and made us feel more rejected than ever. On top of all this, the children were being bullied at school, and people spread gossip about the family.

'The woodwork and dressmaking were never viable and we were getting more into debt. After another two years we had to face facts that it wasn't working and we closed the business and became officially unemployed. After five months we were able to get a job together in London which provided accommodation.

'So were we guided by the Spirit to go to Wales? In the eyes of the world it was certainly a dismal failure and waste of three and a half years. But we are still convinced it was right. The experience taught us that we must not rely on good neighbours, good fellowship, being liked by others, and that it is only on God we can rely. He will never let us down.'

GUIDANCE THAT LED FIRST TO A SPIRITUAL WILDERNESS

' "I'd like you to consider coming through to Bristol with me." That was the bombshell that was to change our lives. After ten years in Oxford, ten very full and fruitful years in which I had become a Christian, got married, had three children, been very involved in a thriving and challenging church, now there was the opportunity to move. My boss, who was also a close Christian friend, had been promoted to a new job in Bristol and had decided to create a post for me. My wife and I set ourselves to pray. Could it be time that we left the nest, left the place where we had been nurtured as Christians, where we knew and loved so many people? Gradually, we came to the conviction that this was the time to move. My boss was delighted. We set ourselves to find where in this massive town of Bristol we should settle. We felt that our priority should be to find the church which we were to join, where we could serve and grow in faith. We went to Bristol to consult with church leaders, denomination didn't matter to us. We struggled to understand the Christian scene and to see where we would fit in. One church particularly impressed us with its openness, vision and strength of community. Bobbie had a vision as we prayed that brought to mind an area of Bristol where we knew this church had a group. Was that where we should go? We were sure enough to step forward. House buying proved relatively simple and soon enough we were there.

'The strange thing was that, despite all our prayers and our attempts to find the right Christian fellowship to join, we found it very hard to settle. Looking back on the experience, it is very hard to know why. There was nowhere where we really felt called and able to throw in our lot. We had always been hundred per centers in our church commitment. If we joined somewhere we had to be wholehearted about it, yet we were failing and we knew it. As the months wore on, my own faith began to grow dimmer and dimmer. I don't know why. I was depressed and the family noticed it. In many ways I had everything others might want, a permanent and good job, working for a man I greatly admired, a good house, family, and so on and yet I did not feel at home with God. My relationship with God had always seemed relatively easy. Now it was dark. I spent days in prayer and fasting to little effect. Sometimes I would get desperate and consider moving again to another part of town. Soon we started going to a local church simply out of obedience. It was right to belong somewhere, so we would, even though we didn't particularly feel at home. For me it was a time of loneliness the like of which I had never experienced before. I felt thrown on to God, yet felt nothing of His presence. I remember one day, on a hillside, I had tried to pray and could not. In desperation I said to God 'I don't feel anything, I don't know anything, I am doubting everything, but I will love you.' For me that was the bottom line; a rock from which I could build. I began to look back and to look forward. What were all those years in Oxford for? All those opportunities we had to learn, to be trained, to lead home groups, to preach, to talk to others about the Lord, what were they all for? This job I am in, is this it now for the rest of my life? I was aware that I was privileged as a scientist to have a permanent post, but something inside made me unhappy at the thought of going on in it for the rest of my days. Gradually through the murk, a new possibility arose. What about ordination into the Anglican ministry? Could that be the way God was leading?

'To cut a long story short, much prayer, discussion and tentative steps have led to today, and I am now a curate serving in the Church of England. To those who knew me in Oxford the news came as quite a shock, because in those days I had little time for denominations and ecclesiastical structures. Perhaps I was stubborn, and God had to lead me through a wilderness before I would even consider the possibility seriously. I don't pretend to understand. What I do know is that both my wife and I would testify to a sense of our lives opening out as we have stepped out in the darkness. We have done things we would never have dreamt of doing; we have new interests, new concerns, new loves. Things are not always smooth, but I don't expect that any longer. Of one thing I am sure, and that is that I am glad that we came this way.'

GUIDANCE THAT LED TO LIGHT AND DARKNESS, AND THEN BACK TO THE LIGHT

'After a few years as a curate in Newcastle upon Tyne, I worked for four years as a parish priest in the Anglican diocese of Lesotho. I remember four factors in the guidance the Lord gave me to get me to Lesotho. First of all, I noticed that Christians I knew in Newcastle who had served overseas seemed to have a clearer vision and perspective of what was happening in Britain then and a freedom to respond creatively, and I wanted that. And then, on a night when I had prayed that God's Spirit would fill me, and knowing

He had, but waiting for the gift of tongues, I opened my Bible at random, and it fell open at Isaiah 49. I read verses 1-6 and each of those verses I believe applied to me. But the verse that struck me was verse 6 which includes the words 'I will give you as a light to the nations that my salvation may reach to the end of the earth'. This 'method' of guidance I should add has never worked for me again in the succeeding twelve years. But the Lord used it then and confirmed it with His Spirit, for as I reflected on the passage, I began to pray and then in tongues.

'Six months later I had a conversation with my bishop about the next step for me, and we considered four possibilities in general terms. They were, rural ministry, urban ministry, ministry in Britain south of Hadrian's wall, or an overseas ministry. Very wisely, the bishop said that he would not want me to be a curate in his diocese if all the time I was wondering if I should have gone overseas. Very supportively, he pointed me in the direction of a missionary society. If the door didn't open, we would think again, together, he said.

'The door did open, and I like the Lord's sense of humour. I had said I would go anywhere in the world except South Africa, and the door that did open was in Lesotho, an independent country that is completely surrounded by South Africa! It was agreed between the United Society for the Propagation of the Gospel (USPG) and the Diocese of Lesotho that I would serve as a parish priest there for four years.

'This was from 1977-1981. They were years of great challenge, much heartache, many blessings and a few signs of the Kingdom of God.

'The time came to return to the UK. I resigned my post, as I wasn't clear whether I should be returning. Returning to the UK was much harder than leaving it.

'Two months after my return I still didn't know whether to ask if I was wanted back in Lesotho or not. It was another African bishop who spoke to me. Festo Kivengere was speaking at a conference nearby. A friend and I went to hear him, and I buttonholed the bishop in the interval. He told me very gently that he did not use European priests in parish situations in his diocese, but did use them for specialist ministries. If I wanted to I could write to him. 'Pray about it' he said. As I lay in bed that night I imagined myself working in Uganda in a teaching capacity as a priest, but I had no peace or joy as I pictured the scene. Needless to say, I didn't write.

'What followed was two years of inner searching. At the beginning of this time I did not want to return to parish ministry in the UK. To some people, this was very easy to explain, to others it was not. For a year I believed that I was not ready and that God didn't want it. And then for another year I was believing that God did want me to return to parish ministry as a curate where I could experience the evangelism and healing ministry. I had seen a few signs of it in Lesotho, but now I wanted to see God at work in Britain. Again, it was difficult to explain to some people why ten years after ordination I was looking for a job as a curate! But I wanted to participate in this ministry without the responsibility of leadership, and also I wanted to ease back into the British church scene, and to get my bearings again. Two posts came up, and the Lord said 'No'. One of them was obviously what I was looking for, but being single was a disadvantage, and there was an accommodation problem. The other was obviously unsuitable, the parish needed a major rethink about its buildings and there was no sign this was going to happen, and there was nowhere for a curate to live. I was getting desperate, but a friend said 'No' to this for me. Finally, after eight months of unemployment, the looked-for opportunity came, and it was through an advertisement in a church paper. This one leaped off the page because of the words 'evangelism' and 'healing'. I spent a morning writing an application, finally deciding to tell the truth that I would not on the evidence of past experience be a 'wow' with the youth group. Now the matter was out of my hands. Well, I was appointed, although not the first choice, but then the Lord never promised to spare our pride. By this stage I weighed a stone less than I had on leaving university twelve years before.

'I remember a couple of months later walking down the street and being quietly grateful that it was here that the Lord had put me. The painful searching and seeking is now a great strength to me as I know from great depths within me, God's will is my life.'

It would be wrong for me to comment at length on these experiences. I wasn't involved in their various struggles except, occasionally, as a spiritual onlooker. I did place the advertisement which emphasised 'Healing and Evangelism' and got a measure of criticism for it! What I can say, is that each couple (for my third contributor found a wife in Shepton, and that is another wonderful story) has a spiritual integrity, a dedication, and a spiritual resilience which has grown through these experiences.

St Paul says 'we see through a glass darkly' and 'now I know in part'. The Christian adventure must involve risk, the Christian adventure must involve being prepared to lose one's life in order to save it (see Matthew 16:25). I don't know why my friends who went to Wales had such a terrible time. As a family, they came through it together. They have learned something of the weakness and the poverty that St Paul writes about (2 Corinthians 8:13). I can see more clearly what my two other sets of friends have learned from their times of darkness. In different ways, they needed the darkness in order to hear God's voice again.

So, too, did Beverley. She came to Shepton to teach, and felt called to help in the evangelisation of one of the most atheistic countries in the world. While on holiday there, she contracted a vicious illness. She was never able to complete her teaching practice. After a period of darkness, she retrained, found a good job, and then married the curate!

Again, the picture is of intense darkness, faithfulness through the tears and the uncertainty, then out into the light of a new relationship, a new family and a new Christian calling.

GUIDANCE IN THE THICK DARKNESS

One of the most memorable days when I was at theological college was led by Bishop Frank Houghton.[1] By then, he was an old and frail man, within a year of death. I don't remember much of his message, but I do remember his presence. He spoke and prayed like a holy man of God. He was insignificant, consequently the light of Christ shone through. Rather fearfully, I went to talk to him. He had spoken on 2 Timothy 1:7 (AV) 'For God hath not given us the spirit of fear; but of power, and of love, and of a sound mind'. He radiated love, in his weakness there was spiritual power, and through his testing experiences, the clearest evidence of a sound mind.

For him, one of the darkest moments in his life was when he, as the leader of the China Inland Mission (CIM), had to withdraw all foreign missionaries in 1949. Their very presence added further perils to the already great problems of the Chinese Christians.

In the midst of this, he wrote this poem:[2]

> When God is silent for a space,
> And thick darkness veils His face,
> Until I hear His voice once more,
> Until I see Him as of yore,
> On this firm ground my feet are set –
> His promise 'I WILL NOT FORGET'.

Two wonderful things happened as a result of this painful decision – a decision taken reluctantly, due to circumstances, and without any obvious word from the Lord. First, the death knell of the CIM became the launch pad of the Overseas Missionary Fellowship (OMF). This famous cable was sent from the directors' conference to all members:

> Lengthen cords! Strengthen stakes!
> While emphasising priority prayer for China Conference unanimously convinced Mission should explore unmet need preparatory to entering new fields from Thailand to Japan. Haggai 2:5

Since then the OMF has begun a remarkable work in many parts of the Far East.

Second, the indigenous Chinese church seems to have become wonderfully established. Despite terrific persecution (or perhaps partly because of it?); despite the death in prison of great Chinese leaders like Watchman Nee, the Chinese church has survived the cultural revolution and appears to be emerging with a strength and vibrancy unmatched in the days of the missionaries.

How Bishop Houghton must rejoice! One of the real tests of great leadership is when things flourish after those particular leaders have left. God often doesn't seem to allow His people to see the real fruit of their best work.

GUIDANCE THAT LEADS NOWHERE

In the cases I've cited above, the ultimate purposes of God have shone through times of personal darkness. But, in all honesty, I must consider situations where guidance has apparently led nowhere. It is difficult to cite examples! People are unwilling to give them; and who am I to add to misery and tension by seeming to judge?

What sort of situation am I thinking of? Someone feels called to Christian ministry; the call isn't recognised, there is frustration, hurt, and waste of time. Someone feels called to move house. Their marriage falls apart and the original guidance looks questionable. Someone moves to serve God in a new city, or overseas, and the experience is an expensive failure. A church feels called to have a Mission, or an expensive social/building project and the resulting chaos takes the parish backwards; and so one could go on.

What has happened? Essentially there are three possibilities. Either the original guidance was wrong, or the circumstances have changed and the plans have been frustrated, or the whole thing is correct even though outwardly it is a complete failure.

We do make mistakes. We think we hear 'God's voice' when actually what we hear is our inner desire to 'hear'. This is particularly likely to happen when other people are receiving guidance, and we want to jump on the bandwagon! Mistakes can always be rectified, by returning to the Lord and admitting them. The difficulty so often is that we are genuinely unsure. Are we to be like Abraham, who despite the circumstances 'did not waver through unbelief regarding the promise of God' (Romans 4:20)? Or are we like the godly King Josiah (2 Chronicles 35:20ff), deaf to God's voice and heading for some sort of shipwreck?

I believe in these situations we must question the original

guidance – using Scripture, prayer and trusted friends. If we honestly conclude the guidance was correct, we must press on believing that, like my friends quoted above, God's light will penetrate the darkness.

'We walk by faith, not by sight' (2 Corinthians 5:7, RSV). We need the faith of Habakkuk who when facing disaster wrote 'Though the fig-tree does not bud and there are no grapes on the vines, though the olive crop fails and the fields produce no food, though there are no sheep in the pen and no cattle in the stalls, yet I will rejoice in the Lord, I will be joyful in God my Saviour' (Habakkuk 3: 17-18). But if we honestly conclude we made a mistake, we need to seek God's guidance in our new situation. God does not abandon us because we make mistakes. Abraham made mistakes, Jacob continually made mistakes, Peter made mistakes; all the great heroes of Christendom have made mistakes. We grow through making mistakes. If we never listen for God's voice, we shall doubtless never be misled. But that sounds suspiciously like the one talent man in the parable (Matthew 25:14ff), and he was none too popular with the Master!

We also need to realise that just because God guided us at the beginning of some venture, it doesn't guarantee that he is still guiding us later on. If that sounds surprising, consider again the marriage of Isaac and Rebekah (Genesis 24)![3]

God called Isaac and Rebekah into marriage. God had great plans for Jacob. But He surely didn't plan the misery of their divided household. However, mercifully, the reverse is also true. Out of darkness and misery, can come healing and light.

GUIDANCE IN THE MUD AND THE MIRE (see Psalm 40)

I was quietly relaxing at a wedding reception. A young man,

whom I knew slightly, came up to me. Could he have a word? His first marriage had broken up — his wife had left him for another man, taking their baby with her. He'd just got engaged to a childhood sweetheart. What was the church's view? Could she be baptised? Could they be married in church?

This situation proved straightforward. The man's marriage was dead. In a very real way, adultery kills a marriage. Of course there can be forgiveness and a restart, but often it is not possible. Matthew 19:9 seems, to me, to permit remarriage in this situation. His fiancée joined him in a real profession of faith, a wonderful baptism, and what promises to be a joyful Christian marriage.

In this case, the mire wasn't too deep. The bride, literally, found a new song in her mouth (Psalm 40:3) and started singing at work! The bridegroom's period of darkness helped him to see God's love in a deeper way.

A crucial principle is that God is concerned with us *today*. 'Today salvation has come to this house' says Jesus to Zacchaeus (Luke 19:9). That very day the woman at the well (John 4) discovered Jesus as Messiah and proved a very effective evangelist (John 4:39). What happened to her uncomfortable marital situation? We aren't told.

The world is concerned with *yesterday* and *tomorrow*, the Lord is concerned with *today*. 'But seek first his kingdom and his righteousness, and all these things will be given to you as well. Therefore do not worry about tomorrow, for tomorrow will worry about itself. Each day has enough trouble of its own.' (Matthew 6:33-34)

God has a word for me *today*. It may involve waiting in our present situation; it may involve radical change; it may involve forgiveness; it may involve freedom; it will involve Him and me. I may feel a prisoner to my past, I may feel like Abraham that I must repeat past mistakes (Genesis

20:17; *cf* Genesis 12: 10-20), I may feel there is no escape from my illness, my career, my marriage, or whatever; but God has a word for me *today*.

Notes and references

1 See poem 'On Freda's Death' in Chapter 14 of this volume.
2 Houghton, Frank. *Faith Triumphant* — an anthology of verse. Overseas Mission, 1973, p 131.
3 See Chapter 11 of this volume.

16

THE SILENT VOICE TODAY

About twenty-five years ago, I read a book called *The Cross and the Switchblade*.[1] I was moved by the accounts of David Wilkerson's work among the drug addicts of New York, but what amazed me was the way in which he seemed to hear God's voice. Time and time again, God's voice came to guide him and to direct him step by step in his new work.

At the end of one term, long before I was ordained, I felt that God was telling me to start a Bible Study Group in the school. It may sound easy, but it terrified me! Who could I ask? What would the chaplains think? What right had I to even consider such a thing? As I prayed, God seemed to speak . . . 'Go to the early morning end-of-term service, a particular boy will be there, ask him.'

The service was at 7.30 a.m. At approximately 7.20 a.m. I woke up, looked at my watch and said 'Sorry, Lord, I'm not going to make it . . .' Something propelled me out of bed, and I found myself dressed and racing towards the little chapel where the service was taking place. I arrived about five minutes late, and I tried to recover my breath and concentrate on the service. There were about fifteen people there – chaplains, masters, a few boys who were leaving, and one other! Somehow, I managed to approach him during the day, and we did form a small group. I don't know how much good it did any of them, but I was walking on air. Suddenly, I believed that God, if He chose to, could speak even to me. I remember visiting Rome a few weeks later, walking around the Colosseum, and the Catacombs, thinking of God who spoke to the apostles and the very ordinary Christians of the first centuries.

As a boy, I had been fascinated by the Venite, Psalm 95, which was always part of Morning Prayer. One verse always stood out 'Today if ye will hear His voice, harden not your hearts' (Psalm 95:8 BCP). The Alternative Service Book renders it 'Today if only you would hear His voice', while the NIV has 'Today, if you hear His voice'. Each translation presumably has merit, and I wouldn't presume to know which is correct. Probably, in a real sense, they all are. But each has a different nuance which I want to explore.

TODAY, IF YOU HEAR HIS VOICE

Ken Matthew was born in York in 1918. He was brought up in a nearby village. His family was very religious, and he was taken into York, a three mile walk, three times each Sunday. Scarcely surprisingly, by the age of sixteen, he hated church. The Revd George Jeffreys was running a series of evangelistic meetings in the York City Art Gallery. An enthusiastic lady came out to Ken's village and, personally, invited him to come to one of the meetings. He refused, but she persisted. Eventually Ken said that he would take her, but not go to the meeting! The lady agreed. When they got to York, Ken parked his bike and deposited her at the meeting. He walked back to his motorbike. He heard a voice saying, 'Go inside'. He walked on. He heard the voice say again, 'Go inside'. He reached the bike. A third time the voice spoke 'Go inside'.

Ken obeyed. He heard the gospel message and responded. He was saved! He also knew that God had called him to be a minister. This meant going to Bible College. The main problem was that he came from a poor family and had no means of raising the fees. He sought the Lord about going to college and the problem of the money.

Some time later, a woman knocked on the door of his house. 'I'm looking for Ken Matthew,' she said. She seemed somewhat amazed to have found him. She told Ken her story. She was a Christian, and that morning while praying, she heard the Lord tell her to go across York, out to his village, find a young man called Ken Matthew, and offer to pay his fees at a Bible College. 'How much do you need?' she asked. Ken replied very calmly, 'If the Lord has told you all that, He will tell you the amount I need!' The lady deposited a sum in his bank account. It was exactly enough to meet his needs.

Perhaps not surprisingly, Ken had a remarkable ministry. He started in the Elim Pentecostal Church, he ended as an Anglican minister. One of the many people whom he was privileged to lead to faith was my friend Fred Smith.

In November 1987, I attended the national Prayer Breakfast. This was a remarkable time of fellowship and prayer, sponsored by an inter-Parliamentary group of Christian members of the Houses of Parliament. During the morning a West Indian group was introduced by a Conservative MP with the quip 'Can any good thing come out of Brent?'

Their story was very moving. Most of them had been in prison, all of them had had a tough and difficult life. One Christmas Eve, one of them was walking across a piece of ground near a large disused bus station. He felt the Lord's presence. He felt an overwhelming call from Jesus, and he felt that it concerned the bus station. He witnessed to his parents of his Christian experience, and he set about the bus station project.

With the help of a group of friends, all new Christians, they set about achieving a project of vision for the transformation of the derelict area. The result can be seen today in the Bridge Park project opened with much celebration by the Prince of Wales in December 1988.

Obviously, I could cite many more examples, but in each of these, there was a decisive call, followed by costly and obedient action. God's voice doesn't call us to a personal glory trip, but to a lifetime of costly service.

TODAY IF YE WILL HEAR HIS VOICE

Do we really want to hear God's voice? Life is complicated enough without seeking the additional stress of listening to God. It is very costly to change. I suspect that there is a sort of spiritual 'inverse square law' which states that for every year over twenty-one, the difficulty of change becomes appreciably harder. One parishioner had a remarkable experience of God ten years ago. It came to her, I think, partly because she was prepared to take the trouble to listen; and, principally through an act of grace:

'This happened when I sat down, probably for the first time in my life with the intention of praying to God for five consecutive minutes without letting my mind wander. The date and the time are not important to me (May 18th 1979 at 2.00 p.m.), but my reasons for doing so are.

Following the first House Groups I ever attended, I read *When the Spirit Comes* by Colin Urquhart[2] and as a result, told God while at the communion rail in Shepton Mallet Church, that I wanted the Holy Spirit "like those people in the book." I had no idea what I was doing! Nothing happened and I forgot all about it. My effort at prayer followed some weeks later after some follow-up seminars.

I fixed God half-way between myself and the clock on the fireplace, closed my eyes, said "I know you're there somewhere" and did my best to think only of God.

After a couple of minutes, I became aware that I was feeling happy, not it seemed, in my mind, but in my body. The feeling was gentle and pleasant at first, but quickly got stronger and deeper; no longer a puzzling happiness, but a joy I could feel deep within me — it was as if it had been poured into me, and I felt it with my body rather than my mind, even to the tips of my fingers.

I stopped trying to pray and wondered what was the matter with me, but after various fruitless thoughts, I turned my mind back to God, but there seemed to be no answer there either.

And then, quite suddenly, I knew. I don't know how I knew, but I knew with absolute cetainty that it was God. It was as if my whole being knew, and the knowledge had come from deep within me — the words dredged up from the depth of my being "It is God, Oh, it is God". And it was as if I had always known. This moment of knowing came as no shock, but gently with a dawning wonder — a fraction of a second which lives forever, outside time, eternal in itself.

And after that, nothing mattered to me — only God mattered and I knew the barrier between life and death was very fine, not to be feared at all and easy to pass through. As I sat there, life with God was the same as being alive with Him, and I don't know which of these states I was in, for they existed together — there was no difference and I knew that in some way I had passed through this very fine barrier and I was dead with God. And all this time, the joy had increased and deepened to such an extent as to be almost unbearable and it had become a love such as I could never have imagined possible — a living, consuming love which filled every part of me, from deep within my soul, to my hands and feet — moving and alive. It was all around me and in me — it was as if God from without had come into me and released a God that was deep within my soul, and the two had come together in an explosion of divine love and the overwhelming feeling was that this love was pouring out of me in a living stream, unending, alive and yet somehow complete.'

Two others who, in different ways, had to respond to God's call are the parish Readers, Joyce and Albert.

For over twenty years, Joyce had served the parish as secretary, and general ear to the parish, under three previous rectors. One day, soon after I arrived, I apparently said to Joyce, 'Working in the office offers you tremendous opportunities for speaking a word about the Faith.' Joyce, who had, and still has, a tremendous listening ear, was horrified! But, obedient as ever, she tried occasionally, feeling suitably embarrassed. Then the silent voice started nagging her to train to be a Reader. This went on for over a year, eventually, fortified by our first lay training course, she spoke to me. I was amazed, and took a little while to see the sense of the suggestion. Joyce consulted the previous rector, who was encouraging, and set out on the course. This eventually led to her retiring from the office and becoming a voluntary Parish Visitor and Reader.

Albert was well established as parish Reader when I came. When I first came, he worked long hours out of Shepton. It seemed impossible that he could get a job in the Prison Service in Shepton. He realised that there were going to be many opportunities for service, listened to God's voice, and prayed for work in his home town. Very quickly, an unexpected vacancy occurred in Shepton. This made a tremendous difference to his availability.

TODAY IF ONLY YOU WOULD HEAR HIS VOICE

Here there seems a great urgency. The situation cries out, something must be done! My mother-in-law, Elizabeth Feilden, has always had a strong social conscience. Her call to faith, from a television broadcast of Archbishop Trevor Huddleston, has led her down many paths – some painful, some wonderful. An empowering experience of the Holy Spirit led her to use her house for a remarkable series of seminars, a friendship with a Polish family led her to Poland with a lorry load of medicines and supplies soon after martial law was declared, a call to Kenya came to her at the age of sixty.

For the last three years, she has led a development project near Oyvgis in Western Kenya. It hasn't been easy; there have been frustrations, mistakes, and natural disasters. But she has had an overwhelming sense of God's call to persist despite the difficulties. Fish ponds have been built, but as yet the fish aren't caught by the right people; new crops are grown and the land is much more productive; desperately needed trees are being replanted; primary health care is being taught; volunteers from Britain are gaining experience of the real problems of living even in a relatively prosperous Third World country; the local Anglican church is supporting and being supported.

How much easier it would have been to remain in Oxford, comfortably supporting a dynamic church, using her catering and leadership gifts in their natural surroundings. But God's voice spoke to her conscience.

If only we would hear His voice. We are so deaf to the needs all around us. We live in a comfortable round of busyness. Will we take time to listen?

Bishop Ban It Chiu was another who needed to hear God's voice. At the end of 1972, he left Singapore to attend an

International Conference in Bangkok. He found much of the conference oppressive, he was dissatisfied with his own spiritual life, worried by the state of his diocese, and perplexed by reports of students experiencing something of the Holy Spirit which sounded fanatical and ridiculous.

An Indian priest, from Fiji, whom he met on a bus, gave him Dennis Bennett's book *Nine o'clock in the morning*.[3] Bishop Chiu[4] writes:

'My rational mind was repelled by the descriptions of "speaking in tongues", "healings", and miraculous happenings.

' "It's a fairy tale — they can't happen today!" was my first reaction. At the same time, I was so fascinated and exhilarated by what I was reading that I could not put the book down. When I finished the book it was time for an afternoon siesta. I prayed a short prayer:

' "Lord, please give me your Holy Spirit as you gave Him to Dennis Bennett and others mentioned in the book." I then dozed off.

'When I woke up I was conscious of a great difference within me. God was suddenly very close. My heart was filled with love, joy and peace, instead of anger, despair and gloom. I burst out with praise and thanked God through Jesus Christ. When I ran out of English words I resorted to Chinese. Soon I was struggling again to to find the words and correct theological thoughts to express myself. The dam of the mind burst and I found myself uttering new sounds and syllables which had no meaning to my mind, but which I knew in my spirit were fluently giving expression to the praise and thanksgiving which was welling up within me towards God. When I went under the shower the syllables winged themselves into song!

'Surprised and a little nonplussed by the experience, I sought out my Indian friend and related to him what had

happened. Later he arrived in my room with a black
American Pentecostal minister and a Mexican Pentecostal
bishop. They asked me to share with them what had
happened. We soon found ourselves on our knees, praying
and worshipping God simultaneously in a harmony of international and spiritual sounds! "Jerusalem on the day of
Pentecost must have sounded like that," I thought. When
it was over my friends assured me that I had been "baptised
in the Holy Spirit" and had been given the "gift of speaking
in tongues". In fact, after the initial cross-examination we
all began worshipping, praying and singing in tongues
together! It was an awesome and reverent, but joyful and
beautiful experience.'

THE PARABLE OF THE DITCH

I used to be in charge of a school nature reserve. On a
Wednesday afternoon, a dozen conscripts who preferred
social activities to military ones were dispatched to help. The
reserve was crossed by a series of parallel, foetid ditches.
Each of them was full of oozing sludge which moved very
slowly towards a fast flowing stream at one side of the
reserve. Each autumn, higher authority decreed that the
ditches were to be mud-scooped. The effect of this
unpleasant operation was that piles of dripping mud were
deposited on the banks of the ditch. The reserve looked
untidy, it smelt, and the ditches flowed minimally faster than
before. Was it all worth it? Was it just a device to occupy
an intelligent group of schoolboys who didn't want to do
military things? One year the new group of recruits had an
idea. 'Why not cut a ditch from the main stream to the head
of the ditch?' It was perfectly possible. The main stream
curved round the top of the reserve, and a loop could be

cut by digging through about thirty metres of chalk and marsh to a point where the stream was closest. The working party really enjoyed the challenge. It was hard work; we had to dig a very deep channel through some high intervening ground, but it worked. A few weeks later, the connection was made. Clear, clean water gushed through the old ditch. Ancient mud was swept into the lower reaches of the stream. By the next day, the ditch had a clear chalk bottom, and a trout was seen swimming up it. The transformation was complete.

Of course, some might say that we had ruined the ecology of the ditch (there were plenty of others, not readily accessible to the treatment), some would have said it was too difficult and not worth the effort, others might have said 'When you're gone we'll fill it in again . . .'

There is an obvious spiritual parallel. The ditch speaks to me of renewal, it speaks to me of one of God's ways of speaking to us. First there was the dissatisfaction with the sluggish ditch. Many have felt similarly with their spiritual lives.

> As the deer pants for streams of water,
> So my soul pants for you, O God.
> My soul thirsts for God, for the living God.
> When can I go and meet with God?
>
> (Psalm 42: 1-2)

My tears have been my food day and night,
while men say to me all day long,
'Where is your God?'
These things I remember as I pour out my soul,
how I used to go with the multitude,
leading the procession to the house of God,
with shouts of joy and thanksgiving

among the festive throng.
Why are you downcast, O my soul?
Why so disturbed within me?
Put your hope in God,
for I will yet praise him,
My Saviour and my God.

(Psalm 42: 3-5)

This longing for God is often the way in which we begin to hear His voice. Then we discover the fast flowing stream, and as we read or hear of other people's experiences, we long to make them our own. We begin to catch the vision of Isaiah.

The desert and the parched land will be glad;
the wilderness will rejoice and blossom.
Like the crocus, it will burst into bloom;
it will rejoice greatly and shout for joy . . .

Then will the eyes of the blind be opened
and the ears of the deaf unstopped.
Then will the lame leap like a deer,
And the mute tongue shout for joy.
Water will gush forth in the wilderness and streams in the desert.

(Isaiah 35: 1-2a; 5-6)

Then, perhaps, God speaks to us. He shows His way for us; His unique path. At that moment the voice of the world is liable to speak: 'Don't interfere with Nature. Leave the ditch alone. It's quite useful as it is. It's how God intended it to be' which means spiritually 'Don't try to change. You're fine as you are. You're doing a good job just as God intended . . .'

But inwardly we know that's not true, God has more for us, He wants us to experience far, far more. The lazy voice of the flesh starts to speak 'It will be too difficult. The ground is very hard in places, and marshy in others. It may not work. Stick to the old ways, they are well tried and much easier' which means spiritually 'You'll look pretty silly if you make all this effort to hear God's voice and experience His presence and nothing happens . . .'

And then the voice of Satan says 'I shall oppose this. I can fill in your connecting channel. I can block it with great stones', which means spiritually 'prepare for trouble. I'll make sure that this listening business gets you into a real confused mess.'

And thus, in a real sense, it must be. If we hear God's voice, it is bound to mean change. It is bound to mean hard work. It is bound to mean opposition. For a time the stream may flow, then it may become blocked. We shall need help and discernment from others to discover the cause. But in the end, the overwhelming testimony of God's people of many differing theological persuasions, is of the sheer wonder of the experience of hearing God's voice and, in a profound way, of encountering God, Himself.

One word of warning from the ditch. I tried, totally unsuccessfully, to connect a second ditch to the main stream. It really was too difficult, too far away, and not suitable. This is a constant reminder to me that God has a unique way of speaking to each of us and that we are not called to be spiritual clones.

HOW DO WE KNOW IF IT IS HIS VOICE?

At the end of Chapter 1 I suggested ways in which 'guidance' could be tested. In the end we cannot be certain, but as Jesus said of prophets and miracle workers 'by their fruit you will recognise them' (Matthew 7:16). By the fruit of the guidance, we shall know the source of the voice.

'I said to the man who stood at the gate of the year
"Give me a light that I may tread safely into the unknown."
And he replied "Go out into the darkness and put your hand into the hand of God.
That shall be to you better than light, and safer than a known way." '[5]

King George VI brought glory to God when, in the depths of Britain's darkest hour, he made this bold affirmation of faith. His word to the nation rang true. In the tensions of unexpected kingship and a bitter war, lay the seeds of his early death. But, by his example, he helped to lead his people, thus fulfilling his coronation vows.

The world's fruit tends to be 'success' and 'power'. Of course, the Spirit does lead Christians into successful and powerful ministries, but more often He leads us into other pathways. Behind each 'successful' church usually lies a period of pain, desolation, prayer, and spiritual heartbreak. In the life of each godly person there also seems to be such periods.

The flesh's fruit tends to be 'I' centred. Great things may happen, but the centre is a personality and not a body. When 'I' moves on, collapse takes place.

Satan's fruit tends to be a short cut to power. His temptations to Jesus illustrate this. Satan can imitate almost everything in Christian experience — except the cross.

'Bear with each other and forgive whatever grievances you may have against one another.Forgive as the Lord forgave you. And over all these virtues put on love, which binds them all together in perfect unity. Let the peace of Christ rule in your hearts, since as members of one body you were called to peace.' (Colossians 3:13-15)

Satan's guidance, as with the story of Madam Zelda in Chapter 13, is spectacular and horrible. Innocent people, including the Madam Zeldas and their modern counterparts, are duped into thinking that they have heard the voice of God.

The Holy Spirit's fruit is quite different. His fruit brings glory to Jesus. As I write, I remember that a number of years ago, Archbishop Luwum was murdered in Uganda. My former rector, Michael Green, used to teach him. I was with him when he heard the news. I remember his tears. But Archbishop Luwum did not die in vain. His death and the triumphant funeral that followed, loosened the grip of a frightful dictator. His death, outwardly the tragic end of a real calling from God, brought glory to Jesus.

'He will bring glory to me by taking from what is mine and making it known to you' (John 16:14).

Here is the ultimate test of all guidance – does it bring glory to Jesus?

POSTSCRIPT

The young man walked along a long, narrow lane. It was a beautiful summer's day. He tried to weigh up the future. He loved his job, but God's call seemed to be to a different kind of service. The world said 'You're needed where you are. There aren't many mathematicians. You're involved in an important educational experiment.' The flesh said 'My great ambition is to be a successful schoolmaster. I'm happy where I am. I'm serving God there.'

Satan said 'Don't be a fool. You're not much good where

you are, but you certainly won't be any better elsewhere.'

The silent voice of God reminded him that He had spoken, and He expected obedience.

'Once God has spoken; twice have I heard this: that power belongs to God; and that to Thee, O Lord, belongs steadfast love, for thou dost requite a man according to his work' (Psalm 62:11-12, RSV).

Twenty-one years later, despite many disappointments, despite many mistakes, that man believes he truly heard 'the silent voice of God'.

Notes and references

1 Wilkerson, David. *The Cross and the Switchblade*. London, Lakeland Press, 1964.
2 Urquhart, Colin. *When the Spirit Comes*. London, Hodder & Stoughton, 1974.
3 Bennett, Dennis. *Nine o'clock in the morning*. Coverdale, 1974.
4 Harper, Michael (ed). *Bishop's Move*. London, Hodder & Stoughton, 1978.
5 Words from Minnie Louise Haskins quoted by King George VI in his Christmas Broadcast 1939.